"The deft analysis of race as it intersects with and challenges genre traditions—the western and speculative fiction—makes this an extremely timely and important book."

—SARA L. SPURGEON, author of *Exploding the Western: Myths of Empire on the Postmodern Frontier*

"By looking at speculative Wests that 'disrupt' authenticity and truth claims latent in the mythos of the western, this book provides another example of the contemporary relevance of the western as part of a hybrid genre that enables meditations on past, present, and future."

—REBECCA M. LUSH, professor of literature and writing studies at California State University–San Marcos

SPECULATIVE WESTS

Postwestern Horizons

GENERAL EDITOR

William R. Handley
*University of
Southern California*

SERIES EDITORS

José Aranda
Rice University

Melody Graulich
Utah State University

Thomas King
University of Guelph

Rachel Lee
*University of California,
Los Angeles*

Nathaniel Lewis
Saint Michael's College

Stephen Tatum
University of Utah

SPECULATIVE WESTS

Popular Representations
of a Region and Genre

MICHAEL K. JOHNSON

University of Nebraska Press | Lincoln

The University of Nebraska Press is part of a land-grant
institution with campuses and programs on the past,
present, and future homelands of the Pawnee, Ponca,
Otoe-Missouria, Omaha, Dakota, Lakota, Kaw, Cheyenne,
and Arapaho Peoples, as well as those of the relocated
Ho-Chunk, Sac and Fox, and Iowa Peoples.

Publication of this volume was assisted by the University of
Maine at Farmington, Office of the Provost.

Library of Congress Cataloging-in-Publication Data
Names: Johnson, Michael K. (Michael Kyle), 1963– author.
Title: Speculative Wests: popular representations of a region
and genre / Michael K. Johnson.
Description: Lincoln: University of Nebraska Press, [2023] |
Series: Postwestern horizons | Includes bibliographical
references and index.
Identifiers: LCCN 2022022446
ISBN 9781496233509 (hardback)
ISBN 9781496234582 (paperback)
ISBN 9781496234810 (epub)
ISBN 9781496234827 (pdf)
Subjects: LCSH: Speculative fiction—History and criticism. |
West (U.S.)—In literature. | West (U.S.)—In mass
media. | Fiction genres. | BISAC: LITERARY CRITICISM /
American / General
Classification: LCC PN3448.S64 J64 2023 |
DDC 809.3/8762—dc23/eng/20220815
LC record available at https://lccn.loc.gov/2022022446

Set in Chaparral Pro.

Contents

SPECULATIVE WESTS

Introduction

A lone traveler makes his way across a barren landscape and arrives at a small frontier town. He silently enters the town saloon, ignoring the silence that falls in his wake and ignoring, as well, the insistence from a local tough that he pay for a spilled drink. The argument escalates, and during the ensuing fight, the traveler violently dispatches the tough and two of his henchmen and then silently goes about his business of apprehending the wanted man who is his bounty.

This is, of course, the opening scene of *The Mandalorian* television series, set in the universe of the science fiction (SF) franchise *Star Wars*, but it's evocative of the western at every turn, with its bounty hunter protagonist (played by Pedro Pascal) and its knowing references to western films.[1] The opening scene replays the introduction of Clint Eastwood's bounty hunter character in the Sergio Leone film *For a Few Dollars More*.[2] Eastwood's terseness of speech is reflected in the Mandalorian's silence. Both Eastwood's character and the Mandalorian use preternaturally quick and skilled violence to take down several opponents. Eastwood's action of silently dealing himself into a game of poker with his target is paralleled by the Mandalorian's mute presentation of his "bounty puck" to his target. The Mandalorian's comment (his only spoken words in the scene) to his bounty, "I can bring you in warm, or I can bring you in cold," repeats with slightly different wording Eastwood's warning to his bounty ("Alive or dead. It's your choice"). We are not in the American West in the speculative science fiction story that is *The Mandalorian*, but we are surely in the western.

The contemporary zombie television series *The Walking Dead* similarly reinvigorates western-genre conventions by placing them within the framework of another genre—the horror story. In the episode "Nebraska," series regulars Rick Grimes (Andrew Lincoln), Glenn Rhee (Steve Yeun), and Hershel Greene (Scott Wilson) encounter two strangers inside an abandoned bar with dust-covered, scattered tables and chairs and an upright piano against one wall.[3] The barroom set would need only slight alterations to be made into a western saloon. A vintage poster on a wall advertises "Pawnee Bill Shows, WILD WEST, Touring America This Season." When the expected gunfight breaks out (with former sheriff Rick Grimes outdrawing two men), it verifies the promise of the poster. Although set in Georgia, in *The Walking Dead* we are metaphorically in the "Wild West," existing under frontier conditions brought about by a viral outbreak of zombies and the subsequent collapse of civilization.[4]

As Miller and Van Riper observe in their introduction to *Undead in the West*, "as the frontier—the meeting point between civilization and the untamed wilderness—has been drawn into the realm of speculative fiction, it has become a shifting construct, no longer fixed in either time or space," representing, for example, the "boundary between the mysterious and the familiar, the worlds of the undead and the living."[5] *The Walking Dead*, Shelley S. Rees writes, conjoins "the traditional Western with the more modern zombie narrative," producing "a grotesque hybrid, a changeling Western, animated yet altered."[6] As Neil Campbell observes in "Post-Western Cinema," various commentators have been declaring the death of the film western for over a century now. However, Campbell argues, "far from being dead," westerns have survived by "traveling across generic boundaries, poaching and borrowing from many different earlier traditions, whilst contributing to the innovation of the genre."[7] Altered but reanimated, the western genre in the twenty-first century continues to amble forward in new hybrid forms, as amply documented in the *Undead in the West* and *Undead in the West II* anthologies.[8] And as the 2020 critical anthology *Weird Westerns: Race, Gender, Genre* underscores, the weird western has a demonstrated potential for including voices and experiences in those hybrid forms that the classic western often excludes.[9]

Speculative Wests investigates both speculative westerns and speculative texts that feature western settings. Looking across the cultural landscape of the twenty-first century that includes literature, film, television, comic books, and other media, we can see multiple examples of what Rees calls a "changeling Western," what others have called "weird westerns," and what I will refer to as "speculative westerns"— that is, hybrid western forms created by merging the western with one or more speculative genres or subgenres (science fiction, fantasy, horror, alternate history, steampunk, time travel, etc.).[10] Moreover, as "western" refers both to a genre and a region (the North American West), my project here involves a study of both genre and place, a study of a "speculative West" (or more precisely, "speculative Wests") that has begun to emerge in contemporary speculative texts: the zombie-threatened California of Justina Ireland's *Deathless Divide*, the reimagined future Navajo Nation of Rebecca Roanhorse's Sixth World series, the complex temporal and geographic borderlands of Alfredo Véa's time-travel novel *The Mexican Flyboy*.[11]

Although my primary focus is contemporary culture, hybrid westerns are not a new phenomenon, and my coinage, "speculative Wests," builds on earlier terms used to describe a generic hybridity that has been part of the western (and part of depictions of the West as a region) for a long time. I give preference to the term "speculative Wests" for several reasons. "Weird Westerns," although often used as a catchall term for any western hybrid, suggests primarily the supernatural, and although it doesn't exclude, for example, science fiction, "speculative" seems a more inclusive descriptor of a variety of popular genre forms. Similarly, the term "speculative" tends to be used to refer more generally to texts with nonrealist elements, including literary and cinematic works that would not necessarily be associated with a particular popular genre. As Shelley Streeby observes, "speculative fiction" is "an umbrella category that draws genre boundaries expansively to encompass heterogeneous forms and genres of writing, notably including science fiction and fantasy," as well as, importantly, "work by people of color" that contains elements of the speculative but that may not have been classified or interpreted in terms of genre connections.[12]

"Speculative," Streeby suggests, opens up interpretative possibilities for considering the work of writers who might otherwise be excluded from conversations about popular genres. As Lysa Rivera points out, "Chicana feminists Gloria Anzaldúa and Chela Sandoval have turned to science fiction as well to theorize Chicano/a subjectivity in the postmodern era," with Anzaldúa describing mestiza subjectivity in terms of "'alien' consciousness," and Sandoval arguing that "colonized peoples of the Americas" possess a type of "cyborg consciousness."[13] As Rivera continues, "These examples point to the existence of an under-examined history of Chicano/a cultural practice that employs science-fictional metaphors to render experiences of marginalization visible and to imagine alternative scenarios that are at once critically informed and imaginative."[14] As an umbrella term, "speculative" opens up the possibility of examining narratives—"at once critically informed and imaginative"—representing a variety of ethnic and racial traditions and experiences without the confinement of narrower and exclusionary definitions of specific genres.

"Speculation," Aimee Bahng observes, also suggests a "modality more fundamentally rooted in inconclusive reflection" and "carries with it a sense of lingering conjecture," "experiment-reveling," and "meticulous inquiry." That is, in addition to providing a categorical term encompassing multiple separate genres, the speculative also suggests not just a genre with shared conventions but a mode of inquiry, reflection, conjecture, and experimentation. Speculative works invent "other possibilities (alternate realities, upside down hierarchies, and supernatural inventions)." The speculative may imagine the future as well as "explore different accounts of the past."[15] Speculative fiction, in the most general terms, "highlights the speculative mode of the 'What if?'"[16] Speculative westerns might pose the following questions: What if we could imagine the western differently? What if we could imagine a different past, present, or future West?

"Science fiction," Catherine S. Ramírez writes—and I would amend, speculative fiction more generally—"can prompt us to recognize and rethink the status quo by depicting an alternative world, be it a parallel universe, distant future or revised past." The status quo that *Speculative Wests* proposes to rethink includes the prevalent approach in both the western genre and regional studies on realist texts. *Specu-*

lative Wests also joins ongoing work in genre and regional studies that questions the centrality of whiteness in studies of the western and the West. If speculative genres such as science fiction have been historically considered "the domain of geeky white boys," Ramírez comments, we have also seen, over the last part of the twentieth and the first two decades of the twenty-first centuries, that "innovative cultural workers," including artists of color, have transformed the field of the speculative "into a rich, exciting, and politically charged medium for the interrogation of ideology, identity, historiography, and epistemology."[17] We have seen a similar transformation in the field of western studies, at least in some areas. *Speculative Wests* proposes the unusual project of bringing the concerns of these fields together, the western and the speculative, a hybridized joining of critical and theoretical concerns that is reflective of the hybridized nature of the texts examined, and one that emphasizes the work of contemporary artists of color who are actively involved in crossing the borders from one genre to another, creating new visions of the American West in the process.

Speculative Wests emphasizes texts by (or featuring) people of color, following the work of critics such as Anishinaabe writer Grace Dillon (who coined the much-used term Indigenous futurism), Adilifu Nama (who has examined race in science fiction film), Aimee Bahng (whose book *Migrant Futures* examines a variety of texts that "play across various geographies of colonialism"), and many others who study an emerging field of inquiry focused on speculative narratives: Afrofuturism, Chican@ futurism, Chican@ speculative productions, postcolonial speculative fiction, Asian futurism, speculative Blackness, and various global futurisms.[18] In *Migrant Futures*, Bahng "sets out to think speculation from below and highlights alternative engagement with futurity emerging from the colonized, displaced, and disavowed," arguing that writers of color have been and are involved in ongoing "affective experiments" that usurp and recast "conventional science fiction tropes" and that "demonstrate how speculation can take the shape of radical unfurling."[19] *Speculative Wests* shares in that project of tracing the interventions made by people of color in the field of speculative literature, but with a particular focus on the point where those speculative texts intersect specifically with the genre western and with, more generally, representations of the American West.

RACE, HYBRIDITY, AND GENERICITY

Hybrid westerns (that is, westerns that are explicitly connected to another genre or genres) have been around for a very long time—from at least as early as Edward S. Ellis's 1868 dime novel *The Steam Man of the Prairies* (in which a steam-powered robot leads the way for western expansion). And hybridity itself is by no means an exclusive feature of weird westerns, science fiction westerns, or speculative westerns. As John Rieder points out, "Pigeon-holing texts as members or nonmembers of this or that genre is intellectually frivolous. . . . This is doubly true because, first, genre itself is an intertextual phenomenon, always formed out of resemblances or oppositions among texts, and second, no individual text is generically pure."[20] Although hybridity—indeed, multiplicity—may be a feature of any genre text, what strikes me about contemporary hybrid westerns is the *self-consciousness* with which the texts draw our attention to their impurity, their hybridity, the audacity of their generic combinations. I am also interested in the way contemporary texts *make use* of the western. That is, when narratives draw our attention to the western elements of their stories, those western elements are usually included as part of an individual text's generic mix with a purpose—often as part of critical commentary on the western.

Writing specifically about cinema, Jim Collins observes that irony, self-consciousness, and hybridity have been notably prevalent features of genre films since the 1990s. As one of his primary examples, he points to director Robert Zemeckis's *Back to the Future III*, the third film in the time-travel series featuring the adventures of Marty McFly (Michael J. Fox) and Dr. Emmitt Brown (Christopher Lloyd), which sends Marty and the DeLorean time-travel machine back into the nineteenth-century West.[21] Collins notes that within the Old West of that film, "we enter a narrative universe defined by impertinent connections, no longer sustainable by one set of generic conventions.

We encounter, instead, different sets of generic conventions that intermingle, constituting a profoundly intertextual diegesis, nowhere more apparent than in the shot of the DeLorean time machine being pulled through the desert by a team of horses, the very co-presence of John Ford and H. G. Wells demonstrating the film's ability to access both as simultaneous narrative options."[22] Such moments of "co-presence" or "simultaneity" in the hybrid genre text encourage us to recognize (and enjoy) the impertinence of such connections. What Collins sees as a feature of contemporary genre films in general, the contemporary hybrid western makes explicit through a variety of strategies that draw our attention to the copresence of the (at least) two dominant genres that inform the story being told. The DeLorean time machine pulled by a team of horses is also suggestive of a convention distinctive to the hybrid western—metaphorical representation within the narrative of its own generic hybridity.

In Cherokee writer Daniel Wilson's *Robopocalypse*, which is usually categorized as a science fiction novel, sentient machines have taken over and started waging war on humans.[23] As is often the case in Indigenous futurist narratives, the apocalypse (whatever its cause, zombies, robots, disease, war, etc.) suggests both destruction and the possibility of renewal. As Rebecca Roanhorse (of Native American and African American descent) writes, "Dr. Grace Dillon (Anishinaabe), inspired by Afro-futurists, coined the term Indigenous Futurisms. Indigenous Futurisms is a term meant to encourage Native, First Nations, and other Indigenous authors and creators to speak back to the colonial tropes of science fiction—those that celebrate the rugged individual, the conquest of foreign worlds, the taming of the final frontier."[24] Implied, if not directly stated, in Roanhorse's formulation is that science fiction and westerns share a similar set of colonial tropes (rugged individualism, conquest, taming of the frontier). More directly, John Rieder writes in *Colonialism and the Emergence of Science Fiction*, "Science fiction comes into visibility first in those countries most heavily involved in imperialist projects—France and England," and "no informed reader can doubt that allusions to colonial history and situations are ubiquitous features of early science fiction plots and techniques."[25] Speculative texts that intentionally and purposefully combine science fiction and western conventions offer the opportunity to speak back to both genres.

"Indigenous Futurism," Roanhorse continues, "asks us to reject these colonial ideas and instead re-imagine space, both outer and inner, from another perspective. One that makes room for stories that celebrate relationship and connection to community, coexistence, and sharing of land and technology, the honoring of caretakers and protectors."[26] In *Robopocalypse*, the rural Osage reservation in Oklahoma, surrounded by prairie, provides an unexpected refuge for humans (Native and non-Native) seeking safety, in part because existing robots were created for mobility in urban spaces. From the safety of a hilltop, the Osage Nation reestablishes itself in the community of Gray Horse, cultivating both cattle and buffalo in the surrounding prairie. *Robopocalypse* maps out an alternate cartography of western space, a future vision of the American West. What emerges at Gray Horse is a postsettler society, one that builds on Indigenous governance traditions, one that follows traditional Indigenous practices of tribal building (by, for example, rejecting blood quantum rules and adopting into the group all that need refuge), and one that provides not only a protected space but a place where humans are able to regroup and plan a counterattack. The reservation, a product of western expansion, is reimagined as a place of refuge and rebirth.

In the novel, the artificial intelligence behind the robot revolution develops new robots with more flexible mobility, and an attack is mounted on Gray Horse. The revitalized Osage Nation, while returning to precybernetic tradition (cultivating buffalo), also proves to be adaptable to new technologies. They use their own technical skills (and scavenged parts from robots), which they combine with Indigenous know-how and a kind of cowboy derring-do and style. When a grade of robots known as stumpers (they attach themselves to human appendages and explode) threatens Gray Horse, the Osage counterattack is aided by the appearance of "the legend himself, Lonnie Wayne Blanton," who seemingly "falls out of the sky." Blanton arrives on "a tall walker—one of Lark's Frankenstein projects. The thing is just two seven-foot-long robotic ostrich legs with an old rodeo saddle grafted onto it. Lonnie Wayne sits up top, cowboy boots pushed into stirrups and hand resting lazily on the pommel. Lonnie rides the tall walker like an old pro, hips swaying with each giraffe step of the machine. Just like a damn cowboy."[27]

Such "Frankenstein projects" are essential elements of speculative westerns, as the process of material assemblage of mismatched parts, of grafting materials from one genre ("seven-foot-long robotic ostrich legs") to another ("old rodeo saddle"), provides a metaphor for and metacommentary on the writer's process of genre hybridization. Ultimately, Lonnie saves the day with another western relic. The heat of human bodies causes the stumpers to trigger, and as Lonnie looks out on all the stumpers swarming through the prairie grass, he pulls out an "antique Zippo lighter," which he drops into the hand of narrator Cormac Wallace. Cormac observes, "A double R symbol is painted on the side, along with the words 'King of the Cowboys.'" With a smile, Lonnie says, "Let old Roy Rogers help ya out."[28]

In this speculative western, out on the Oklahoma prairie of the future, an Osage Roy Rogers rides tall in the saddle on a robotic horse—the Indigenous cowboy supplanting the white hero of the classic western. This scene provides an exemplary moment of simultaneity, of belonging to multiple genres at once, and the pure fun of the scene comes from its intentionality, its recirculation of the tropes of the western in a way that is parodic but that also draws on their mythic qualities. Scenes such as this one are signature moments in the narratives of the speculative West.

William Handley and Nathaniel Lewis observe in their introduction to the anthology *True West*, "There are few terms at play in the history of this vast region that have as wide a reach and relevance, and there is no other region in America that is as haunted by the elusive appeal, legitimating power, and nostalgic pull of authenticity."[29] As Nathanial Lewis demonstrates, notions of western authenticity emerge in the 1830s, when writers such as Timothy Flint and James Hall "were energetically voicing the need for a recognized literature of the West" and, in their writing, actively constructed a concept of western literature in opposition to the emerging writing of the American Renaissance—

the imaginative romantic tradition of Hawthorne, Poe, Sedgwick, and Longfellow. "If," Lewis writes, "authorship in eastern writers increasingly emphasized the individualized authorial personality and imaginative genius, authorship in the West revolved first around the perceived *authenticity* of the work and *authority* of the writer." What defined the quality of an authentic and authentically western text was "not imaginative originality but the stunning and even original presence of western landscape and people."[30] That speculative works (which are, almost by definition, works of "imaginative originality") are not regularly included in discussions of western writing is at least partially a result of this enduring philosophy of what constitutes authentically western art.

Quoting Jacques Derrida, Campbell argues that the western's "'living on' in new or altered forms" involves "'a sort of participation without belonging—a taking part in without being part of.'"[31] In narratives of the speculative West, subordinating the western to another genre helps create a critical distance from the form, potentially creating a "space of reflection, a critical dialogue with the form, its assumptions and histories."[32] As Joanna Hearne observes, "The pedagogic work of Westerns is closely related to the genre's emotional involvement in telling stories about history. Often targeted toward children and marketed as family fare, Westerns teach history by claiming frontier realism, even within the genre's more melodramatic modes of storytelling."[33] Speculative westerns, by intentionally bringing the fantastic and the futuristic to the form, undermine the western's claim to "authenticity" and "frontier realism" and challenge the "stories about history" that westerns have told.

In *The Politics of Aesthetics*, Jacques Ranciére writes, politics "revolves around what is seen and what can be said about it, around who has the ability to see and the talent to speak."[34] Society "polices" what "can be seen and said" in multiple ways that reinforce social hierarchies. In the context of the study of genre, the "rules of genre" (the identifiable conventions, characters, and iconography of a given genre) set the guidelines for what can be said within that genre, often reflecting the larger political strictures and hierarchies of society. The rules of the captivity narrative and the western, for example, define what is seen and said in those stories, in part by establishing racial and gendered roles for the participants in those narratives. White women are captives, white men are heroic rescuers, and Native Americans are villainous captors.

As Ranciére argues, "maps of the sensible" (which include such things as the rules of genre and other aesthetic forms and conventions) restrict and limit what can be said and what can be done and restrict and limit *who* can be involved in the saying and doing, but aesthetic forms also provide a means to "reconfigure the map of the sensible."[35] It is possible to disrupt, break, rupture, and subvert those rules and roles and, by so doing, to intervene and potentially alter the social order. In *Migrant Futures*, Aimee Bahng points out that "the critique leveled by postcolonial speculative fiction writers examines some common science fiction tropes . . . and questions to what extent the genre itself reproduces the social and political ideologies of a system of science that has historically operated in close conjunction with imperialist and neocolonial enterprises."[36] For writers and artists of color, or for writers coming out of specific ethnic heritages, or for women (whose participation in male dominated genres has often been limited or, as Victoria Lamont pointed out in her women's history of the western, whose participation has been active but ignored by the processes of canonization), participation in dominant-culture narratives often involves a process of revising, remaking, and reconfiguring forms and genres and, by so doing, using the "potential power of the literary imagination to call forth new political economies, ways of living, and alternative relational structures; and different sorts of subjects into the world."[37]

Drawing on the work of Ranciére and on Deleuze and Guattari's idea of "minor literature," Campbell writes, "The 'distribution of the sensible,' therefore, constitutes the 'major' language through which we come to know the West-as-region, *speaking* its myths, *circulating* its established discourses, and *approving* its ideologies. What is possible, however, is to unearth and experience what Deleuze and Guattari called the 'minor' at work alongside and within the major, not as a subsidiary or an insignificant language, but rather one that exists '*to send the major language racing*.'"[38] "Minor literature," Campbell writes, "is a foreign language operating *within* the dominant language because it asks questions of genres and how forms solidify and reinforce certain approved or presupposed values."[39] Similarly, I argue here that the speculative western performs as the "'minor' at work alongside and within the major," the straightforward "authentic" realist western, speaking against its myths, disrupting its claim to authenticity, interrupting its ideologies. Or at least, by creating a critical distance from the western through its explicit deployment of other genres, by deliberately introducing the foreign language of other genre conventions into the approved forms and defined structures of the western, the speculative western offers the potential for such disruption.

SPECULATIVE REGIONALITIES

Speculative Wests is located at the intersection of fields of study and the work of theorists not often considered together: the revisionist genre histories of Victoria Lamont's *Westerns: A Women's History*, Michael K. Johnson's *Hoo-Doo Cowboys and Bronze Buckaroos: Conceptions of the African American West*, and Joanna Hearne's *Native Recognitions: Indigenous Cinema and the Western*; the critical regionalism of Neil Campbell's *Post-Westerns* and *Affective Critical Regionality*; the speculative perspective of Aimee Bahng's *Migrant Futures*; and the emerging areas in race and ethnic studies attentive to Afrofuturism, Indigenous futurism, borderlands science fiction, and Latin American and Hispanic speculative literature.[40] *Speculative Wests* locates a discussion of the speculative within the framework of critical regionalism, as well as within genre studies, following an approach suggestive of what Neil Campbell refers to as the study of "the *regionalities* of the American West," an investigation of western places as involving the "intersection of many entangled lines," rather than the more traditional approach of "understanding region as straight lines, neat borders, simple rootedness, or fixed points."[41] "The West," Campbell writes, is "mired in a universal claim to centrality and dominance," to the idea of manifest destiny, to the centrality of whiteness in the telling of western history. Regionality, Campbell argues, instead "places the emphasis upon process and becoming rather than established ground and invariance so that the circled unanimity is challenged by multiple processes, little refrains, local histories."[42]

We see a similar understanding of region as regionality in Emily Lutenski's *West of Harlem: African American Writers and the Borderlands*, particularly her way of conceptualizing the borderlands, which she understands both as a specific geographic region encompassing the U.S. Southwest and northern Mexico and as a more general area defined as much by its multiethnic demographics as by its geographical place.[43] In her discussion of Arna Bontemps's *God Sends Sunday*, she notes that Bontemps describes a Los Angeles neighborhood that is "both African American and multiethnic," a place of complex networks of relationships between "African Americans, Mexican Americans, Filipinos, and whites" who live in a western place, which, she argues, constitutes a borderlands of multiethnic communities, one "that fosters a racial egalitarianism."[44] That is, Lutenski imagines an approach to regionalism that is grounded in specific concrete places but not limited by the traditional lines, boundaries, and geographies that generally inform place studies. The emphasis instead is on the borderlands created by complex networks of relationships.

Although Aimee Bahng does not situate *Migrant Futures* in western studies, she notes the importance of a specific western place to her own development as a reader of speculative works: "The project emerges in many ways from my particular affiliation with Pasadena, California," home of NASA's Jet Propulsion Laboratory and Caltech, as well as "black speculative fiction writer Octavia Estelle Butler," and adjacent to the sprawl of Los Angeles and the "'imagineering' ethos of Disney and Hollywood." As an Asian American growing up in a western city with "a racially tense and divided environment," Bahng found "a sense of outsider commiseration in the video arcades and comic book stores."[45] In a description that uses language that will be familiar to anyone involved in critical regional studies, she observes, "The realm of science fiction was also a bustling contact zone for urban youth of color whose interests in popular media affiliated with science fiction . . . constituted one of the few opportunities for cross-ethnic solidarities in an otherwise segregated and gender-normative landscape." Against the official maps of social organization created by "racially unequal systems of housing, fissured with decades of redlining practices and the dismantling of public transportation, libraries, education, parks, and other meeting places," Bahng and her friends created their own map of Pasadena and Los Angeles, one that centered the importance of video arcades and comic book stores and one that encouraged a complex network of relationships in the form of "playful assembly in the literary, gaming, and role-playing worlds associated with science fiction."[46] As does Campbell, Bahng places the emphasis on "process and becoming rather than established ground and invariance," on the "multiple processes," the "many entangled lines," the "little refrains," and the "playful assemblies" (to borrow Bahng's phrase) that constitute an alternate cartography of place.

In *South of Pico: African American Artists in Los Angeles in the 1960s and 1970s*, Kellie Jones practices a critical regionalism that centers on African Americans and African American migration to the West generally and to California particularly.[47] However, Jones places that specific migration within the larger context of global Black migration, arguing that "the West became interchangeable with other locales that African Americans imagined offered prosperity and freedom from brutality and second-class citizenship. Was it a space in this country or a space in the world? Was it California, Africa, or Kansas?"[48] African American western migration, Jones writes, is a history of constructing place through "spatial movements," a history made visible by a cartography attentive to mapping bodies in motion "creating new paths to selfhood and enfranchisement." Such movements, Jones argues, are "assertions of space" that create "place, whether actual sites in the world or positions in the global imagination."[49]

Jones's emphasis on movement and imagination as constructive of place suggests a potential connection between the domains of western history, critical regionalism, western cultural studies, and place-oriented theoretical approaches to African American studies and the work of writers and artists of color involved in the rapidly expanding speculative and futurist fields. Contemporary speculative artworks similarly explore new concepts of space and place, past and future, conceived as both "actual sites in the world" and positions in the imagination, as a real history of bodies and spatial movements and an exploration of possible histories and places existing outside the limitations of the here and now and the here and then. Taking together Jones's idea of the West in the African American imagination as "interchangeable with other locales," Lutenski's imagining of the borderlands as a concrete place defined as much by the network of relationships it contains as geographic location, and Campbell's "emphasis upon process and becoming rather than established ground and invariance," *Speculative Wests* shifts away from a critical regionalism grounded in the analysis of realist works to posit a *speculative regionality* involving imagined, fantastic, and future western places.

At the center of Maurice Broaddus's young adult steampunk novel *Buffalo Soldier* is a kind of Jamaican cowboy, Desmond Coke, whom we first meet sitting beneath a cottonwood tree and "under the strange western sky" of the Tejas Free Republic, rolling a cigarette.[50] The *Buffalo Soldier* title is a playful double reference, both to the specifically African American history of the American West that the phrase suggests (the late nineteenth-century Black cavalry troops who served in the American West, the Ninth Cavalry, stationed in West Texas, and the Tenth Cavalry, based in Kansas) and to the song "Buffalo Soldier" (also commemorating the Black western troops), written and performed by Jamaican reggae artist Bob Marley. Coke is, in a sense, the "buffalo soldier" of the book's title and of Marley's song; like the hero of the song, Coke is journeying through "the heart of America," "fighting on arrival" from his Jamaican homeland, and "fighting for survival" as the story advances.

Unlike the usual western cowboy, his cigarette is actually a marijuana-filled spliff. When offered a cigarette with "Carolina-grown" tobacco, he declines, saying, "I have my own," and "with quite the production, he took a long hit, held the smoke for several heartbeats before letting loose a thick cloud of smoke." "An unusual odor, I must say," someone observes. "It's not from Carolina," Coke explains.[51] And unlike the usual western cowboy, he prefers a more colorful style of dress, "a light red shirt, mostly hidden by a yellow cross-hatched vest, topped with a green bow tie," which, he ultimately realizes, makes him stick out too much, "ever the *obroni*, the outsider, as his people called him." And he observes, even after changing to a drab outfit "with no flamboyant shading," "he was still too brown, with too much accent."[52]

Coke is not a cowboy in the traditional sense of the word, although he is easily identifiable as the outlaw-hero character type often associated with the western. Coke is, or was, a member of "a Jamaican dissident group, the Order of the *Niyabingi*," specially trained "to fight imperialism wherever we find it."[53] He has left Jamaica with a child named Lij, helping the boy escape from the plans the Jamaican ruling class have for him. The novel traces their westward journey to California through a reimagined United States of competing territories: Albion (in the novel's version of history, still a colony of England and serving the crown and occupying a geography similar to the United States without Texas, the southwest, and the Pacific Coast states); the Tejas Free Republic; and the Assembly of First Nations, which occupies a large swath of western territory carrying the name California. The novel's time period is also not the traditional nineteenth century of the western. Though not exactly stated, the time seems to be roughly contemporary, although the novel combines nineteenth-century technology (steam power), contemporary technology (solar panels), and futurist technology (pulse weapons).

As a science fiction subgenre, alternate or alternative histories present "a version of the past in which some historical event yields an outcome other than what we know," creating thereby "alternative versions of our present moment and possible futures."[54] "These imagined interventions in actual historical events," Spurgeon writes, "can offer a fruitful method for thinking through current and past systemic realities and injustices" and, by so doing, can provide "a means of resistance to contemporary social, political, and economic structures by insisting on the historical contingency, rather than the supposed inevitably, of such structures." Alternative histories of the American West, which play against a dominant historical narrative that insists on the "manifest destiny" of the contemporary social, political, and economic structure of the United States, can perform "a decolonizing function by subverting the presumed naturalness and inevitability at the heart of colonialist histories of the sort frequently found in westerns."[55] Alternative histories that reimagine the history of the American West while also engaging with the western form may function to decolonize and to subvert both history and genre.

If the genre western is particularly noted for the repetition of the trope of the "vanishing Indian," *Buffalo Soldier* speculatively imagines an American West with a coalition of sovereign nations at its center.[56] The Assembly of First Nations is a powerful political entity, a home to ecological and technological innovation, and a bulwark against the white supremacist (and slaveholding) Albion Empire. Escaping from a saloon fight that breaks into a gun battle in the Tejas town of Abandon, Coke and Lij arrive in the border city of Wewoka, an alternate-history version of the capitol of the Seminole Nation, established in nineteenth-century Oklahoma Territory. This version of Wewoka is in what is called California, located on the border between the First Nations and Albion. Reflective of the actual history of the relationship between Seminoles and people of African descent, Coke and Lij seek refuge with the Seminole Nation, and by the end of the novel, they have become part of a mixed-race community.

Referencing Deleuze and Guattari's discussion of Franz Kafka, Campbell notes that Kafka "created minor literature without a standard notion of the 'the people' as already defined and established by state and nation, myth and representation, and instead voiced the potential of an unformed 'people to come.'"[57] Because of the nature of speculative artworks, particularly science fiction narratives and works that speculate about the future, they are often about the "people to come," at least in some sense. In books such as *Robopocalypse*, a catastrophic event (the robot uprising) fragments the "standard notion of 'the people' as already defined and established by state and nation," and the book's speculative project involves imagining how the survivors emerge and coalesce as a new group, the "people to come." Consistent with the speculative works examined here, the "people to come" in *Robopocalypse* are not predominately of European descent. In his short story "A History of Barbed Wire," Wilson imagines a world in which the Cherokee Nation, surrounded by a "Sovereign Wall," has become a refuge from a United States taken over by corporations, which has left many people impoverished and desperate—so desperate that they purchase DNA-altering medical procedures to create "a DNA signature that links to the Dawes Rolls" in an attempt to get tribal ID and access to the protected space of the Cherokee Nation.[58] European descent, a marker of privilege in the current configuration of the United States, is no longer desirable. For the "people to come" in Wilson's story, being Cherokee (or becoming "Cherokee") is so desirable that non-Natives are willing to alter their genes and risk everything to make it beyond the "Sovereign Wall."

Buffalo Soldier suggests, if not the "people to come," then the people who might have been, basing that speculation on the real historical existence of mixed-race communities such as Wewoka. The community that emerges in Buffalo Soldier centers on a coalition of Native American and First Nations groups, but it also comes to include migrants such as the Jamaicans Coke and Lij. If the futurism of Robopocalypse explores what might be, then the alternate history of Buffalo Soldier shows us a map of what might have been: if Jamaica had emerged as a rival power to European empires; if Texas had successfully resisted incorporation into the United States and thereby thrown "a cog into Albion's Western Design dream: a coast-to-coast version of the United States"; if Indigenous peoples had adapted the strategy of the coalition of sovereign nations and moved westward to occupy California and established a well-defended boarder that prevented the territory of the United States from reaching the Pacific Ocean.[59] Buffalo Soldier demonstrates that western expansion was neither manifest nor destined and, by extension, suggests that other political and geographic configurations of what is now the United States are possible in the future.

Speculative regionality emerges in Buffalo Soldier and in other speculative works not just demographically ("the people to come") but cartographically—through descriptive maps of the past, present, and future of western places. Buffalo Soldier uses the science fiction subgenre of alternate history to also suggest an alternate cartography, a remapping of the American West, one that both acknowledges and disrupts the real history of westward expansion and one that reimagines another possible outcome to the colonialist and imperialist impulses that created the currently existing map of North America.

In his discussion of the writing of Rebecca Solnit, Campbell observes, "Solnit is fascinated by maps and, most importantly, the desire to 'remap' and thereby shift perceptions and alter perspectives which have too readily become taken for granted through established, dominant cartography and their 'supposedly seamless relations between unifying geographical accounts and systems of representation.'"[60] In science fiction, alternate history is similarly fascinated by maps and by the possibilities of remapping—of undoing the "unifying geographical accounts" and "displacing the [dominant] narrative(s)" as part of a larger project of exploring the contingency of the political and social arrangements in the world we know.

In Karen Tei Yamashita's *Tropic of Orange*, the latitudinal marker the Tropic of Cancer physically moves northward, the literal shift (rather than a remapping based on alternate political configuration) of that geographical marker causing "a physical disruption of space that intensifies the ramifications of both natural and manufactured borders on peoples and nations."[61] As the Tropic of Cancer moves north, it brings along with it "a new, normally excluded or contained population." The science-fictional concept of shifting continental movements rearranging the physical world figures the political alterations created by human migration in the real world. The figure of a changing geology and geography enables Yamashita to "imaginatively and provocatively [remap] the space of the West" to reflect "contemporary globalization through Los Angeles, the region-West, and its multiple relations with the world."[62] The "multiple experiences and stories of diverse peoples, moving across borders and frontiers," become in *Tropic of Orange* "an alternative atlas of affective performance, of region as relational, alive, still forming, shifting, and collapsing."[63]

Speculative writing offers the opportunity to represent literally the more figurative and ephemeral processes, perception shifts, and perspective alterations that Campbell describes in *Affective Critical Regionality*. Or rather than a literal rendering of metaphorical concepts, perhaps what happens in speculative art, as Seo-Young Chu argues in *Do Metaphors Dream of Literal Sheep? A Science-Fictional Theory of Representation*, is the creation of a "high-intensity variety of realism," in that such art has the "capacity to generate mimetic accounts of aspects of reality that defy straightforward representation."[64] *Tropic of Orange*, Bahng observes, "is a story whose geography remains in constant motion," creating "an elasticity of borders" that suggests through its physical metaphors (a literal and physical moving and changing of the landscape) aspects of reality (the "constantly shifting and contested dynamics of social power") that defy straightforward representation.[65] Maureen Moynagh makes a similar point in discussing the speculative elements of Caribbean Canadian writer Nalo Hopkinson, arguing that the "political purchase of the fantasy and science fiction in Hopkinson's novels lies in their staging of the fantastic histories and equally fantastic relations that structure diasporic lives in the Americas."[66]

"Speculating from the margins," Bahng states, writers of color in speculative fields have become in the twenty-first century "the genre's emergent cultural producers."[67] Through their participation in speculative genres, contemporary writers of color are also intervening in the genre of the western and in the field of western regional writing, recasting western history and the history of the western, prompting us to rethink place, history, and genre. Emergent speculative writers, Ramírez writes, are transforming science fiction "into a rich, exciting, and politically charged medium for the interrogation of ideology, identity, historiography, and epistemology."[68] The speculative texts that I examine here are simultaneously and similarly transforming the western and narratives of the American West into a "rich, exciting, and politically charged" interrogation of the western genre and western history, geography, place, and region.

Speculative Wests is not alone in noticing the connections between the American West, the western, and speculative literature, as has been documented in the *Undead in the West* and *Undead in the West II* anthologies.[69] And as the recent critical anthology *Weird Westerns: Race, Gender, Genre* underscores, the hybrid western has a demonstrated potential for including voices and experiences that the classic western often excludes.[70] Additionally, recent critical studies that have focused more specifically on science fiction include Carl Abbott's *Frontiers Past and Future: Science Fiction and the American West* and William H. Katerberg's *Future West: Utopia and Apocalypse in Frontier*

Science Fiction.[71] *Speculative Wests* adds to these studies by focusing specifically on race and racial themes and by emphasizing works by or featuring African Americans, Indigenous people, and people of color. *Speculative Wests* differs from other studies by centering a framework that draws from critical regionalism as much as from genre studies and by paying greater attention to works featuring African American artists and writers and Latin American and Hispanic writers.

Speculative Wests differs from all the works mentioned above by adopting a narrower and more contemporary chronological focus. At least one central text in each chapter was published, produced, aired, or dropped in 2016 or later—2016 being the year that science fiction writer N. K. Jemisin became the first African American writer to win a Hugo Award for Best Science Fiction Novel (for *The Fifth Season*, the first book in the Broken Earth series), a defining landmark event for the current moment of speculative innovation.[72] I contextualize and situate these texts through reference to and analysis of a wider chronology of texts, but my central emphasis is an extended study of a particular moment in time, from 2016 to 2020, when BIPOC (Black, Indigenous, and people of color) writers and artists are emerging as major figures in speculative fields and when, simultaneously, there seems to be new interest among these writers and creators in reimagining the American West and the western through the framework of the speculative. In the spirit of "playful assembly," I juxtapose here texts from a variety of media: literature, film, and television, for the most part, but also comic books and music. Although I'm attentive to the distinctive formal elements of each medium and the different ways readers, viewers, and listeners experience those media, my approach follows my teaching practice and my everyday experience, both of which frequently join together novels and films, television and comic books, and other combined art forms. Individual chapters may focus on works in a particular medium, but I also move back and forth between one thing and another.

Three central themes weave in and out of the chapters of the book. First, I argue that speculative texts engage with the western as a means of genre critique, often including the western as part of a mix of influences as a way of commenting on the genre, as a means of drawing attention to its ideologies, silences, and absences and therefore to its claims to authenticity. Second, narratives of the speculative West explicitly address a history of trauma and the transmission of trauma. As Keith Clavin and Christopher J. La Casse comment, the western in general "is itself a genre defined by the post-traumatic," often populated by "soldiers and damaged psyches" and often involving "a man's quest for a reconciliation of a difficult or mysterious past through the use of violence and guns."[73] Many of the narratives of the speculative West discussed here center on investigating the trauma of western history, on examining the individual and collective effect of trauma, post-traumatic stress disorder, and transmission of trauma. Third, a study of the speculative West involves "meticulous inquiry" into western history.[74] As such, the western texts that I examine are often crossed with science fiction subgenres particularly attuned to the investigation of history: alternate history, future history, and especially time travel, a science-fictional trope that is particularly useful for speculating about history, its contingency as well as its intractability, and especially as a narrative device for uncovering the truths about historical events that conventional histories distort, conceal, or ignore. One of the surprises of this project was the volume and variety of western time-travel narratives, and thus *Speculative Wests* frequently follows the complex paths these narratives track through western time and space.

Chapter 1, "Race, Time Travel, and the Western," investigates speculative texts that involve time travel to the nineteenth-century American West. The chapter provides an overview of the time-travel western as a hybrid genre, one that appears in a variety of media (literature, film, television, comic books) and one that has developed its own set of conventions, while at the same time drawing on familiar tropes of the two (and sometimes more) genres that it combines. I argue that the time-travel western re-creates the western form to appeal to the sensibilities of a twenty-first-century audience—by bringing, for example, currently popular genre character types, such as superheroes, into an Old West setting. Contemporary television series such as DC's *Legends of Tomorrow* on the CW and the NBC series *Timeless* also bring a gender-balanced and multiethnic cast to the Old West setting of their time-travel adventures. This chapter also sets out the theories of genre and reviews the genres that ground the book as a whole, as well as providing definitional overviews of science fiction and the western as genres.

Chapter 2, "Trauma, Time Travel, and Legacies of Violence," continues with the theme of time travel. The first part of this chapter sets out some of the parallels between narratives of trauma and narratives of time travel, before turning its attention to a series of western texts that take us back in time to moments of traumatic violence in western history. Ultimately, the chapter focuses on the 2019 HBO adaptation of the *Watchmen* graphic novel, as the series transforms Alan Moore's story of masked crime-fighting vigilantes into a story of the speculative West by resetting the primary location to Tulsa, Oklahoma, and by centering the story on the ongoing effects of the 1921 Tulsa race massacre (and the continuing threat of white supremacist violence) as they are felt in the 2019 present of the story. In a key episode of the series, slipstream time travel takes us back to 1921 to experience those violent events firsthand. As the second chapter of the book, "Trauma, Time Travel, and Legacies of Violence" provides the framework for understanding trauma and the representation of trauma that informs the remainder of the book.

In chapter 3 I argue that to reclaim Native space, Indigenous artists use the hybrid genre of the speculative western to remap western places and to rewrite the western, intervening in both geography and genre, thereby creating an alternate cartography of the West and the western. My focus here is the representation of the desert Southwest and, more specifically, the Navajo homeland, Dinétah, as that space is depicted in a variety of texts by Native American artists, including the 2012 film *The 6th World: An Origin Story*, by Navajo filmmaker Nanobah Becker, and two novels by Rebecca Roanhorse (Native American and African American), *Trail of Lightning* and *Storm of Locusts*, which are part of a series of books set in a Dinétah of the future.[75] These texts combine the western with elements of Indigenous futurist conventions, themes, and philosophies, creating opportunities for investigating the western from a position that is both inside and outside the genre and offering an opportunity, as well, for intervening in representational practices related to the western landscape. This chapter continues the investigation of the western as genre, adding to that discussion an analysis of the western as trauma. Finally, this chapter further develops the concepts of speculative regionality and speculative cartography sketched out in the introduction, in turn establishing a framework for the specific investigation of speculative borderlands cartography in the chapters that follow.

Chapters 4 and 5 examine the science-fictional representation of life in the borderlands—of living in the social space of a contact zone. These chapters bring together many of the threads of the book as a whole: genre hybridity, time travel, representations of post-traumatic stress disorder, and speculative regionality. Chapter 4 focuses on Rudolfo Anaya's ChupaCabra novel series, which is set in the twenty-first century and employs such speculative elements as mythical creatures, flying saucers, genetic experimentation, and time travel to imaginatively explore a borderlands experience that mixes together folkloric and science-fictional creatures from different cultural traditions and that ultimately collapses the boundaries between past and present. In chapter 5 I look at two time-travel narratives that explore trauma and post-traumatic stress disorder through the broader geographical concept of the borderlands.

The Amazon Prime series *Undone* plays out in the specific place of San Antonio, Texas, using its geographical location to suggest main character Alma's larger connection to the sociology of living in the borderlands. Alma's geographic mobility in the story is paralleled by her growing ability to travel temporally, as she goes back in time to investigate a history marked by personal trauma. In Alfredo Véa's *The Mexican Flyboy*, main character Simon Vegas travels through time in order to rescue victims of violence throughout history.[76] As does Rudolfo Anaya in his ChupaCabra books, *Undone* and *The Mexican Flyboy* extend the concept of the borderlands as a contact zone by connecting it to the science fiction trope of time travel, reimagining a cartography of the borderlands that emphasizes the dimension of temporality, the exploration of the frontiers and crossroads of time as well as space. The necessary fluidity of living in the social, political, and geographical place of the borderlands is reflected in the time traveler's ability to move temporally. Or we might say that both *Undone* and *The Mexican Flyboy* use the device of time travel to actualize the lived experience of borderlands temporality.

Chapter 6, "Speculative Slave Narrative Westerns," examines multigenre texts that bring together elements of Afrofuturism with two popular genres that both have their source in nineteenth-century American literature: the slave narrative and the western. This chapter suggests that the specifically African American genre of the slave narrative has proven to be as durable and as flexible a genre form as the western, science fiction, fantasy, and horror. As Campbell writes of the western, the slave narrative has continued to live on as a vibrant and productive form by "traveling across generic boundaries, poaching and borrowing from many different earlier traditions," and by combining in unexpected ways with other types of narratives.[77] My focus for this chapter is speculative western narratives that explicitly engage slavery, the slave narrative tradition, or both, as those elements also reimagine the American West of western tradition through a science-fictional or fantastical frontier setting. Those works fall into several categories in their relationship to the western: science fiction westerns, as in the film *The Brother from Another Planet*, where the reimagined setting is Earth itself, which is experienced as a new frontier by a new arrival (the titular "Brother" from another planet); fantasy westerns, stories that are set in a fantastical other world that is identifiably and explicitly built on the model of the Old West, as in Charlotte Nicole Davis's *The Good Luck Girls*; and SF-horror westerns, as in Justine Ireland's *Dread Nation* and *Deathless Divide*, which take place in the traditional setting of the nineteenth-century American West, which has been speculatively altered by the presence of monsters—zombies, to be precise.[78] While science fiction and western hybrid texts continue to be central to the discussion, chapter 6 also branches out to include more emphasis on the fantasy and horror genres, thus shifting the discussion toward other hybrid formulations of the western and pointing toward future directions for investigating the speculative West.

Speculative Wests has been inspired by the rich outburst of speculative western stories that have appeared during the period in which much of the book's writing occurred: 2016–20. In the afterword, I reflect back on a period of time spent writing about the speculative in a historical moment that too often felt science-fictional. I look back through the lens of Mike Chen's 2020 novel *A Beginning at the End*, published early in the year 2020, just as global awareness of COVID-19 was starting to expand, and set (seemingly prophetically) in a postpandemic San Francisco six years after a devastating disease.[79] In the reimagined near-future (2025) American West of Chen's novel, his characters guide us toward a more hopeful future, building on a mythology of western transformation to imagine a new world emerging from disaster that is inclusive and humane.

Speculative Wests emphasizes close readings of a select group of texts, and it offers only a beginning, a sample of speculative work about the American West, and one that leaves large swathes uncovered. As new work continues to be published and created, as possible cartographies continue to be imagined, as we make new discoveries in the past about the predecessors of the twenty-first-century artists examined here, we will hopefully see new maps—and new mappings—of the speculative West continue to emerge.

Race, Time Travel, and the Western

Although the western no longer dominates the television schedule as it did in the 1960s and 1970s, twenty-first-century television continues to find ways to bring the venerable genre to contemporary screens, most creatively, perhaps, through hybrid generic forms. In several contemporary television series, the science fiction trope of time travel provides the means of joining the SF and western genres. By mixing genres, the time-travel western re-creates the western form to appeal to the sensibilities of a twenty-first-century audience—by bringing, for example, currently popular genre character types, such as superheroes, into an Old West setting. These contemporary television shows also bring a gender-balanced and multiethnic cast to a genre that in its classic form has repeatedly been critiqued for lacking those qualities.

This chapter provides an overview of the time-travel western as a hybrid genre, one that has developed its own set of conventions, while at the same time drawing on familiar tropes of the two (and sometimes more) genres that it combines. Although television time-travel westerns will be at the center of the discussion, I will also provide a larger context by talking about some time-travel westerns in other media, such as literature, film, and comic books. The chapter also outlines a discussion of race in science fiction and the western (and in popular genres generally). Although there are comic book precedents (weird westerns being a comics staple) for almost every chapter topic, comic book history seems particularly important here, because several of the television shows that I will discuss involve adaptations of characters first created for comic books.

For my primary examples, I will focus on the first seasons of two television shows, DC's *Legends of Tomorrow*, a time-travel superhero series airing on the CW, and the NBC series *Timeless*. *Legends* follows the adventures of time master Rip Hunter (Arthur Darvill), who (in season 1) chases supervillain Vandal Savage (Casper Crump) through time, trying to prevent Savage from murdering his family and, by the way, preventing him from bringing about the end of the world. To aid in his quest, Rip recruits a team of superheroes (and super-villains turned hero). The team is inclusive in terms of gender and race, a diversity accomplished in part by casting African American and mixed-race actors for what in the comic books were originally white characters. In the episode "The Magnificent Eight," the group goes back in time to the fictional town of Salvation, in the Dakota Territory in the 1870s, a setting to which they return several times, including in the episodes "Outlaw Country" and "The Good, the Bad and the Cuddly."[1]

In *Timeless*, a trio of time travelers—an African American pilot and scientist (Rufus), a white female historian (Lucy), and a white male soldier (Wyatt)—journey through time chasing a villain (Garcia Flynn) who is attempting to change history. Two episodes from the first season address western history: "The Alamo" and "The Murder of Jesse James."[2] Similar to contemporary movies such as *Hidden Figures*, *Timeless* is attentive to recovering the "hidden figures" of history, especially the women and people of color who have been left out of dominant narratives.[3] Thus, "The Murder of Jesse James" focuses on the highly accomplished (but largely unknown) African American deputy U.S. marshal Bass Reeves. Although the prime directive of the time traveler is "don't change history," the goal of *Timeless* is to change the way we *see* history, by making visible some of history's hidden figures. "The Murder of Jesse James" revises both history and genre. As the episode depicts the actual historical figures Bass Reeves and Jesse James, it also evokes the character types, conventions, and iconography of the western, intervening in and commenting on the classic versions of the genre by placing an African American lawman at the center of the narrative and as the embodiment of western justice.

There are so many literary, comic book, cinematic, and televisual narratives that involve time travel to (and from) the Old West as to constitute a genre in itself, one that has developed its own set of conventions, character types, and iconography—as well as taking advantage of the full menu of conventions made available by the genres it brings together. In television, time-travel westerns feature in every era, from episodes of *The Twilight Zone* (1959–64) to *Voyagers* (1982–83) to *The Adventures of Brisco County, Jr.* (1993–94) and *Sliders* (1995–2000) to the recent *Timeless* (2016–18).[4] Many science fiction–oriented series have included an episode or episodes involving time travel—virtual or real—to the Old West, including *Star Trek* and *Doctor Who*.[5] The time travel sometimes involves a time machine (as with *Doctor Who*) or other device (as with the mysterious orb in *Brisco County, Jr.*). Or as with *Star Trek*'s holodeck adventures, it may involve a virtual West that the characters enter; or as in the case of *Sliders*, it may involve parallel universes, with the movement being between dimensions rather than through time, as such.

Time travel in general is a frequent trope in superhero comics, and everyone from Wonder Woman to Superman to the Black Panther have journeyed back in time to the Old West. In the *Black Panther* comic series, the two-volume story "Saddles Ablaze" takes T'Challa, via the aid of a pair of magical golden frogs, to the Old West town of Aberdeen, Texas, where he lands with his fellow travelers (including a doppelganger version of himself) in the sort of wide dusty street that provides the setting for many a gunfight—with startled horses in the background, along with visible signs of iconic western structures, such as a saloon and a barbershop.[6] Among other adventures, he meets Marvel western comics characters the Two-Gun Kid and the Rawhide Kid; for good measure, Thor and Loki show up as well. As the combination of Black Panther, the Two-Gun Kid, the Rawhide Kid, Thor, and Loki suggests, part of the appeal of frequent time-travel adventures in comics is to create the possibility of crossover stories between different comic lines (such as between superhero and western series). The marketing appeal of such crossovers is the opportunity to bring fans of the Rawhide Kid over to stories about Black Panther (and vice versa).

As with the television series *Timeless* and *Legends of Tomorrow*, the example of Black Panther suggests the way time travel can work as a strategy for introducing African American characters into western stories, as well as, in this case, offer an opportunity for an African American writer like Christopher Priest, primarily associated with superhero comics, to write a Black western. Likewise, when Justice League members are transported through time back to 1879 in the *Justice League Unlimited* animated television series episode "The Once and Future Thing, Part One: Weird Western Tales," African American writer Dwayne McDuffie has an opportunity to write a western story involving another Black superhero, the Green Lantern (voiced in the episode by African American actor Phil LaMarr).[7] When Green Lantern is transported to the Old West with fellow Justice League members Batman and Wonder Woman, they are met by a trio of outlaws, including an African American gunman whose costuming (including a distinctive black hat) and facial features seem to be modeled after actor Woody Strode and the outlaw character he played in *Once upon a Time in the West*.[8] In addition to giving Green Lantern a chance to display his gun-spinning skills (as he smoothly holsters a pistol taken from the would-be outlaws who tried to hold them up), the episode (through this brief appearance of a Black outlaw character) provides an opportunity to pay homage to one of western film's most important African American actors—one who played roles in multiple John Ford westerns as well as in Sergio Leone's classic spaghetti western.[9]

The 1966 television series *The Time Tunnel* featured a building-sized cornucopia-like device that time travelers walked into in order to begin their trips through time. Two of the scientists associated with the development of the time tunnel (code named Project Tic-Toc), Tony Newman and Doug Phillips, enter the device before it's fully tested and become lost in time. The Project Tic-Toc scientists remaining at the home base are able to monitor and eavesdrop on Tony and Doug; in moments of danger, they manipulate the device to cause them to shift elsewhere in time. But they can't control where or when Tony and Doug land and are therefore unable to bring them back to their own time. Thus, each episode sees the travelers in a different moment in time.

The Time Tunnel includes several western adventures, including trips to the Alamo and to the Battle of the Little Bighorn. As will be explored in a later chapter, time travel to a western site of violence, trauma, or massacre is a repeated convention of the time-travel western—with the Alamo and the Little Bighorn in particular serving as frequent destinations. Another repeated convention of the time-travel western is the encounter with famous western figures, especially those western outlaws and lawmen made famous through genre westerns. In the *Time Tunnel* episode "Billy the Kid," Tony and Doug encounter that famed western outlaw in a prison cell.[10] When the Kid escapes and threatens Tony's life, Doug shoots him. Added to the guilt he feels as a generally nonviolent scientist, Doug is devastated because he fears that by killing Billy, he has altered the time line, the big taboo of time travel. When the Kid later shows up alive and well (saved from the bullet by his large belt buckle) and set on revenge, Doug is so enthusiastically glad to see him—much to Billy's puzzlement—that he even reveals the truth about his being a time traveler (which also puzzles Billy and angers him because he thinks Doug is lying to him). Later in the episode, the Project Tic-Toc scientists project their voices into the past, fooling Billy into believing he is surrounded by a posse and allowing Doug and Tony to get the jump on the distracted Billy. The conversation between the characters serves as a metacommentary on genre, and much of Billy's anger in the episode occurs when Tony and Doug fail to play by the rules of the western. "Don't make the same mistake I did," Billy advises as they tie him up rather than killing him. "Blaze away!" When Doug reveals that there's no posse, only "a voice from the future," a dejected Billy grumbles, "There you go with that time talk again," and hangs his head in disappointment, as if he would much rather take a bullet that ends his life (which he finds acceptable because it follows the genre rules he expects) than have to deal with the inexplicable rules and conventions of time travel.

If these stories send contemporary characters back to the Old West, others do the opposite, bringing a character from the past into the present. In the 1986 television series *Outlaws*, an entire gang of outlaws, along with the sheriff chasing them, is transported from 1886 to 1986 via a lightning strike.[11] In Marvel's *Red Wolf: Man out of Time*, the Cheyenne character Red Wolf travels from 1872 in the town of Timely in the New Mexico Territory, where he has taken over the job of the town's sheriff, to the contemporary Santa Rosa, New Mexico, where he similarly finds himself involved in law enforcement (but with supernatural and cybernetic villains).[12] A central figure of weird western comics, Jonah Hex has traveled (backward and forward) through time on multiple occasions, often in the company of other members of the Justice League of America; in "Crisis from Tomorrow," he even engages in a gun battle with a Tyrannosaurus Rex.[13]

In time-travel narratives in general, the means of time travel varies, although it is usually via scientific (a time machine) or supernatural means. Marty McFly famously travels through time in a scientifically modified DeLorean. In *MacGyver*, Richard Dean Anderson falls asleep to wake up (a popular means of time travel, as is being knocked unconscious) in the Old West town of Serenity.[14] *A Modern Day Western: The Sanchez Saga* posits perhaps the most unique means of time travel. Outlaw Reno Sanchez escapes hanging in 1884 Texas by chewing on the worm from the bottom of a tequila bottle, which transports him to contemporary America.[15] In the official video for Lil Nas X's "Old Town Road" (featuring Billy Ray Cyrus), outlaw hero Lil Nas X escapes in 1889 on his fast horse from a posse and from a homesteader with a rifle by jumping through a cellar door into a long underground tunnel that somehow transports him to California in 2019.[16] In the time-travel western, the means of time travel may be virtual (e.g., *Star Trek*'s holodeck); technological (i.e., a time machine); supernatural or magical (e.g., a shaman, golden frogs, or the intervention of a supernatural entity like an angel or demon); or natural, if somewhat strange (e.g., a lightning strike, sleep, a blow to the head, a mysterious tunnel or portal). Or it may be the effect of some other plot device (e.g., a tequila worm).

Sometimes intersecting or adjacent to the time-travel western, a science fiction subgenre that is specifically in tune with Indigenous speculative fiction is what Grace Dillon terms "Native slipstream, a species of speculative fiction within the sf realm, [which] infuses stories with time travel, alternate realities and multiverses, and alternative histories."[17] Slipstream stories may involve time travel without a time machine, or the movement in the story may not be so much backward or forward in time as from one reality, dimension, or universe to another (in which case, the different reality may represent a different time period than that of the traveler, but the movement is from one dimension to another, rather than to different points on the same time line). Native slipstream, Dillon notes, "replicates nonlinear thinking about time and space" and suggests an understanding of time that is not necessarily science-fictional but is in keeping with Indigenous concepts of time and thus "models a cultural experience of reality" rather than (or in addition to) a set of genre conventions.[18] Dillon discusses slipstream in both Native and non-Native contexts, with the non-Native use of the term seeming to have originated with writer Bruce Sterling in 1989 as "an attempt 'to understand a kind of fiction . . . that was not true science fiction, and yet bore some relation to science fiction.' Notably absent from Sterling's original list of 135 so-called slipstream writers" were any Indigenous writers, despite "the abundance of slipstream elements in the works of" Gerald Vizenor (Anishinaabe), Thomas King (Cherokee), and many others.[19]

In Vizenor's *Custer on the Slipstream*, reincarnation serves as the figure for time travel, as we follow both General George Armstrong Custer and Crazy Horse in various incarnations through time, exhibiting the same character traits and attitudes, whatever body each inhabits.[20] In Sherman Alexie's *Flight*, protagonist Zits (his nickname) travels through time by slipping from one body to another, at one point experiencing moments from the Indian Wars (at Little Big Horn and, in another embodiment, at the site of another massacre, perhaps Wounded Knee) from within the bodies of both Native and white participants.[21] In the multivolume graphic novel *A Girl Called Echo*, written by Katherena Vermette (Metis), a thirteen-year-old Metis girl (Echo Desjardins) finds herself repeatedly traveling back in time to "Qu'Appelle Valley, North-West Territory (Now Saskatchewan), 1814," visiting a Metis camp, observing a buffalo hunt, as well as experiencing firsthand battles between Metis and settlers (the Pemmican Wars in the title of the first volume).[22] As she slips from one time period to another (sometimes while sleeping, sometimes while reading), what she learns about the past contributes to the reparation of her relationships in the present, especially as discussing moments of Metis history reconnects her with her estranged mother. As Dillon observes of Native slipstream in general, the genre "appeals because it allows authors to recover the native past, to bring it to the attention of contemporary readers, and to build better futures."[23] As a mode of time-travel western, Native slipstream also enables Indigenous writers to approach the history (and the historical figures) often placed at the center of genre westerns from a critical perspective, one that isn't necessarily constrained by the genre conventions (as a time-travel western might be) of either the western or science fiction. Chapter 2 will return to Native slipstream stories, with a particular interest in Alexie's *Flight*.

In the works I'm classifying as time-travel westerns, particular western locations stand out as frequently visited settings. Tombstone features prominently in time-travel westerns that take contemporary characters back to the western past. In *Doctor Who*'s "A Holiday for the Doctor," the Doctor visits Tombstone seeking Doc Holliday's help with a toothache.[24] The contemporary *Doctor Who* series has had frequent episodes set in the American West (because Stetsons are cool). "A Town Called Mercy" is not set in Tombstone, but the typical structure of such a story is a town tamer, during which the stranger in town, the time traveler, takes on the Wyatt Earp role of protecting the town from a group of outlaws—or as in "A Town Called Mercy," a single cyborg gunfighter.[25] *Back to the Future III* follows a similar pattern (with Hill Valley, California, as the threatened town).[26] It also establishes the trope of the contemporary character adopting a familiar name—not of a historical western figure but of a western actor: Clint Eastwood, Marty McFly's adopted western name.[27]

As naming oneself Clint Eastwood suggests, the Old West of the time-travel western is often not the West of historical reality but the mythic West of the western. In this sense, time travel serves as an engine for genre mixing. Jim Collins observes that "hyperconsciousness" (such as knowing references to other films) and hybridity have been prevalent features of genre films since the 1990s. Using *Back to the Future III* as a primary example, he notes that within the Old West of the film, "we enter a narrative universe defined by impertinent connections, no longer sustainable by one set of generic conventions. We encounter, instead, different sets of generic conventions that intermingle, constituting a profoundly intertextual diegesis, nowhere more apparent than in the shot of the DeLorean time machine being pulled through the desert by a team of horses, the very co-presence of John Ford and H. G. Wells demonstrating the film's ability to access both as simultaneous narrative options." Such moments of "co-presence" or "simultaneity" in the hybrid genre text encourage us to recognize and enjoy the impertinence of the connections they make.[28]

Thus, in the *Black Panther* story "Saddles Ablaze," the title is just one of the many references to the comedy western *Blazing Saddles*—perhaps the best known western to feature an African American hero (Cleavon Little as the new sheriff of the decidedly racist western town of Rock Ridge).[29] The *Black Panther* references to *Blazing Saddles* don't just suggest an awareness of the western but specifically point to the *Black western* as a reference point. Time-travel narratives are often metanarratives that comment explicitly on their status as genre stories, in part by making obvious allusions to other texts in the genre, such as explicit references to western films, like naming oneself after a western actor rather than a western historical figure, or the inclusion of science-fictional figures, like H. G. Wells, author of *The Time Machine*, as a character in the story (and Wells appears frequently in both time-travel and science-fictional stories).

In "Tempus Fugitive," an episode of *Lois and Clark: The New Adventures of Superman*, an alien named Tempus kidnaps H. G. Wells and his time machine as part of a plan to travel back in time to the day of Kal-El's arrival in Smallville, Kansas, in order to kill him as a vulnerable infant. In the present, Wells manages to tip off Clark Kent, who, with Wells's instructions, builds his own version of the time machine.[30] Due to a miscalculation, Tempus lands in the nineteenth century, at the time when Smallville was a frontier town and at a moment when Jesse and Frank James happen to be visiting the town saloon (which is operated by the great-grandmother of Jonathan Kent, who is married to the local sheriff, Jonathan's great-grandfather). The historical figures of Wells, famous in the world of science fiction, and the James brothers, famous in western history and western legend, signal the copresence of the episode's genres. When Clark intervenes in a saloon shoot-out by using his superpowers to capture the James brothers, there is another moment of simultaneity, as the tropes of each genre (gunfights versus superpowers) intermingle in the same scene. Clark does what many a western hero has done before him, disarms and captures the outlaws, although he uses his superspeed rather than his accurate gunfire to do so. Likewise, taking the wounded Sheriff Kent to the doctor (using his superpower of flight) is exactly what the cowboy hero would do. But it's also an action that is in keeping with the conventions of time travel; Clark preserves the time line by making sure that the ancestor of Jonathan Kent doesn't die before he's supposed to.

In the episode "The Good, the Bad, and the Wealthy," the dimension shifters of *Sliders* enter a parallel world where the Republic of Texas has expanded to the West Coast, and they land in a late twentieth-century version of San Francisco where the code of the Old West has been adapted to the field of business.[31] Lawyers are literally hired guns, contract negotiations are gunfights, and a hostile takeover might involve a challenge to a fast draw contest from Billy the Kid. Above the bar inside the Wall Street Saloon (in what otherwise looks like a typical western saloon) is a digital display reporting stock market prices. Three-piece suits with bolos, cowboy hats, and holstered pistols are the company dress code. The episode is sprinkled with characters named Bullock, Dalton, and Sutter.

The journey here is to an alternate-history version of the present, rather than time travel to the Old West, but the episode follows the conventions of the time-travel western. That we are traveling into the western genre rather than to an actual western place is indicated both by the title (alluding to Sergio Leone's *The Good, the Bad, and the Ugly*) and by specific references to two western films in particular: *Shane* and *The Man Who Shot Liberty Valence*.[32] Just as Shane famously emerges out of the wilderness and rides up to the Starrett homestead watched by young Joey Starrett (Brandon De Wilde), the sliders emerge from the nothingness of the portal to arrive before the amazed eyes of young Jamie Hardaway. And just as Joey watches the climactic gun battle between Shane (Alan Ladd) and Jack Wilson (Jack Palance) by peeking beneath the saloon doors, Jaime watches the fight between series star Quinn (Jerry O'Connell) and gunslinging lawyer Jed Dalton (Barry Levy) while crouched outside and looking through a windowpane—and in the final scene of the episode, we have a close-up of Jaime after the sliders have departed, crying out, "Quinn, come back! Quinn!" Quinn, who tries to avoid the fight in the first place, becomes an instant legend by defeating Jed, but as is the case in *The Man Who Shot Liberty Valence*, the legend is not the same as the truth. The killing bullet was actually fired surreptitiously by Jaime's mother, Pricilla (Karen Lorre), as is the case in *The Man Who Shot Liberty Valence*, where Jimmy Stewart's Ransom Stoddard is credited with killing outlaw Liberty Valence (Lee Marvin), a shot actually fired by Tom Doniphon (John Wayne).

Although the American Civil War between the North and the South took place in this reality, the Republic of Texas remained neutral, concentrating on expanding its border westward instead. The fact of slavery in Texas is overlooked by the episode, which features an African American gunslinger-lawyer, Billy Ray Bledsoe (Kent Faulcon), who stylishly wears a black cowboy hat; easily bests another lawyer in a quick-draw contest (or contract negotiation); and although he works for episode antagonist Jack Bullock, eventually reveals that his allegiances (despite his black hat) are ultimately for the forces of good, as he steps out of the crowd to stand in front of Quinn to shield him from Bullock's gunfire. And in contrast to other western Black men who act selflessly to protect the white hero, he does not die in doing so—as he is merely the first of several townspeople, who follow his selfless gesture, to protect Quinn. Series regular Rembrant Brown (African American actor Cleavant Derricks) also takes part in the western action—sitting in for Pricilla Hardaway in a trading session (that is, a poker game) and demonstrating his skill at the western art of poker by winning several hundred thousand dollars of stock options for her company.

Thus, the time-travel western provides a means of incorporating African American actors into a western story, giving them important (if secondary) roles in the plot and in the action, although it does so by positing a postracial society in which Brown and Bledsoe are not marked as different. No one raises an eyebrow when the African American Rembrant sits down at the poker table, and no reference is made to either man's race during the episode. As Madhu Dubey writes, "Some critics have regarded the raceless futures of U.S. science fiction as evidence of the socially progressive tendencies of the genre," although others have pointed out that "the erasure of racial distinctions in science-fictional images of future societies might be indicative of an evasion of the race problem rather than a solution."[33] Questions related to race that the episode might have raised (such as: How did this version of Texas somehow not become entangled with slavery?) are simply not addressed, "an evasion of the race problem," rather than an attempt to grapple with it.

GENRE AND RACE

The Old West episodes of *Legends of Tomorrow* and *Timeless* are both western and science fiction and, as such, participate in two genres generally regarded as being unfriendly to African American authors, characters, and stories. African Americans, as authors, as actors, as directors, have nonetheless participated in each of those genres—with Pauline Hopkins's 1902 novel, *Winona: A Tale of Negro Life in the South and the Southwest*, being one of the first Black westerns.[34] Additionally, African American characters have appeared in both genres, particularly in film and television, from the earliest examples onward. And as critics Adilifu Nama and Isiah Lavender have pointed out, race has always been an important element of science fiction, even if racial issues are represented in allegorical form—with green-skinned aliens, for example, as a representation of an otherness that is coded as racial.[35]

As Andre Carrington argues in *Speculative Blackness*, because of the dominance of white writers and white readers in the world of science fiction, there is a "presumption of Whiteness" in the genre. Even allegorical explorations of race frequently replicate contemporaneous racial hierarchies by opposing the white hero against the alien other. Science fiction is as saturated "with race thinking as any other variety of popular culture, [and it has the tendency] to reproduce conventional understandings of race."[36] The presumption of whiteness, Carrington argues, goes a long way to explaining why many Black writers and Black readers experience alienation from the genre. Nonetheless, Carrington argues, and his argument here could just as easily be applied to the western or to most any other popular genre, "Black people's significance for speculative fiction— and sometimes our alienation from it—can be the point of departure for understanding in a more profound way what genre has to do with racial identity."[37] "Every cultural form invented by Black people in the diaspora," Carrington writes, "from the sorrow songs to break dancing, demonstrates complex and potentially liberatory uses of existing cultural forms."[38] Even though "the overrepresentation of Whiteness and the comparatively limited involvement of Black people in producing speculative fiction both have a significant impact on what it means for Black people to locate ourselves in the ranks of the genre's authors and its audiences," African American artists may make "exemplary interventions in speculative fiction."[39]

Although *Timeless* has at least one African American staff writer, actor and screenwriter Anslem Richardson, who is one of the credited writers for the episode "The Murder of Jesse James," television is a collaborative medium, and we cannot lay claim to any television episode (even one with a credited Black writer or director) as a Black-authored text in the same way we would a novel. However, a television episode may nonetheless make an "exemplary intervention" in both science fiction and the western.

Even if there is not an identifiable African American writer involved, a text is still open to racial meanings and racial readings. Drawing on Stuart Hall's theory of preferred, negotiated, and oppositional readings, Nama writes that "intentionality does not restrict the meaning of a film nor is the message of a film passively consumed by an audience." Although there may be preferred meanings that a media text authorizes, "from an audience-centered perspective, the racial meaning of any SF film is up for grabs."[40] A television show is also a collaborative work, and the presence of African American actors in that work suggests at least a degree of African American input in the creation of the text. For television in particular, performance is central to the spectator's experience of the story. An actor or actress may suggest additional readings—open up possibilities of meaning making—through physical presence and performance that potentially go beyond those scripted by the writers, directors, costumers, set decorators, and other involved parties whose work is part of the collaborative text a television series creates.

A central text in studies of African American presence in science fiction has been *Star Trek: Deep Space Nine* (*DS9*), which featured African American actor Avery Brooks as Benjamin Cisco, Starfleet commander and head of the *Deep Space Nine* space station. Although not a western, the *DS9* episode "Far beyond the Stars" is a precursor to *Timeless* and *Legends* in terms of using time-travel conventions as means of addressing issues of race. Carrington's analysis of the episode helps sketch out a framework for thinking about race in other popular genre texts.[41] In "Far beyond the Stars" (which Brooks also directed), Cisco goes back in time (through mysterious means) to 1950s New York to live the life of Benny Russell, a science fiction staff writer for *Incredible Tales* magazine (whose race is unknown to the readers). During the episode, an inspired Russell writes a speculative story about a Black commander of a space station—a future that literally cannot be imagined in the 1950s, as indicated by the publisher's decision to destroy the issue rather than send it to the newsstand.

The major actors from *DS9* are recast in the episode as the individuals who populate Benny's world. Among the *Incredible Tales* staff writers, Nana Visitor plays Kay (pen name, K. C. Hunter, with the name and character being a nod to writer C. L. Moore, who likewise used initials to conceal her gender). When the editor announces that the publisher wishes to print a photograph of the writers, he also observes that Benny and Kay "can sleep late" that day. As Carrington writes, "The portrait of science fiction writers that 'Far beyond the Distant Stars' offers contends that women and people of color have been present as a creative force throughout the history of science fiction, but their contributions have disappeared."[42] *Timeless* in particular employs a similar ethics of critically examining the oppressive racial and gender formations of the past, and it likewise uses the science fiction trope of time travel to make that "disappeared" history visible.

Science fiction practitioners and advocates have pointed to the genre's utopian visions of the future as evidence of exceptionalism regarding race and ethnicity. *Star Trek* espoused an egalitarian view of the future that, however, it only rarely achieved in practice. By traveling back to the "golden age" of science fiction in the 1950s United States, "the episode would raise troubling questions about the inspirational rhetoric of science fiction—and *Star Trek* in particular—by situating the dynamics of racial conflict squarely within the history of the genre."[43] The episode shows the genre's complicity with—rather than transcendence of—white supremacy. "Far beyond the Stars" uses one of the science fiction genre's conventions (time travel) to critique the racial assumptions of the genre itself. Both *Timeless* and *Legends* similarly use genre stories to critique (implicitly or explicitly) the long-standing assumptions of the genres in which they participate.

"THE MAGNIFICENT EIGHT"

What Collins sees as a feature of contemporary genre films in general, the time-travel western foregrounds through its explicit interest in juxtaposing two time periods in a way that also draws our attention to the copresence of the two dominant genres that inform the story being told. Time-travel narratives are often Oedipal in nature; they return to the primal scene, to the place of origin.[44] Although science fiction, fantasy, and horror narratives that have western roots may conceal those roots (by replacing six-guns with ray guns, outlaws with zombies), the time-travel element makes that hybridity explicit in its juxtaposition of two historical moments (which also represent two different but related genres). The Oedipal return to the origins is also a return to genre origins, a means of explicitly acknowledging the western roots of what on the surface seems to be primarily science fiction, fantasy, or horror. In *The Time Tunnel*, the frequent (and cost-saving) use of stock footage suggests how much time travel in the series is also travel into movie and television history—as the characters immerse themselves not so much in a particular historical moment as in the remnants of old film footage. As Tony and Doug shift from one time period to another, their journeys are not so much from one historical moment to another as they are from one costume drama to another.

As the episode title "The Magnificent Eight" suggests, the western roots of *Legends of Tomorrow* go directly to the western film *The Magnificent Seven*, as indicated by Rip's recruitment of a team of misfits and sometimes ne'er-do-wells.[45] Rip Hunter has his own long history in DC comics—one not connected to the western. In contrast, this version of Rip has a backstory rooted in the western, and the episode takes us back to those origins, to a moment when SF hero Rip Hunter was a western hero. Rip's "magnificent" team includes Dr. Martin Stein and Jefferson Jackson (who merge together to become the superhero Firestorm), Sara Lance (aka Canary, who was trained by the League of Assassins), Ray Palmer (aka the Atom, clad in a robotic suit), Kendra Saunders (who becomes Hawkgirl), Leonard Snart (whose technological superpower is a freeze ray), and Mick Rory (who's handy with a fiery blaster). The superhero team is mostly white men but is inclusive of two women, one African American man (Jefferson Jackson, played by actor Franz Drameh), and the ethnically Egyptian Kendra Saunders (played by actress Ciara Renée, who identifies as ethnically mixed: African American, European, Native American, and Indian).[46] Although the Dr. Martin Stein half of Firestorm comes from the DC comics incarnation of the character, Jefferson Jackson is a new character created for the televisions series—and the pairing of the white Dr. Stein with the African American Jax is a new element as well.

The character Kendra Saunders is rooted in western comics. Kendra started out as Kate Manser, who first appeared in 1978 in *Weird Western Tales*. After her father's death, she adapted the persona of Cinnamon, trained as a gunfighter and martial artist, and sought revenge against the bank robbers who killed him. As her story plays out in the comic books, we learn that she has been incarnated in many different times in different forms, as Cinnamon, as Shiera Saunders-Hall, and as (her earliest incarnation) Egyptian princess Chay-Ara. She is immortal, sort of—in that she can be killed but she is always reincarnated—as is her paramour, Hawkman (Egyptian prince Khufu in his original incarnation, aka Carter Hall), although they don't always recognize one another in each new life.[47]

Kendra's roots in DC's western comics are a significant part of "The Magnificent Eight" episode, which alludes to her western origins as much as it reveals Rip's connection to the Old West. Kendra meets Cinnamon in the town saloon. She later visits Cinnamon's camp and realizes that she has, in fact, met her older self (or an older version of one of her selves). Cinnamon (a white character in the comics) is played by African American actress and writer Anna Deavere Smith, a casting choice that contributes to the episode's diversification of both the western and the superhero genres and that also references the historical reality of African American pioneers. Best known as the writer-performer of *Twilight: Los Angeles, 1992*, about the Los Angeles riots in the wake of the acquittal of the officers in the Rodney King case, Smith brings to the episode by her presence another layer of possible meaning, an evocation of more contemporary African American western history that is suggested allusively rather than explicitly.[48] Cinnamon also tells the story that connects *Legends'* superhero characters to their roots in the western. Not only does Kendra meet her western self (in the form of the character that was her first comic book incarnation), but Cinnamon also describes the western roots of Hawkman, whom she knew in his nineteenth-century incarnation as Hannibal Hawkes (aka Nighthawk). As Green comments on the character, "The evolution of the Western masked crimefighter known as Nighthawk into a superhero" is typical of the way many western comic book heroes were either retired or transformed "to make them relevant to a contemporary readership rooted in superheroes, science fiction and fantasy."[49] Hannibal Hawkes, a western hero who rides a horse and wears a costume with a hawk-wings insignia on the chest, essentially develops into a superhero when the artists remove the symbolic hawk wings and transform them into actual wings. The scene with Cinnamon, and her story of Hannibal Hawkes, provides the means of acknowledging the western roots of his contemporary incarnation, Hawkman—a character whom we eventually meet in later episodes of *Legends*. This episode, in the guise of a time-travel western, is also a lesson in comic book history.

The revelation of Rip Hunter's western origins, although different than the character's comic book origins, allegorically reflects the more general transition of comic book characters from one genre to another. In *Legends*, Rip Hunter's belonging to the western genre, even before "The Magnificent Eight" makes that connection explicit, is already indicated by his costuming, with his long brown duster, and by his choice of weapon, which looks like an old-fashioned revolver. He is the one character who doesn't change into western gear to fit in with the locals when the episode takes us back to the 1870s. Rip's costume is one way that the series signals its hybridity, its status as a speculative western. Rip has been in the Old West—and in the town of Salvation—before, and if he is not literally walking in the boots of one of weird western comics' best-known characters, he is literally wearing his coat. Jonah Hex and Rip Hunter are old friends who have fallen out. When they parted, Rip took Jonah's duster along—and named his son Jonas after him as an homage to his friend. The larger homage of the episode is to the weird western itself, acknowledging that hybrid genre's influence on *Legends*, and thus the inclusion of Jonah Hex (Johnathan Schaech) as a character in the story, acknowledging the best-known comic book weird western hero as the model for this version of Rip Hunter.

After a failed raid on the outlaw's ranch (in which each side takes a captive), the heroes and outlaws decide to settle things through a showdown on Main Street. Rip goes up against the outlaw leader. Whoever wins the gunfight also wins the release of the captive. This scene, from the elements of the mise-en-scène to the action, belongs to the genre of the western. The two men face each other in the middle of a muddy street, their pistols holstered, while spectators tensely watch from the sides. There are hip-level close-ups of hands poised above holstered pistols, intercut shots of spectators' faces, close-ups of the gunfighters' faces as they stare intently at one another. Both men draw, and the outlaw falls dead.

What happens next reflects the series' awareness of itself as a self-consciously hybrid generic form. Two genres require two fight scenes, so we have a second showdown. The setting remains that of the western—the muddy street of a frontier town—but the action belongs to the superhero genre. Three men in body armor march into town and start shooting laser-like bolts from their gauntleted hands. The Legends switch out their six-shooters for their own energy-powered weapons. Kendra takes off her western duster, exposing her hawklike wings, and takes flight. Jackson and Stein combine to become the red-and-gold-costumed Firestorm, thrust into the air by columns of fire shooting out of his legs—and literally returning fire by shooting it from his hands. This scene exemplifies hyperconscious hybridity. The action is both a full-scale western gunfight and a superhero action sequence, simultaneously, and the pleasure of the scene is the intermingling and copresence of the two genres: some characters in western costume, some in high-tech superhero gear, guns firing, lasers blasting, all playing out in the same western street that had just provided the setting for a quick-draw gunfight.

The first showdown celebrates the traditional western (and the bravery and skill of the single heroic male gunfighter). The second showdown suggests a critique of the first. In the first showdown, the African American character is tied up, held hostage, the object rather than the agent of the action, a typical scenario in westerns (or other genre works) with African American characters. Jackson, in fact, is a failure as a western hero. During the raid on the outlaw camp, all he manages to do is get himself captured, making possible—even necessary—the white male heroism of Rip. In the second showdown, in the persona of Firestorm, Jackson contributes to the action and the mayhem. Similarly, the whole team, male and female, are involved in the action, rather than simply watching the cowboy hero. If Jefferson Jackson and Kendra Saunders don't quite belong in the classic version of the genre western, this episode suggests, there is certainly a place for them in the speculative West.

"THE MURDER OF JESSE JAMES"

More so than *Legends of Tomorrow*, *Timeless* shares some of the same qualities and areas of emphasis as African American speculative fiction, in large part because of the centrality of Rufus, the African American scientist and time-ship pilot (one of three central characters rather than a member of a large ensemble). Additionally, *Timeless* is consistently attentive to African American points of view—and not just the individual point of view of Rufus (Malcolm Barrett). As Carrington points out, "Interpretations of the past shaped by attention to racial oppression as a driving force in history differentiate some SF works by Black authors from those writers focusing on the present, the future, and alternate realities from other points of view."[50] With some consistency, *Timeless* uses the character of Rufus to draw our attention to the presence of racial oppression as a driving force in the historical periods he visits. *Legends* does so as well but less frequently. Black speculative fiction, Carrington writes, can intervene in the larger generic field by "situating conventional subject matter in alternative frames of reference," by, for example, juxtaposing the conventional science fiction trope of time travel with the history of American slavery.[51] Through time travel, Rufus confronts various levels of American racial oppression, from slavery to segregation. He must dress, act, and respond differently than his white companions in certain time periods. That is, *Timeless* does not follow the strategy of some science fiction (and western) texts of creating multiracial casts but positing postracial characters. *Timeless* offers Rufus as many opportunities for heroic action as it does his white companions, but it continually makes the audience aware of how race affects his experience in different historical contexts.

Of the various science fiction conventions that have been evoked and reimagined in African American speculative fiction, the time-travel trope has been particularly important. For example, Octavia Butler's novel *Kindred* and director Haile Gerima's film *Sankofa* both feature contemporary protagonists who travel back into the past of American slavery.[52] As Womack observes, time travel serves, in both these narratives, to "ingrain the realities of slave life and the ensuing sense of responsibilities into their protagonists. They used time travel to encourage connections to a painful past."[53] "Travel, escape, and mourning" in Afro-Atlantic speculative narratives, Michelle Commander writes, "are taken up as forms of resistance against narratives of progress and the supposed healing properties of the passage of time, of forgetting." The history of slavery is also experienced as a "felt reality" rather than an abstraction.[54] The trope of travel (temporal or geographic—or both) is central to Afro-Atlantic speculative fiction, Commander argues, evoked frequently by metaphorical, actual, and supernatural "flights." Such "flights of the fictive literary and filmic imaginations propel the traveling protagonist toward the past to engage with historical realities, which arm her with the necessary understanding of the prior events and institutions and perhaps even improve her and other Black Americans' chance at realizing social life in the present."[55]

Timeless, on more than one occasion, takes Rufus back to slaveholding times—he is, at one point, chained and held captive. However, the "felt reality" of slavery for Rufus also includes the reality of resistance. Prior to his time travel to the American South, Rufus knows and fears, at least intellectually, the brutal realities of chattel slavery. He is surprised, however, to find collective resistance.[56] That discovery alters his character's behavior in the present, as he becomes more assertive in his resistance to his employer's instructions and as he begins to realize that the "freedom" he experiences in the present may be more limited than he originally thought. Although *Timeless* tends to posit a more harmonious racial present, it does, in keeping with Black speculative fiction generally, acknowledge that there are continuities between past and present rather than simply "comparing a deficient racial past to a promising future."[57] During his trips into the past, Rufus proves adept at applying African American survival skills such as masking and exploiting his "invisibility" (no one notices a "Black chauffeur" stealing a car, for example), suggesting, at least, that such survival techniques are a part of his present as well.

African American speculative narratives also draw on specific elements of African American culture and history. One of the most famous African American folktales involves a fantastic story of flying Africans. In some versions, the Africans are newly brought to America, take one look at what is going on around them, and immediately ascend into the air and fly back to Africa. Commander argues that "African descendants in the New World have extended the legacy of Flying Africans" through the lens of "Afro-Atlantic speculation: a series of imaginings, including literary texts, films, and geographic sites, that envision return flights back to Africa."[58] The desire for flight—

returning to Africa, escaping to the North, traveling westward—has been an essential element of African American cultural forms, visible in slave narratives, folktales, spirituals, and twentieth- and twenty-first-century forms like fiction, film, nonfiction, and travel narratives.

By creating the character of the pilot as African American, *Timeless* (knowingly or unknowingly) participates in the extensive fantastic legacy of flying Africans. Naming the character Rufus suggests some familiarity with African American texts, as the character name may allude to a central character in Octavia Butler's *Kindred* (the white ancestor of main character Dana—whom she travels back in time to save from death on several occasions throughout his life). Coincidental or intentional, these parallels suggest the possibilities of finding new meanings in *Timeless* by juxtaposing it with African American texts such as *Kindred*.

"The Murder of Jesse James" begins with a famous western death—Jesse James (Daniel Lissing) shot in the back while dusting (or hanging or straightening) a picture on the wall on April 3, 1882. That death is interrupted by series villain Garcia Flynn (Goran Visnjic), who arrives on the scene just as Jesse turns his back. Flynn shoots and kills Robert and Charles Ford, their guns already in their hands, saving Jesse's life and enlisting his aid in guiding Flynn through Indian Territory to seek out a fellow time traveler stranded in the nineteenth century. Lucy (Abigail Spencer), Wyatt (Matt Lanter), and Rufus—our intrepid historian, soldier, and pilot trio of heroes—chase after Flynn and James. Historian Lucy realizes that they will need help, and she suggests they enlist the aid of Bass Reeves (Colman Domingo), "arguably the best lawman in the Old West," the man who, "they say," was the inspiration for the Lone Ranger. Lucy's use of the phrase "they say" (suggesting a vagueness of sourcing) may reflect the screenwriters' awareness of just how speculative and dubious attempts to connect the historical figure Reeves with the fictional Lone Ranger have been.

Lucy does not mention that Reeves is African American. His first appearance on screen is likely to be as surprising to viewers as it is to Rufus and Wyatt. In staging the introduction of Reeves as a surprise, *Timeless* evokes a television convention for introducing a Black cowboy on-screen that goes back at least as far as guest appearances by Sammy Davis Jr. and Woody Strode in *The Rifleman* and *Rawhide* series from the early 1960s.[59] This scene is often staged so that the white actors who are series regulars serve as audience surrogates— staring in wonder and amazement at the unexpected appearance of an African American figure in a western.[60] In the *Timeless* version of this scene, however, it is Rufus, the African American series regular, who serves as the audience surrogate—decentering the perspective of the white cowboy hero more usually at the center of television westerns. When Reeves steps on his porch to greet his visitors, the camera cuts to Rufus's reaction, which shifts from dumbfounded surprise to pleasure: "The Lone Ranger is Black? That's . . . awesome!"

Rufus brings a perspective to the Old West that is contemporary (his pop-culture references provide the sense of hyperconscious inter- textuality) and African American, as revealed through his responses and comments throughout the episode. It is indeed awesome that an African American lawman is at the center of *Timeless*'s western episode. While the series often takes pains in terms of historical accuracy, "The Murder of Jesse James" is more about genre than his- tory. Musical and visual cues throughout suggest that we have not so much traveled into the past as into the western's version of history as legend. In his first appearance, the camera lingers on Reeves, who is filmed from a low angle as the music swells, suggesting a mythic rather than realistic portrayal. That is, Reeves is presented to us as the cowboy hero of the western.

Place and time are refracted through genre traditions. Part of the western mythmaking in the episode is the claim that Bass Reeves is the inspiration for the Lone Ranger. We view the historical figure Reeves through the lens of his supposed fictional descendent.[61] When Reeve's Cree-descended friend Grant Johnson (Zahn McClarnon) arrives to guide them through Indian Territory, Rufus exclaims, "It's Tonto," to which Johnson, without any knowledge of twentieth-century popular culture, takes offense: "This guy called me foolish."

There is no evidence that any of the individuals involved with the creation of the Lone Ranger radio show had ever heard of Reeves, much less based the character on him.[62] "The Murder of Jesse James" seems to adopt the western genre's attitude toward history; "This is the

West, sir," as newspaper reporter Dutton Peabody (Edmond O'Brien) famously states in *The Man Who Shot Liberty Valance*, "when the legend becomes fact, print the legend." The episode chooses legend over historical fact to assert a countermythology—an origin story for one of the most famous fictional characters of the twentieth century, the Lone Ranger, that is demonstrably untrue but in keeping with the episode's embrace of the genre western as a mode of storytelling is undeniably an "awesome" idea. "This is the western, sir," the episode seems to say, so let's "print (or film) the legend."

Although we learn a few details of Reeves's personal life, the character is primarily defined by his relationship to the law, and he represents the very embodiment of justice itself. When Wyatt suggests they go in with guns blazing and kill both James and Garcia, Reeves responds, "This ain't the 1820s. We capture him and bring him to justice. Alive." When Wyatt argues that "shooting on sight would be easier," Reeves responds that capturing James is "what's right. . . . Who the hell ever said easy and right were the same thing?"

As Daw-Nay Evans writes in "The Duty of Reason: Kantian Ethics in *High Noon*," the sheriff in the classic western often embodies a philosophic position similar to that espoused in Immanuel Kant's moral theory, an adherence to the belief that "doing the right thing requires us to do our duty despite any intended or negative consequences that might follow."[63] Reason "commands us to abide by principles rather than consequences." The "Kantian moral agent" seeks "to do what reason dictates rather than what our instincts desire."[64] That is, our instinct for self-preservation might cause us to desire to shoot on sight, but allegiance to the principle of justice enables us to transcend personal desire to do what is objectively right. Guided by "a maxim of standing against lawlessness," the lawman of the classic western will act "to achieve justice regardless of the consequences to [his] person, [his] friends, [his] family."[65] His actions will not be influenced by desires for safety, for personal revenge, or consideration of the possible consequences of taking the right action (such as the possibility that the captured outlaw might escape prison and cause further havoc). Like Marshal Will Kane (Gary Cooper) of *High Noon*, Reeves is a "Kantian moral agent," one who acts according to principle and reason and who refuses to be swayed by others who urge him to act against that principle—even if that means that by the end of the episode, he walks away in disgust from his comrades and, in a gesture that recalls Kane's famous tossing of his badge into the dirt at the end of *High Noon*, refuses to accept the bounty money for the capture of Jesse James, turning his back when Lucy tries to hand it to him.[66]

When the travelers return to their own time, Wyatt tells Rufus that he used to watch westerns as a child and admired the clear sense of right and wrong advocated by cowboy heroes such as Gary Cooper and John Wayne, but experience in war taught him a different lesson, one more about uncertainty and ambiguity in deciding matters of right and wrong. He finds himself shaken by encountering Reeves, whose commitment to justice recalls those silver-screen cowboy heroes of his childhood. Rather than a necessarily realistic and complex rendering of the historical figure of Bass Reeves, *Timeless* offers us something perhaps even rarer: an African American western hero whose commitment to the cause of justice and doing the right thing is unwavering.

Other elements of the episode suggest an awareness of participating specifically in a story of the African American West. The surprising reveal of the African American cowboy hero is a repeated feature of Black westerns, as is the strategy of revealing the existence of racism through the African American character's initial arrival in a town.[67] In the blaxploitation western *Boss*, for example, star Fred Williamson (who plays Boss) and D'Urville Martin (Amos) ride down Main Street as townspeople stare at them:

> AMOS: Sure is funny the way they think we is the devil.
> BOSS: Folks always fear the things they don't know much about, Amos. I reckon people in this town ain't ever seen Blacks before.[68]

Blazing Saddles memorably riffs on the convention by showing the comically exaggerated racist reactions of the townspeople of Rock Ridge when Cleavon Little's Sheriff Bart rides into town.[69] There's a similar moment in *Django Unchained* when King Schultz (Cristoph

Waltz) and Django (Jamie Foxx) ride into town, with Shultz asking, "What's everybody staring at?" and Django responding, "They ain't never seen no n—— on no horse before."⁷⁰ In *Timeless* we begin with a long shot of Reeves's posse riding into town, and we then observe the townspeople noticing their presence.

WYATT: Why is everybody looking at us like they want to kill us?
REEVES: Because the two of us are Black and one's an Indian.
RUFUS: Huh, so it's like the scary version of *Blazing Saddles*.

Timeless references all three of the earlier movies here, with the white character Wyatt's question echoing that of the white character (Schultz) in *Django Unchained*. Significantly, "The Murder of Jesse James" alludes more directly to the versions of this scene played out in *Boss* and *Blazing Saddles* than it does to *Django Unchained*, pointing toward an affiliation with the two films that have not only African American actors but African American screenwriters (Fred Williamson, who not only stars in *Boss* but receives sole credit for the screenplay, and Richard Pryor, one of several screenwriters of *Blazing Saddles*). *Blazing Saddles* receives a shout-out in the dialogue, but the staging and camera placement in the scene come directly from *Boss*. When viewing the riders, the camera consistently stays to their front and to their left (as is the case with *Boss*). In both *Timeless* and *Boss*, camera placement and angle suggest that we are alternating back and forth between the perspectives of the riders (the camera placed in the center of the street looking down and at an angle toward the sidewalk) and the townspeople (the camera positioned at various places on the sidewalk, angled up to view the mounted riders). The camera's movement matching the speed of the horses further suggests that we are viewing the gaping townspeople from horseback. The rhythm and pattern of the editing also follows that of the *Boss* sequence (although the *Timeless* sequence is shorter, with fewer cutaways to the staring townspeople). Although one of the white characters, Wyatt, contributes to the conversation, the camera remains centered on the two Black men, Rufus and Reeves, as it does on Boss and Amos.

The climactic scene of the episode is the expected showdown with Jesse James, who has been armed by Flynn with a twenty-first-century automatic weapon. Although not as playful in its evocation of hyperconscious hybridity as *Legends*, the image of James with advanced weaponry is one such moment of copresence—an intentional break from the story's adherence to the realist conventions establishing time and place in the western. Grant Johnson, Reeve's Cree friend, is killed by James (and thus the sole Native American character vanishes from the story, reinscribing rather than revising a trope of the classic western). The death of Johnson sets up an expectation of revenge. However, in keeping with the episode's characterization of Reeves, he sets aside revenge for the sake of justice. As a Kantian moral agent, he acts according to reason and principle rather than desire (for vengeance). He gets the drop on James and places him under arrest, but just after James puts down his weapon and surrenders, the historian, Lucy, shoots James in the back. James dies on the day he is supposed to die, and in the way (more or less) that he is supposed to die (shot in the back). The moment also provides another allusion to *High Noon*. Kane's wife, Amy (Grace Kelly), shoots one of the outlaws in the back—a surprising moment there, as it is in *Timeless*, of a female character as the agent of western violence.

An exploration of the ethics of violence—as justified or even necessary—is a central theme of the western. *Timeless* uses this western episode to bring that theme to the forefront of the series, as it's a question that the time travelers will continue to grapple with for the rest of season. The "Murder of Jesse James" represents a different form of simultaneity than does the showdown in *Legends*. Lucy's killing of James, shooting in the back a man who is in the act of surrendering himself to the law, is morally dubious from a Kantian (and classic western) perspective. On the other hand, in terms of the science fiction genre, she acts according to principle (to preserve the time line). That principle involves the consequentialist thinking that the classic western rejects, but it is perfectly in keeping with the exploration of the murky morality of changing the past (or trying to restore changes already made), which is the central ethical question of the time-travel narrative. This is half the fun of the time-travel narrative—to entangle the characters in crisscrossing time lines, to force them to consider a headache-inducing multitude of unintended consequences and an array of befuddling ethical and moral dilemmas. Lucy's killing of James belongs equally and simultaneously to both genres—the violent climax of the western resulting in the outlaw's death, as well as the attempted preservation of history that belongs to the time-travel narrative. How we judge Lucy's actions may depend on which generic context we situate them in.

That judgment is further complicated by the action's failure to accomplish the goal of preservation. James dies on the day he is supposed to die, but credit for the capture of the outlaw Jesse James goes to Bass Reeves—despite Reeves's refusal to accept the bounty money and his attempt to reject that credit. The body of James upright in a coffin accompanied by a sign that reads "The Vile Outlaw Jesse James Brought to Justice" comments ironically on Reeves's stance on the injustice of unnecessary killing. Rufus tries to convince Reeves that taking the credit for the capture is important to the future, that people will want to know his story and will find inspiration in that story—in the heroic actions of an African American lawman. "If you don't tell your story," Rufus warns, "some white dick in a mask might end up a legend instead of you. People are going to want to know your story. Today. Tomorrow. Maybe even a hundred years from now." "I'm not doing this for them," Reeves responds, before riding out of town on his white horse, his allegiance, as it has been throughout the episode, to doing his duty as a lawman—unconcerned with the potential consequences of his actions "a hundred years from now."

As the episode closes, Lucy is reading a historical article about the death of Jesse James on her tablet—one that begins with a photograph captioned, "U.S. Marshall Bass Reeves with lawman Grant Johnson, who gave his life bringing down the murdering outlaw Jesse James." The article states that "Reeves and his posse delivered the lifeless body of Jesse James to the St. Joseph's Sheriff's office," and it concludes with a photograph of James in his coffin—and a startled-looking Lucy in the foreground at the edge of the frame. Rather than being forgotten, Reeves, in this version of history, becomes a central figure in it. The time travelers violate their prime directive to leave history unaltered, but in so doing, they make visible a history that has been invisible, bringing an African American figure to the forefront of history and to the center of the genre western.

From the perspective of genre, the time-travel trope offers a similar possibility, an opportunity to revisit the western and make visible the histories that the genre itself has obscured—the stories of Black lawmen, bounty hunters, and outlaws that the western has failed to mythologize in the way it has their white counterparts; the stories of Black cowboys who historically participated alongside their white fellows in nineteenth-century cattle drives; and the stories of African American settlers who, like Cinnamon in "The Magnificent Eight," made lives for themselves in western towns like Salvation. *Legends* and *Timeless* critique the western by participating in it, remaking the traditional genre via the hybrid form of the speculative western.

2

Trauma, Time Travel, and Legacies of Violence

The central traumatic event in the film *See You Yesterday* is the death of Calvin Walker (played by Astro), the brother of protagonist Claudette Walker (Eden Duncan-Smith), as the result of police violence—another incident of what Eve Ewing calls the "recurring nightmare" of young Black men killed by police or by white vigilantes in twentieth-century and contemporary America.[1] A teen science prodigy, CJ (Claudette's nickname) has invented a device that enables time travel in a limited capacity. There's only enough power to return to the recent past, although, as she discovers, improving the power source enables travel slightly further back in time. With her time-travel device, CJ repeatedly goes back in time to the moments surrounding her brother's death, as she tries and repeatedly fails to prevent that death from happening. In *See You Yesterday*, "trauma's otherworldly temporality"—in this case, the recurring cycle of violence in a targeted community—is "externalized and validated" as objective fact through the time-travel trope of the unalterable past, in which the same events occur despite the time travelers' best efforts to prevent them, even if some of the details change.[2] And with the one trip back in time when CJ *is* able to prevent Calvin's death, her actions result in the death of another Black man—CJ's friend Sebastian (Dante Crichlow), who is killed by the same white police officer. Even when CJ manages to alter the past to save her brother, she can't stop the violence, which continues unabated, collecting another victim in her brother's stead.

Poet Eve Ewing reflected on the 1919 death of Eugene Williams, a seventeen-year-old Black boy, which was the catalyst event for a riot in Chicago that resulted in thirty-eight deaths: "Time is always folding in on itself or moving in a more circular fashion. And so what does it mean for us to have the story of Eugene Williams, . . . which then becomes the story of Emmett Till, which then becomes the story of Laquan McDonald? What does it mean for us to be constantly living this kind of recurring nightmare?"[3] The feeling *See You Yesterday* evokes is similar to Ewing's reflection on Williams's death and the experience of "constantly living this kind of recurring nightmare" throughout time. Through the science fiction trope of time travel, time in *See You Yesterday* is literally experienced as "folding in on itself" and "moving in a circular fashion," as the film renders objectively the subjective individual and collective experience of Black Americans caught in the "recurring nightmare" of such violent incidents—which happen over and over again despite repeated efforts to halt the cycle of violence. In Ewing's terms, the story of Eugene Williams becomes the story of Emmett Till, which becomes the story of Laquan McDonald, which in *See You Yesterday* becomes the story of Calvin Walker, which then becomes the story of Sebastian Thomas.

As Seo-Young Chu writes, "The appeal of time travel, alien abduction, and other SF motifs as strategies for narrating traumatic experience lies in their capacity to substantiate metaphors for psychological trauma. In science fiction, figurative expressions surrounding trauma are granted literal veracity: trauma is literally an out-of-body experience, the traumatic event is literally relived in time."[4] Viewed as CJ's individual story (rather than as, or in addition to, an allegorical narrative of collective experience), *See You Yesterday* neatly illustrates how time-travel stories can parallel narratives of post-traumatic stress disorder (PTSD). "Many traumatized persons," van der Kolk and van der Hart write, "experience long periods of time in which they live, as it were, in two different worlds: the world of the realm of trauma and the realm of their current, ordinary life. Very often, it is impossible to bridge these worlds."[5] In time-travel stories that address themes of traumatic experience, the science-fictional device of time travel serves as a means of journeying between the world of the past ("the realm of trauma") and the world of the present ("the realm of their current, ordinary life"). For individuals suffering from post-traumatic stress disorder, "insistent reenactments of the past" (often "in the form of intrusive thoughts, nightmares, or flashbacks") are a signature symptom of post-traumatic stress disorder.[6] This symptomatic subjective experience associated with PTSD is rendered objectively in time-travel narratives in which "the traumatic event is literally relived in time."[7]

Although *See You Yesterday* is not a western text since it is set in Brooklyn, it effectively illustrates the parallels between time-travel stories and narratives of trauma, both of which center on "insistent reenactments of the past." The traumatic event keeps happening because the time traveler literally keeps returning to the moment of trauma, as each time jump CJ makes results in her repeatedly reliving the trauma of her brother's death. *See You Yesterday* also suggests the way PTSD can be a phenomenon that is experienced both individually and collectively. The first part of this chapter sets out some of the parallels between narratives of trauma and narratives of time travel before turning its attention to a series of western texts that take us back in time to moments of traumatic violence in western history, from the "insistent reenactments of the past" we see in time-travel stories that take us back to the scene of heroic last stands to the traumatic violence of the 1921 Tulsa race massacre as represented in the HBO series *Watchmen*. I will return to this topic in chapter 5, which will take us into the geographical borderlands of the American Southwest and the temporal remapping of those borderlands as spaces of traumatic experience in the Amazon Prime television series *Undone* and Alfredo Véa's novel *The Mexican Flyboy*.

The best-known science fiction text that explores the intersection of PTSD and time travel is no doubt Kurt Vonnegut's *Slaughterhouse-Five*, in which protagonist Billy Pilgrim becomes "unstuck in time."[8] The World War II bombing of Dresden, which author Vonnegut experienced as a prisoner of war, is at the center of Billy's traumatic experience. Time-travel stories are often vehicles for exploring paradox, and we might say that time travel in narratives of trauma functions to literalize the paradoxical nature of traumatic experience. As with the case in *See You Yesterday*, Billy's time travel suggests the literal reenactment of past trauma. However, as Chu observes, Billy's time travel might also be interpreted as the exact opposite, as a psychic defense that prevents him from getting too close to the traumatic memory—propelling him elsewhere in time before he gets to the core of the memory.[9] That is, paradoxically, time travel in the novel represents both an insistent return to the past and a forceful escape from it.

The metaphor of time travel also suggests further paradoxes in relation to PTSD. On the one hand, Billy's time travel is a symptom of his PTSD, an involuntary return to (or conversely, movement away from) the traumatic memory. On the other hand, we might also interpret Billy's time travel as a kind of therapy—an attempt to go back to the moment of trauma in order to understand it and ultimately move beyond it. An experience that has not been integrated into consciousness, Caruth writes, "continually returns" in symptomatic forms (reenactments, nightmares, hallucinations, etc.) unless (or until) it has been transformed "into a narrative memory that allows the story to be verbalized and communicated."[10] Through therapeutic treatment, patients return to the traumatic memory as part of the process of integration, transforming unspeakable trauma into narrative. In another seeming paradox, the treatment for PTSD—return to the traumatic memory—is also a symptom of PTSD. Similarly, the metaphor of time travel might be interpreted either as a symptom of PTSD (an insistent reenactment) or as a possible therapeutic practice (providing the necessary bridge between the two worlds as part of the process of closing the distance between the two). Studies of PTSD suggest that both may be true at once. Time-travel stories in general—which thrive on exploring paradoxes and contradictions, on disrupting chronology and examining the constructed nature of the way we experience time—provide a particularly apt narrative form for exploring the paradoxes and complexities of traumatic experience.

The model of trauma and the representation of trauma set forth above follows Cathy Caruth's *Unclaimed Experience: Trauma, Narrative, and History*, as well as other subsequent texts in the field of cultural trauma studies.[11] However, as Keith Clavin and Christopher J. La Casse write, this theoretical tradition "has been challenged from numerous angles," even as "the paradigm [Caruth] created has largely remained intact, particularly among popular depictions of trauma."[12] The Caruth model, for example, has been criticized as "narrow," despite its claims of universal application. More recent theorists, as Michelle Balaev observes, "seek to construct a 'pluralistic model [that] accounts for variability of experiences and social contexts that construct meaning and values.'"[13] Nonetheless, "Caruth's model has had a lasting effect in the cultural realm. Critics have noted that the paradigm is as much prescriptive as descriptive, with fiction writers possibly aware of and replicating the markers of trauma theory," even as those theories have been challenged by more recent psychological models. As part of their discussion of the HBO series *Westworld*, Clavin and La Casse note, however, the continued usefulness of the Caruth model, in part because of its apparent influence on fictional representations of trauma and PTSD: "Our interest in this essay is not to weigh in on this debate but, rather, to highlight where the show engages with these theories and explore how certain literary and cultural markers of trauma are used to convey the notion of political awakening through the hosts through an engagement with narrative awareness."[14]

Similarly, I would claim that the Caruth paradigm remains an effective means of analyzing the narratives discussed here, as that model seems in keeping with the understanding of trauma articulated in those texts. Creators may have become aware of that model from a variety of sources, including numerous Vietnam War narratives (such as Tim O'Brien's well-known *The Things They Carried*), as well as Art Spiegelman's influential Holocaust narrative and graphic memoir series *Maus*.[15] The narrative and aesthetic techniques that Spiegelman uses in *Maus* (the paradoxical combination of cartoonish unreality and detailed realism, the self-awareness and metacommentary, the continual questioning of representational choices, the various visual techniques he uses to combine or juxtapose past and present as coexisting in the same temporal moment) have also been widely adopted as formal strategies in narratives of trauma.[16] In *Contemporary American Trauma Narratives*, Alan Gibbs notes the general codification of aesthetic strategies in trauma narratives, which often involve "fragmented, non-linear chronologies, repetition, shifts in narrating voice, and a resultantly decentered subjectivity," all qualities familiar, as well, to time-travel stories.[17] The effect of all these techniques is to "produce a disruptive reading experience that attempts to approximate traumatic experience," a combination of narrative and aesthetic techniques that is as visible in HBO's *Watchmen* as in *Westworld*.[18] In time-travel narratives of traumatic experience, the emphasis on paradox may serve a similar function, an aesthetic choice that attempts both to tell the story of what happened and to preserve the "event's essential incomprehensibility."[19]

Specific to the science fiction trope linking time travel and trauma, the repetition of similar techniques across a variety of texts also suggests the enduring influence of Kurt Vonnegut's *Slaughterhouse-Five*.[20] Following Clavin and La Casse, I would emphasize here that my interest is not to promote a particular model as a valid or preferred psychological theory but rather as an appropriate lens for understanding elements of the fictional texts examined, as that model seems to have informed the understanding (and aesthetic choices) of the creators of those texts—whether the influence comes directly from Caruth or from the multitude of late twentieth- and early twenty-first-century texts that have used similar techniques to represent traumatic experience. Following Clavin and La Casse, my interest is "to explore how certain literary and cultural markers of trauma are used" in these texts to convey meaning, how, as in the example of *See You Yesterday*, the "markers of trauma" are linked to the story's political argument—as a means, much like the use of time-travel conventions, of representing and articulating aspects of experience that, in Chu's phrase, "defy straightforward representation."[21]

TIME TRAVEL AND THE LAST STAND

That stories set in the American West frequently address traumatic events in the western past is not surprising—western history is a history of conquest, of violence, death, and massacre. Violence against individuals and against groups are both part of western history, and both are central to the stories told in fictional narratives of the West. Also, unsurprisingly, time-travel westerns and time-travel stories set in the West with some frequency take us back to specific traumatic events, like to the Battle of the Little Bighorn; to the conflict at the Alamo; or to the assassination in Dallas, Texas, of President Kennedy.

In the 2016 Hulu miniseries *11.22.63* (based on the Stephen King novel of the same title), protagonist Jake Epping (James Franco), at the behest of diner owner Al Templeton (Chris Cooper), goes back in time to 1961 with the ultimate goal of stopping the assassination of John F. Kennedy in 1963.[22] The traumatic event is not Jake's personal trauma, and we might regard *11.22.63* as a narrative of the transmission of trauma (which will be discussed in more detail later in this chapter), as it is Templeton's traumatic cultural memory of this historical event that Epping attempts to resolve—by taking on Templeton's mission as his own and working to change the past so that the traumatic event does not occur. However, as Templeton tells Jake in preparing him for the journey, the "past pushes back." That is, as the PTSD sufferer is pushed away from directly confronting the trauma that was too intense to be assimilated by narrative memory, so is the time traveler (whether Jake or Templeton) prevented by the past itself from getting too close to the traumatic moment that he seeks. An unexpected car crash, a suddenly angry group of men, loud noises that prevent the time traveler from hearing crucial information, and in Templeton's case, the sudden onset of terminal cancer—these are just a few of the events that happen to prevent the time traveler from either knowing the truth that he seeks or successfully disrupting the chain of events that result in Kennedy's assassination in Dallas.

In *11.22.63* the initial setting of the story is Lisbon, Maine, and the wormhole (or whatever we want to call the passageway into the past that is hidden in the back room of Templeton's diner) is purely temporal. Jake walks into the passage in the present and exits in Lisbon, Maine, of 1961. His journey afterward, however, is a journey west, as he makes his way to Dallas, where he sets about trying to determine if Lee Harvey Oswald indeed acted alone to assassinate Kennedy— because killing or otherwise stopping Oswald will only prevent the assassination if he is the sole agent. Jake's friend Templeton believes that the death of Kennedy was a turning point in American history, one that took that history in a dark direction. When Jake eventually prevents the assassination and returns to what's left of Lisbon, Maine, in the present, he discovers that the opposite was true—that the world in which Kennedy lived ended up being much worse than the one in which he died.

As Constance Penley has written, time-travel stories often suggest "primal scene" fantasies, the "name Freud gave to the fantasy of overhearing or observing parental intercourse, of being on the scene, so to speak, of one's own conception."[23] Summarizing and quoting Freud, Penley writes, "The child uses fantasies to disguise the history of his childhood, 'just as every nation disguises its forgotten prehistory by constructing legends.'"[24] On the national level, the time-travel narrative revisits the primal scenes of history, the formative moments of the nation, or the moments that have been transformed from a nation's prehistory into significant moments, legendary moments. Time-travel narratives may indulge the fantasy, "working in the service of pleasure . . . a pleasure that depends upon suppressing conflicts or contradictions," or the narratives may challenge those constructions, returning to the past to uncover a truth about one's origins.[25] The miniseries *11.22.63* raises questions about the narratives surrounding Kennedy, the belief that the disruption of the fantasy of Camelot prevented another version of manifest destiny, of an American exceptionalism that was intended to be if only this one event hadn't happened.

Many time-travel narratives that visit traumatic moments in the past, however, especially ones that have become symbolic fantasies of national origins, such as the battles at the Alamo and the Little Bighorn, often work "in the service of pleasure," repeating national myths rather than uncovering historical truths. As Raúl Ramos writes in "The Alamo Is a Rupture,"

> The Alamo has come to represent Texas and its story. It is a symbol synonymous with courageous last stands. The mission statement for the [2019] redevelopment plan for the Alamo . . . makes the claim that the battle at the Alamo was not only for the state or nation, but for the hemisphere. "The thirteen days in 1836 that culminated in the ultimate sacrifice of 189 heroes changed the course of history, leading to the creation of the Republic of Texas,

followed by the state of Texas, ultimately defining the geopolitical structure of the Americas."[26]

Referencing the work of anthropologist Richard Flores, Merla-Watson observes that the Alamo has functioned as a "master symbol" that reinforces "Anglo superiority and Mexican inferiority within the US imagined community," representing a "racialized and gendered mythos of Texan and US individualism, freedom, and liberty" while simultaneously standing as "both discursive and physical testimony to the ongoing colonization of native peoples and subjugation of Mexican@s and Chican@s."[27] "The story of the Alamo should be widely studied," Ramos argues, "but it should be the real history, the one that intersects with and embodies the nation's history of enforcing a racial order through violence, and the campaigns of white supremacy and slavery that accompanied America's expansion."[28]

When the trio of time travelers in *Timeless* visit "The Alamo," the episode repeats this mythology rather than engaging with the "real history" that Ramos describes.[29] The episode centers on the time travelers' efforts to ensure that William Travis's famous "To the People of Texas and All Americans in the World" letter (or, at least, a version thereof), with its "victory or death" closing, makes it out of the Alamo before it falls, thus ensuring that the mythic story of the courageous last stand becomes the dominant story of the Alamo. The values of freedom and independence are articulated by various characters, but the episode only obliquely suggests that the right to hold slaves is one of the "freedoms" at the center of the conflict and thus conceals one of the contradictions at the heart of American nation building. When Rufus (the African American man who pilots the time machine, played by Malcom Barrett) observes two African American men, Lucy (Abigail Spencer) comments that they're free men, because slavery was illegal in Mexico. Suggested, but not directly stated in Lucy's commentary, is that such would not be the case if Texas was no longer Mexican territory and that by protecting the time line, the time travelers are ensuring the legality of slavery in Texas (an implication that Rufus seems to miss).

Nor does the episode mention that William Travis (David Chisum) himself was a slave owner and that an enslaved—not a free—man named Joe was with him at the Alamo and was one of the few survivors of the battle. If one of the two men observed by Rufus and Lucy was Joe Travis, he was not, in fact, a free man, despite Mexican law. The importance of slavery to the development of Texas and to the western history that follows the eventual defeat of Santa Anna is further concealed by the cross-racial friendship that develops between Rufus and Davey Crockett (Jeff Kober). The Alamo part of the episode ends with a close-up of Jim Bowie (Chris Browning) standing upright (not, as would have been historically accurate, bedridden due to illness), a look of determination on his face, a gun in each hand, and both guns blazing. "The Alamo" episode embraces the mythology of the last stand rather than interrogating it.

We see a general repetition of this pattern in depictions (whether they involve time travel or not) of the Battle of the Little Bighorn. As Roberta E. Pearson observes in "The Twelve Custers, or, Video History," the battle was "an encounter of military insignificance but great symbolic resonance."[30] Ric Burns's documentary *The Way West*, for example, asserts (through a voice-over prologue) that "what happened there would haunt forever the imagination of the American people and define the character of the American nation for centuries to come."[31] Central to the idea that the battle became a defining element of "the American character" is the association with the imagery of the heroic last stand. Historical evidence, however, "questions the hallowed image of the gallant Last Stand, soldiers in an ever dwindling circle, steadfastly fighting to the last man. Native American oral histories and archaeological evidence from the battlefield suggest that the overwhelming numbers of Indians caused the rapid disintegration of morale and discipline among the cavalry troopers."[32] In the face of overwhelming Sioux numbers, soldiers broke and ran, and some may have killed themselves to avoid capture. "Cowardice, panic and suicide clash radically with what the United States military considers its glorious history," Pearson writes, "and with the exception of *Little Big Man* (1970), film-makers have been reluctant to depict such behavior."[33]

Time-travel narratives that return to such primal scenes of American history, scenes of traumatic violence that have been transformed into mythic stories of the formation of the American nation, have been similarly reluctant to question that mythology. In *The Twilight Zone* episode "The 7th Is Made Up of Phantoms," present-day National Guard soldiers in South Dakota are participating in training maneuvers near the site and on the eighty-eighth anniversary of the Battle of the Little Bighorn.[34] Hearing strange sounds (e.g., horses running, war cries), the soldiers decide to investigate further; as the episode plays out, they find themselves transported in time back to the moment of the battle. Rather than returning to their own time, they choose to join the battle. Back in the present, their fellow soldiers puzzle over their disappearance, until noticing their names listed on a battlefield monument along with the names of Custer's men. Their individual embodied humanity disappears from view to be replaced by an abstracted version of themselves, their names printed on a stone memorial, a monument to heroism and heroic self-sacrifice that conceals and displaces from consideration the reality of violent death.

Such transformation of traumatic events into monuments and memorials closes off historical investigation. Rather than confronting the history of racial violence that accompanied westward expansion (of which Little Bighorn was only one battle), *The Twilight Zone* episode ignores the reality of Native American deaths, choosing to mourn the deaths and celebrate the bravery of only the white soldiers. In the context of a discussion of Holocaust documentation, Charlson points to the danger of texts depicting traumatic events that "may be characterized . . . as in one form or another versions of Habermas' 'closed and organic images of history.'"[35] "Such texts," Charlson continues, "attempt to cut off the process of individual and collective mourning prematurely, whether through officially sanctioned interpretations of the past or through narratives that rely on sentimental, pornographic or banal modes of discourse."[36] Texts that embrace the mythology of the last stand suggest such "officially sanctioned interpretations of the past," both in the way they conceal the reality of violent death and in the way they displace or foreclose an understanding of the larger history surrounding those traumatic events, failing to engage with what Ramos calls "the real history" of the American West, "the one that intersects with and embodies the nation's history of enforcing a racial order through violence, and the campaigns of white supremacy and slavery that accompanied America's expansion."[37]

The Time Tunnel television series includes episodes set at "The Alamo" and at the "Massacre" at the Little Bighorn.[38] The episodes are more ambivalent in their approach to this violent history than either *Timeless* or *The Twilight Zone*. In both episodes, time travelers Tony (James Darren) and Doug (Robert Colbert) attempt to convince the antagonists of the folly of their actions, and the episodes characterize both Colonel Travis (Rhodes Reason) and General Custer (Joe Maross) as shortsighted, ill-tempered, and intent on committing folly. In "Massacre," a Sioux historian, Charles Whitebird (Perry Lopez), is brought into the headquarters of Project Tic-Toc and helps the scientists extract Tony and Doug from this moment in history.[39] Tic-Toc commander Lieutenant General Heywood Kirk (Whit Bissell), after watching Custer's actions, observes, "Who was the savage, and who was the civilized man?" And White Bird responds, "There were savages on both sides," undermining the developing critique of Custer and of U.S. actions through a retreat to "both sidesism." Likewise, the episode portrays Crazy Horse (Christopher Dark) as the mirror image of Custer, ill-tempered, hotheaded, impossible to turn away from bloody and violent actions. In both episodes, Tony and Doug, along with a few allies they make, like Sitting Bull (George Mitchell) in "Massacre" and Captain Reynerson (John Lupton) in "The Alamo," contrast with the battle leaders on both sides of each conflict in their efforts to alleviate the human suffering of the individuals outside those command structures.

Nonetheless, elements of the myth of the last stand remain. When Colonel Travis is accidentally brought to Tic-Toc headquarters, Kirk tells him that even though his defense of the Alamo was destined to fail, "it was a grand and glorious gesture." In the final scene of "Massacre," Tony and Doug, before they are projected elsewhere in time, walk through the aftermath of what looks like a traditional version of Custer's Last Stand. The company flag remains firmly planted in the ground, with Custer's body positioned next to it and the bodies of his last remaining soldiers arranged roughly in a circle around Custer and the flag. Even with that heroic staging, though, when Tony and Doug walk through the scene, they do so with a pronounced lack of affect, their eyes cast elsewhere, as if they can't bear to observe the tragedy. For Tony and Doug, anyway, it's clear that they do not view the results of Custer's action as "grand and glorious" in any way.

Unsurprisingly, Indigenous writers who have included Custer, the Battle of the Little Big Horn (known to the Lakotas as the Battle of the Greasy Grass), or other incidents of violent encounters between settlers and Indigenous inhabitants have even more explicitly questioned and contested "officially sanctioned interpretations of the past" that have gathered around those battles. As just one example, Sherman Alexie's young adult novel *Flight* uses the device of slip-stream time travel to revisit and reconsider past violent trauma.[40] The allegorically named character Justice convinces and trains protagonist Zits to seek revenge for the personal and collective ("I think of the millions of dead and dying Indians") traumas he's experienced, by committing mass murder at a bank.[41] In the midst of the murder spree, a bank guard shoots Zits in the head, which propels him on a journey through time, slipping from one body to another, with each person he inhabits being involved in committing an act of violent revenge that they believe is just. A mixed-race character, Zits finds himself embodied in both white and Native individuals—as (in two of his several incarnations) both an Oglala Sioux teenager at the Battle of the Little Bighorn and a U.S. Cavalry soldier in another battle.

In contrast to *Timeless*'s "The Alamo" and *The Twilight Zone*'s "The 7th Is Made Up of Phantoms," both of which emphasize the preparation for battle and both of which emphasize the moment when the heroes bravely face the foe (but neither of which depicts the final battle itself), *Flight* focuses on the aftermath of war. Zits hears but does not see the battle, only arriving on the battlefield to find "hundreds of dead cavalry soldiers," stating, "Bloody corpses are everywhere."[42] Rather than a courageous last stand, he observes "Indian men, women, and children . . . desecrating the bodies of dead white soldiers," stripping off their clothes or gouging out their eyes so they will "be naked and ashamed in the afterlife" or "blind in the afterlife" and thus unable "to find heaven."[43]

The body that Zits inhabits has a huge scar on his neck, and he is unable to speak as a result of the injury. When Zits finds the boy's father, the man is among a group torturing six surviving soldiers, and he encourages Zits to seek revenge for that injury by cutting the throat of one of the soldiers. The moment leaves Zits feeling a variety of emotions, his own as well as those belonging to the boy whose life and body he inhabits:

> I feel the anger building inside of me. I feel the need for revenge. Maybe I'm only feeling the old-time Indian kid's need for revenge. Or maybe I'm only feeling *my* need for revenge. Maybe I'm feeling both needs for revenge.
>
> And then I wonder if that's the reason I killed all the people in the bank.
>
> Did I want revenge? Did I blame those strangers for my loneliness? Did they deserve to die because of my loneliness?
>
> Does this little white soldier deserve to die because one of his fellow soldiers slashed my throat?
>
> If I kill him, do I deserve to be killed by this white soldier's family and friends?
>
> Is revenge a circle inside of a circle inside of a circle?[44]

Time travel in *Flight* is both symptomatic and therapeutic, as Zits becomes unstuck in time in a way that causes him to experience a series of traumatic situations that mirror his own experiences of trauma—the guilt of his violent actions in the bank and also the traumatic events prior to that point that made him susceptible to manipulation by Justice. Unable to process his own traumatic memories, he is nonetheless able to get closer and closer to those memories by experiencing the traumatic moments of others and to experience, as well, the dilemmas around the ethics of justice and revenge they felt. When the moment becomes too much, he shuts his eyes and is transported to another body. After the Little Bighorn, he finds himself in the body of an elderly soldier named Gus, who (despite

Zit's ineffective efforts to stop him) leads a raid against an Indian camp: "These are not my thoughts. This is not my sadness. This all belongs to Gus, and his grief and rage are huge, so my grief and rage are huge, too."[45]

In contrast to science fiction stories that use a time machine as a time-travel device, slipstream stories such as *Flight* make possible an experience of radical intersubjectivity, which complicates the way Zits and we as readers experience those events and which complicates the way we usually experience subjectivity in fiction. We are not one person but two, both the twenty-first-century Zits, who observes from a slight distance, and the nineteenth-century individual who experiences the events and emotions directly. The fact that the unnamed teenager, Zits, and Gus all three experience the same emotions (grief, rage, sadness), albeit from different causes, further entangles their subjectivities.

The fact that Zits both becomes and observes the person he inhabits enables him to also experience conflicting emotions over the ethics of "their" actions. He comes to understand the emotions that drive those actions, but his own resistance (through shutting his eyes in order to initiate time travel elsewhere or by attempting to control the body he inhabits) suggests a desire to step outside the circle of revenge. Each moment of time travel demonstrates how deeply entangled in one another are notions of justice and revenge, and each experience of resisting the drive for revenge within the consciousness he inhabits contributes to his resistance to the impulses that propel his own reactions when he returns to his own body. Ultimately, time travel in *Flight* is therapeutic, as Zits is able to work through the traumatic past that has driven his action in the present. He returns to his own body before the fateful moment in the bank; rather than doing as Justice demands and continuing the circle of violence, he walks out of the bank, thinking, "Maybe we're all lonely. Maybe some of them also hurtle through time and see war, war, war. Maybe we're all in this together."[46]

Flight does not sanitize the violence of the past by concealing it through narratives of heroism, and it does not minimize the "the nation's history of enforcing a racial order through violence." But by looking from two positions simultaneously, it complicates how we interpret those moments of violent interaction—resisting the closure offered by the concept of justice and performing, instead, the ethical work of both understanding and critically examining the justness of the motives that inspire violence.

SLIPSTREAM TIME TRAVEL, THE TULSA RACE MASSACRE, AND *WATCHMEN*

One of the more infamous examples of twentieth-century racial violence in the American West occurred in Tulsa, Oklahoma: the Tulsa race massacre of 1921, when white mobs attacked the so-called Black Wall Street, the prosperous African American–populated Greenwood section of Tulsa. Somewhere between dozens and hundreds of African Americans were killed (accounts vary widely), the Greenwood section was destroyed and burned, and around ten thousand African Americans were left homeless. Contributing to the traumatizing effect this event had on the surviving African Americans was the subsequent silence surrounding it, as the massacre was removed from history—or from the telling of history—until a 1996 commission was formed to study the event.

The 2019 HBO adaptation of the *Watchmen* graphic novel takes Alan Moore's story of masked crime-fighting vigilantes (and the ambivalence they inspire) and transforms it into a story of the speculative West by resetting the primary location of Moore's superhero story to Tulsa, Oklahoma, and by centering the story on the ongoing effects of the 1921 Tulsa race massacre (and the continuing threat of white supremacist violence) as they are felt in the 2019 present of the story. A key element of the story is the return of a survivor of the massacre, Will Reeves (Louis Gossett Jr.), to Tulsa, where his granddaughter (Regina King) Angela Abar (unaware at the beginning of the story of her grandfather's existence and of her own connection through him to the trauma of the massacre) has likewise returned. Or more precisely, since she was born in and lived most of her life in Vietnam (which, in this alternate history, has achieved American statehood), she doesn't so much return to Tulsa, as she is drawn there by events, as if she is also being simultaneously drawn, unconsciously, to the scene of a trauma that she only realizes in the story's present is part of her own history. In a temporal paradox, she returns to a place she has never been before, and she returns to a traumatic memory that is not her own but that nonetheless belongs to her and has shaped her life without her awareness.

The *Watchmen* series emerges out of a contemporary context in which specialists in post-traumatic stress disorder have become increasingly aware of the phenomenon of "intergenerational transmission of trauma."[47] As numerous studies, starting in the late 1990s and continuing into the twenty-first century, have demonstrated, a distinctive element of post-traumatic stress disorder is the continuing effect of trauma even on those who did not experience that trauma directly. As Fromm writes, "There seems to be an almost inevitable outcome to trauma cut out of social discourse; the next generation must deal with it and sometimes represent it."[48] If that trauma continues to resist representation, if it remains outside social discourse, if the trauma is "the truly traumatic"—that is, if it is the type of catastrophic event that affects not just an individual but an entire group of people and, as such, if it "cannot be contained by one generation"—then it "necessarily, and largely unconsciously, plays itself out through the next generation."[49] "What has been traumatically overwhelming, unbearable, unthinkable," Fromm writes, "falls out of social discourse but very often on to and into the next generation as an affective sensitivity or a chaotic urgency."[50]

"What cannot be contained, mourned, and worked through in one generation," Stein writes, "is transmitted, for the most part unconsciously, as affect, mission, and task to the next generation."[51] What studies of intergenerational transmission of trauma have examined is "trauma, and a family's efforts through time—in a way out of their awareness and out of their control—to deal with it."[52] This is, essentially, the plot of *Watchmen*. What has not been contained, mourned, or worked through by the generation who experienced the Tulsa race massacre directly is transmitted intergenerationally as both affect and mission. Through the story of three generations of the Reeves family, we see that family's efforts, acting in ways often outside conscious awareness, at attempting to deal with that trauma. Although such a story of intergenerational trauma could certainly be told within the conventions of realism, *Watchmen*, with its narrative involving masked vigilantes, advanced science, and slipstream time travel, uses science-fictional and superhero motifs to externalize and validate as objective fact that "which in the world of realism must be characterized as occurring subjectively inside one person's mind," the psychological experience of the transmission of intergenerational trauma.[53]

That Angela, in effect, comes home to Tulsa, to a place she has never been, figures the paradox of the transmission of a trauma that was both experienced and not experienced. *Watchmen* also suggests the effect of inherited trauma through objectively rendering psychological experience in the form of concrete lived experience. Although she is living in Saigon, traumatic events that parallel those her grandfather experienced in Tulsa uncannily repeat themselves in her life: the violent death of her mother and father (Will Reeve's son), the experience of being orphaned by violence, a decision to join law enforcement as an adult in order to serve justice as a way of righting a past wrong done to her family, and ultimately, the development of a double identity as a costumed superhero (i.e., her Sister Night persona, which echoes her grandfather's superhero identity as Hooded Justice).

Both Sister Night and her grandfather, Hooded Justice, who meet for the first time in the story's twenty-first-century present, respond in the same symptomatic way to the "unthinkable traumatic experience" of the 1921 Tulsa race riot (and its uncanny repetition in Angela's present, the "White Night," white supremacist attacks in Tulsa that result in the police adopting masks to conceal their identities from the white vigilantes who targeted them). Both characters develop split personalities, alternate personas as costumed crime fighters. Both are driven to uphold justice as a kind of memorial to those who never received justice in the past—the victims of racial violence whose experiences have been "cut out of the social discourse" by the concealment and cover-up of a violent massacre. Although efforts at mourning and memorialization have taken place in the story's present, through a museum about the massacre and through an established process of reparations for the victims and their descendants, *Watchmen* suggests that elements of that story still need to be brought into representation—as demonstrated through the difficult process of telling the story of Will Reeves and his descendants. It is a story that insists on being told, although it comes to us in fragments, in bits and pieces of fact and memory, and ultimately can only be transformed into narrative memory through the device of time travel.

That *Watchmen* is a story of the African American West is emphasized by the focus on two African American characters, Will Reeves and Angela Abar. In addition to the explicit connection to the Tulsa race massacre, the westernness of the adaptation is also underscored by the immediate reference to two western texts at the beginning of episode 1, "It's Summer and We're Running Out of Ice": a silent film western short featuring a character based on African American U.S. deputy marshal Bass Reeves that is disrupted by the rioting outside the theatre in 1921 and a present-day, all-Black-cast production of the musical *Oklahoma* that one of the characters is attending.[54] *Watchmen* may be a superhero drama featuring masked vigilantes, but it is also very much a story of the African American West, and of central importance to that story is the iconic figure of African American western hero Bass Reeves—who, as he does in the Jesse James episode of *Timeless*, symbolizes the ideal of ethical and objective justice.[55] That Will Reeves adopts the last name of his silent film hero suggests the way that the figure of Bass Reeves has started to emerge in the twenty-first century as a central element of a "usable past," an African American role model and touchstone for contemporary reconstructions of the African American West, and one who seems to have a particularly important place in speculative stories of the African American West.[56]

In the silent film ("Trust in the Law") that young Will Reeves watches while his mother plays piano accompaniment, a figure in a black hood and riding a black horse chases another man on horseback. Will later describes the film:

There's a sheriff on a horse. He's shooting at somebody riding after him. It's a man all in black. . . . He's got a lasso, and he throws it at the sheriff. Pulls the sheriff right off his horse. They're in front of the church now. The doors burst open, and all the townsfolk come running out. . . . The man in black tells them the sheriff's no good. . . . They ask him who he is. He throws his hood back, and it's Bass Reeves, the Black marshal of Oklahoma. He shows his badge. The townsfolk cheer.

Although the townsfolk begin shouting in favor of hanging the sheriff, "Bass Reeves won't have it. 'There'll be no mob justice today. Trust in the law.'"[57] The first episode of *Watchmen* begins with this silent film, and we see clips of it throughout the series, with an extensive replay in episode 6 as Will narrates what he remembers of the film, which we see as he talks—projected on the wall beside him. Bass Reeves is identifiable by his distinctive mustache, and a close-up of his badge reinforces his identity, although viewers unfamiliar with the history of Bass Reeves might not realize that identity until Will names him and reveals, as well, the connection to his own choice of last name.

As discussed in the previous chapter, the DC's *Legends of Tomorrow* episode "The Magnificent Eight" is a kind of comic book history, as it brings to our attention the connections between the western hero comic book series popular in the middle of the twentieth century and the later superhero comic books that transformed and in many cases replaced those western heroes.[58] In the alternate history that *Watchmen* constructs (e.g., Bass Reeves was never a silent film cowboy hero, not even in the world of independent Black film production and segregated theaters), we also get an alternate comic book history, one that demonstrates the intertwining of Black western heroes and Black superheroes. That costumed crime fighter Will Reeves (with his black cloak and hood) bases his superhero persona, in part, on his memory of heroic Black western lawman Bass Reeves suggests a parallel transformation of Black heroism—from Black westerner to Black superhero.

The parallels between Black western experience and superheroes is further emphasized by a conversation Will has with a newspaper salesman who is reading a copy of the June 1938 issue of *Action Comics*, which famously introduces the character of Superman: "A boy, a baby, his father puts him in a rocket ship and sends him to Earth just before his planet explodes." Will's identification with the story is indicated by the intrusion of a biplane flying above the street where they're standing, a fragment of memory from the massacre, and by Will's memory of his own father putting him in a car to send him away as his world figuratively exploded around him. This is, in a sense, Angela's origin story as well, since her world also exploded around her, as a terrorist bombing in Saigon killed her parents and left her an orphan. *Watchmen* intertwines these origin stories, joining together Black western history, silent film, Superman, and costumed crime fighters. In the *Watchmen* universe, the doubly masked Hooded Justice (beneath his hood, he wears makeup around his eyes to conceal his racial identity) is the first superhero, the inspiration for the Minutemen, who follow his method of costumed crime fighting. *Watchmen* slowly reveals the truth as it happened in this alternate world—the hidden African American origins of superheroes, with the influence of the model of Bass Reeves and the true racial identity of the believed-to-be-white Hooded Justice.

Uncovering these truths becomes the mission of Angela Abar. "One task of transmission," Fromm writes, "might be to resist the dissociation of that heritage and to bring its full tragic story into social discourse."[59] Angela's dissociation is indicated by her geographic dislocation from her heritage, her birth in Saigon, and by her lack of conscious awareness of her connection to the massacre and of the existence of her grandfather (which is eventually revealed through a DNA test). In a crucial episode of *Watchmen*, "This Extraordinary Being," the trope of time travel literalizes the psychological process of dissociation, resistance to knowing, the painful therapeutic process that guides the patient to an encounter with the traumatic past, and finally, the understanding of what happened that makes possible the eventual representation of the "full tragic story" as part of social discourse.[60] Through a version of time travel, Angela literally goes back to the key traumatic moments of Will's life. Through her actions, we come to understand what happened; importantly, the narrative of her moving through distinctly separate moments in time knits those fragments of traumatic memory into a coherent story.[61]

The device that accomplishes this narrative task is a drug called Nostalgia. As FBI agent Laurie Black (Jean Smart) describes it, "They insert these little chips into your brain, and they harvest your memories. They put them in a little pill, and then you pop one, and you get to experience that shit all over again." Although Agent Black imagines that one would only harvest pleasant memories, Nostalgia also is capable of creating an experience similar to PTSD ("you get to experience that shit all over again"). Nostalgia was once (in the nineteenth century) the name given to a psychological disorder with symptoms similar to PTSD, especially as associated with soldiers who had experienced warfare, so naming the drug Nostalgia seems hardly coincidental.

The Nostalgia pills in the episode were manufactured for Will Reeves, harvesting his memories; when Angela Abar takes the pills instead, she experiences Will's traumatic memories. Psychotherapists who specialize in intergenerational trauma "suggest that the unthinkable traumatic experience of the preceding generation lodges itself in highly charged but chaotic fragments in the troubled mind of the patient."[62] In the science-fictional universe of *Watchmen*, this is literally what happens, via the Nostalgia drug, as the "highly charged but chaotic fragments" of Will's traumatic memories lodge themselves in the troubled mind of Angela, whose suffering from the overdose of Nostalgia induces in her a nearly catatonic state from which she is almost unable to recover. As a therapeutic treatment, Nostalgia replaces the therapist, guiding Angela to the scenes of trauma from her ancestral past, bringing, for the first time, those dissociated events to conscious memory.

Through the version of time travel that's been called slipstream, Angela moves through the past events of her grandfather's life. Although she may not be moving through time physically (as with a time machine), she is nonetheless experiencing the past as a present happening, effectively traveling back to those moments in time. Nostalgia brings the unconscious trauma to the surface as she experiences directly—lives the story as a narrative event that is understandable—the unprocessed traumatic experience that has been transferred to her from earlier generations. It is only when she relives each traumatic event in Will's life (and thereby achieves an understanding of her own life and experiences) that she is able to recover from the catatonic state. "You may be confused about who you are right now, or when, or where," Agent Black tells her at one point, but by the end of the experience, for the first time, Angela knows exactly who, when, where, and, importantly, why she is. No longer dissociated from her traumatic heritage, Angela is able to move forward into the present.

As the drug kicks in, we share Angela's point of view. We experience a disconnected series of images and sounds—multiple voices speaking, the sight and sound of a snare drum, the sound of a piano playing—and then we see the image of a woman at the piano, her back to the camera, and then a snippet of a black-and-white image from a silent film. Initially, these sounds and images from the past intrusively enter the present—as indicated by the way they are visually and aurally incorporated into the present-day mise-en-scène. The woman at the piano can be seen over Agent Black's shoulder outside Angela's jail cell. The voices from the past mix with Black's speech from the present. As the drug completely takes over, however, Angela finds herself transported completely into the past, landing, as it were, in a seat among other police officers at a 1938 ceremony for a graduating class of cadets. The image changes from color to black and white, and the mix of confusing sounds shifts to the dominant sound of the snare drum. The camera revolves around the scene before returning to Angela; sitting in her place, we see a young Black man who, like Angela before him, is the only Black face among the cadets. Angela has not been physically transported back in time, we realize, but she has been placed inside the memory of Will Reeves, her consciousness slipping into his body to experience the events of the past as he experienced them. Throughout the episode, we are made aware of the simultaneous existence of the past and the present— the slipstream time-travel experiences of Angela, who encounters these events for the first time, in the memories of Will Reeves, for whom these events are part of his past. The shifting back and forth in the mise-en-scène between actress Regina King as Angela and actor Jovan Adepo as Will as a young man suggests this simultaneity, as the character who experiences these moments is both Angela as we know her from 2019 and the Will of 1938.

As the episode progresses, we slip from one memory to another, using a variety of techniques to make us aware of the time missing between these transitions. At the end of the ceremony, Angela steps toward the camera, which pans to Will sitting down in a restaurant. As a slipstream narrative, rather than as a time-machine story, we experience more than just the events in Will's life. Instead, we both see those events objectively (via a camera that consistently observes him from a third person perspective) and share his subjective experience of those events, with the episode employing a variety of techniques to suggest that psychological perspective. The intrusiveness of the thoughts, images, and sounds that Will experiences is conveyed, for example, through intrusive editing that interrupts the flow of a scene through introducing on-screen a disconnected series of sights and sounds: the sound of rainfall, which becomes the sound of an airplane motor, a brief image of Will being hugged by his father inside the silent film movie theater, a brief glimpse of an airplane above a city street, a chaotic street scene with a body on the ground and another falling as we hear the sound of a gunshot, all experienced by Will as a series of fragmented memories occurring during a moment's pause in a conversation. The memories from the Tulsa massacre are sepia toned, marking a visual difference with the black-and-white film stock of the 1938 scenes. This visual difference (as does the black and white in contrast to the full color of the 2019 scenes) suggests unassimilated memories. As a visual metaphor for the transformation of traumatic memory into narrative memory (or the failure to do so), the differences in film stock cause these images to stick out, as they are not part of the present-day narrative flow, nor do they conform to the representational visual conventions used to depict nonsubjective reality.[63]

As the conversation in the nightclub continues, we hear the sound of gunfire and shouts, and we see behind Will, in an aisle between tables, a white man in a Klan robe push a Black woman to the ground and shoot her. "That was a long time ago," Will asserts, even though, as we see, psychologically, it is still happening. The device of the Nostalgia drug makes concrete the temporal distortions symptomatic of the subjective experience of trauma, as we experience three moments in time simultaneously: Will's past experiences in the 1930s, Will's traumatic experiences from 1921 (which continue to be part of his present 1930s experiences), and Angela's present-day experiences as she encounters multiple parts of Will's past. When Will is cut down at the last moment after being nearly hanged to death by his fellow officers, it is Angela whom we see on the ground, trembling and gasping, her face bloated and bloody. The trauma of Will's near-death experience becomes Angela's as well, as she experiences the physical and emotional suffering from this act of violence. Because we as viewers share Angela's point of view, we also experience the journey of someone who suffers from the transmission of intergenerational trauma. We follow along with her as she experiences the pain of that trauma; as a result, the unspoken becomes known as part of the story that is unfolding before us, as Angela takes Will's fragments of memory and slowly puts together a coherent narrative of what happened.

One truth that is revealed to Angela is that the actions of Hooded Justice (and, by extension, her own actions as Sister Night) might be interpreted as symptomatic behavior rather than as objectively reasoned actions taken for the sake of justice itself. "The experience of trauma must be communicated," Fromm writes, "or at least be communicable, if the traumatized person is to carry on as a whole person. When it cannot be communicated in words that carry genuine emotion, it is transmitted through action, a kind of unspoken, unspeakable speech."[64] Unable to communicate the trauma in words, Will literally cannot "carry on as a whole person" and thus develops a second identity, one that "speaks" (through action) what he cannot otherwise communicate. His desire to make sense of a senseless event (the massacre of innocent people) is articulated as a series of actions that attempt to translate trauma into a meaningful story of heroism and rescue. However, the continuation of white supremacist violence in Will's present—and the experience of new traumatic events— makes it difficult for Will to move from a position of transmitting trauma through action to one of communication.

His costume, which consists of a black hood and a knotted rope that he wears around his neck, recalls the racial violence of the Tulsa massacre as well as a later traumatic event—when his fellow officers cover his head with a black hood, tie a rope around his neck, and hang him before cutting him loose at the last second. The creation of Hooded Justice is both an attempt to move beyond those traumatic events and a repetition of them. Although the black hood recalls Bass Reeves, the black hood and rope also belong to the trauma of the near lynching. In connection to that violent act, Hooded Justice is, ironically, a symbolic representation of an injustice, and even Hooded Justice's social task as a crime-fighting vigilante is an uncomfortable repetition of the very social evil—vigilantism—that he seeks to rectify. Departing from the advice of Bass Reeves, Hooded Justice does not "trust in the law" but acts outside the law to punish lawlessness. His costume suggests that he is simultaneously hero, victim, and victimizer. For Angela to be able to transform Will's raw experiences into a story that can be communicated, she must come to terms with Will's actions in all three roles—including his participation in the extralegal hanging death of her friend and fellow police officer (and secret white supremacist) Judd Crawford (Don Johnson).

Nostalgia, and the slipstream time-travel experience it initiates, makes it possible for Angela to become unstuck in time in a way that is ultimately therapeutic, as she discovers the truth behind the unconscious drive that has pushed both her grandfather and herself into the role of costumed crime fighter. Angela's time-travel experience brings to conscious awareness the unconscious trauma that has been transmitted to her generation. Her experiences also serve a therapeutic function for her grandfather, as she plays the role of witness to his testimony, with Nostalgia operating as a medium through which he can communicate his traumatic experiences so that they can be observed, understood by another, and thus be brought into representation and into narrative memory.

In the final episode, "See How They Fly," we return to the primal scene, the Greenland Theatre, an architectural survivor of the Tulsa race massacre, the place in the past where Will's childhood ended when the riot interrupted his enjoyment of the silent film, and the place in the present where the Black-cast production of *Oklahoma* had been performed.[65] Will's former place of comfort and refuge becomes again a haven rather than a site of trauma, as Angela takes shelter there from a damaging and deadly rain of frozen squid. Inside the theater, she discovers her grandfather seated in his old seat ("I was sitting in this exact same spot almost a hundred years ago"), as well as her adopted children (all three of whom have been brought there for safety by their grandfather). When Angela affirms that she did indeed take his Nostalgia pills, Will responds, "Now you know everything. My origin story." And Will, at last, is able to tell the story himself: "My momma played the piano right over there, and it burnt too. Last thing I saw before my world ended . . . was Bass Reeves, the Black marshal of Oklahoma, fifteen feet tall in flickering black and white. 'Trust in the law,' he said, and I did. So I took his name after Tulsa burned. He was my hero. That's why I became a cop. Then I realized—there's a reason Bass Reeves hid his face, so I hid mine too."

Importantly, Will communicates not just what happened but the emotions he felt (anger but also "fear, hurt") and his eventual understanding that healing could begin only after the mask—which both revealed and concealed those emotions—had been removed, because "wounds need air." That the trauma has been worked through, that healing has begun, is indicated by tentative steps toward rebuilding a family disrupted by trauma—by the presence of the three children, by Angela's invitation to Will to join them as a guest in her house. They leave the theater together, walking slowly through the disastrous aftermath of the squid fall accompanied on the soundtrack by *Oklahoma*'s "Oh What a Beautiful Morning." Although the juxtaposition of sound and image may be ironic, the image of the family together suggests a more hopeful future. That possible American future is represented by this reconstituted mixed-race family, brought together despite trauma and loss, acknowledging and remembering the racial violence of the past and the present, passing through the wreckage to what they hope will be a better day.

Alternate Cartographies of the West(ern) in Indigenous Futurist Works

In his discussion of the work of Rebecca Solnit, Neil Campbell observes her interest in maps and remapping as a means of "shift[ing] perceptions and alter[ing] perspectives which have too readily become taken for granted through established, dominant cartography."[1] Westerns have offered their own maps of the American West, which have contributed to settler colonialism through "representational appropriation of territories through landscape images," a cinematic western cartography that misrepresents and misuses Indigenous places.[2] For Indigenous futurist artists, undoing dominant cartographies and displacing the dominant narratives those cartographies realize is part of a larger project of decolonization, of remapping Indigenous space, reclaiming Indigenous lands, and imagining Indigenous futures. As a subgenre of Indigenous futurism, the speculative western both remaps western places and rewrites the western, intervening in both geography and genre, thereby creating an alternate cartography of both the West and the western. And perhaps no Indigenous western landscape has been used more frequently in both western and speculative genres than Tse Bu Ndzisgai, the Navajo place known in English as Monument Valley.

   In the early scenes of *Back to the Future III*, we find Marty McFly and Doc Brown at a kitschy 1950s-era Indian-themed drive-in theater.[3] Beneath the movie screen, there is a painted panorama depicting a group of generic "Hollywood Indians" charging forward. Behind the panorama is a real western scene—the distinctive rock formations of Monument Valley. As the DeLorean time machine hurtles toward the movie screen, the screen disappears as Marty goes back in time. Scenic Monument Valley remains, and to Marty's dismay, the western scenario depicted in the panorama comes further to life when he finds himself suddenly in front of a group of "Indians" charging toward him and the DeLorean. Marty's journey is temporal rather than geographic, as he shifts from 1955 to 1885 while staying in the same location. The film, however, engages in a geographic rearrangement of the American Southwest. Monument Valley, located in the traditional Navajo homeland near what is now the Arizona-Utah border, is nowhere near the California location of Hill Valley, Marty's hometown, the frontier version of which is his destination in the film. Such dislocation of place is not exclusive to the science fiction western. Despite the western's explicit appeal to realism and authenticity, one western location frequently substitutes for another. In John Ford's films, for example, Monument Valley is the shooting location for movies set in multiple places, ranging from Texas to Oklahoma to Wyoming to Tombstone, Arizona. Because of the popularity and influence of Ford's westerns, Monument Valley "became generic."[4]

As Salma Monani writes, "Most non-Indigenous audiences recognize Monument Valley (Tse Bu Ndzisgai, as it is known to the Diné) not by its geographic specificity" as part of current-day Navajo land "but as an iconic feature of the landscape in John Ford's mid-twentieth century Hollywood westerns."[5] Sergio Leone's *Once upon a Time in the West*, filmed primarily in Alameda, Spain, includes a sequence shot in Monument Valley. The director traveled there with his actors to film on location, not because the location shooting was necessary for a realistic portrait of an actual place but because of its iconic and generic westernness. As Barton Palmer writes, "The Monument Valley landscapes that were introduced to national and global filmmakers in *Stagecoach* immediately established themselves as archetypally 'western' in a general sense, so thoroughly did they conform to the long-developed cultural stereotypes of the region's wide open spaces."[6] This is the role of Monument Valley in *Back to the Future III*, a film that, like many a time-travel western, journeys not to a particular western time and place but to the mythic time and place of the genre western.

"Much of what we don't know about" Monument Valley, Monani writes, "is because its landscape has served as a *generic* setting for stories of frontier expansion. Ford used the valley as a backdrop for settler conflicts with various tribes—Apache, Comanche, Cheyenne, Arapaho, etc. It didn't matter which tribal group had in fact lived in the valley historically."[7] Ford's "disregard for actual geography in his films," a disregard that has been replicated in other cinematic evocations of western landscapes, ultimately treats "representation of Indians and even Western landscapes as abstractions," a practice that further contributes to social and political "discourses of Indian absence that characterize the genre itself."[8] Although I argue in chapter 1 that the time-travel western offers the opportunity to revise dominant representations of the West, the trope of erasure (of Indigenous peoples and histories) and replacement (with stereotypical representations) is repeated (rather than challenged) in films such as *Back to the Future III*.

In the *Justice League Unlimited* animated television series, the episode "The Once and Future Thing, Part One: Weird Western Tales" transports several Justice League members (Batman, Green Lantern, and Wonder Woman) to the western town of Elkhorn, Oklahoma, in 1879.[9] The landscape background, even in cartoon form, is identifiably based on Monument Valley. As Palmer observes, "An image 'quote' of the valley is all that is needed to reference the thematic and cultural value of that most resolutely national of studio film types."[10] In the HBO series *Game of Thrones*, the central battle scene in the episode "The Spoils of War," although set in the imaginary world of Westeros, is distinctively western in its staging, including CGI landscape features that evoke the buttes of Monument Valley.[11] The continued insertion of Monument Valley into westerns, space westerns, time-travel westerns, virtual reality westerns, and fantasy worlds is part of "the persistent representational violence of such cinematic genres. From the films of John Ford to the related colonial anxieties of sf, the Western has stereotyped or erased Indigenous peoples and their ecological ways of knowing."[12]

Because of the western's erasure of Indigenous peoples, an Indigenous counterdiscourse often involves "embedding a contemporary Indigenous presence in those landscapes."[13] In the short film *Opal*, Navajo filmmaker Ramona Emerson tells a girl-power story of young Opal Shorty's battle against bullies and for the bike-riding rights of girls that directly parodies Leone's *Once upon a Time in the West* by "signifying on stylistic conventions made famous by Leone, such as the alternation of extreme close-ups and wide-angle landscapes. . . . Trading horses for bikes, the two girls [Opal and her friend Bunny] underscore that *Opal*'s affective power resides in its canny juxtaposition of familiar and unfamiliar cinematic Wests. The film relies on viewer recognition of Western tropes in order to disrupt and redirect their meanings."[14] The film also briefly parodies the Charles Bronson revisionist western *Chato's Land*.[15] In addition to parodic commentary on a film in which a white actor plays a mixed-blood Apache character, we also see that Opal finds in the Bronson character, Chato, a kind of inspiring role model who informs her decision to fight back against the bullies who assert that girls aren't allowed to use a community bike ramp. A contemporary western that addresses themes of justice and injustice, that centers on conflict and vengeance, all played out within a narrative of boys and girls and bicycles, the film builds to a showdown between Opal and antagonist Arnold—who settle their differences in a bout of competitive bike jumping on the disputed territory of the bike ramp.

As Bernardin observes, "In purposefully reclaiming the Western genre, Emerson makes a perhaps surprising case for the continued use-value of the Western cinematic genre—in its varied incarnations—for Native filmmakers. As we see with her embedding of a scene from *Chato's Land*, Emerson draws from Westerns a story of strength, toughness, and resilience, the very markers of Indigenous survival that she forwards in her own films."[16] In *Native Recognition* Hearne extensively documents Indigenous artists finding use value in western films, from "Indian dramas" such as director James Young Deer's (Nanticoke) *White Fawn's Devotion* (1910) and "sympathetic westerns" such as *The Squaw Man* (1914) and *The Vanishing American* (1925) to independent films such as *House Made of Dawn* (1972) and director

Chris Eyre's (Cheyenne/Arapaho) films *Smoke Signals* (1998) and *Skins* (2002).[17] *Opal* is part of history, stretching from the silent era to the present, and part of Native American critical engagement with the western form, a practice that involves "appropriating dominant cinema's conventions and images for autonomous political purposes."[18]

In *Opal*, both the contemporary story and the focus on children (which suggests that these Native Americans are not vanishing but growing) assert a continuing Indigenous presence in landscapes associated with the cinematic West. The intentional references to *Once upon a Time in the West* draw our attention to the misuse of those landscapes in mainstream western films as part of the film's project of "wresting control over the visual territory of iconic Westerns."[19] In contrast to the dislocation in the western of places such as Monument Valley, *Opal* very carefully centers the southwestern landscape as part of Navajo space. Filmed on location in the Navajo Nation (in Tohajiilee, near Albuquerque), *Opal* includes a scene of Opal and Bunny biking along Indian Route 7041—the image of the road sign specifically identifying the film's local setting in contemporary Indigenous territory. As Bernardin observes, "The panoramic shot that follows the lingering focus on the road marker sweeps across land synonymous with the Southwest: red rock, dramatic sky, cactus. Yet . . . the presence of youth riding bikes familiarizes this space as home, community, and center."[20]

A contemporary western rather than a speculative western, *Opal* provides a good example of a deliberate practice of a contemporary Indigenous filmmaker speaking back to the western and to the western's use of Native landscapes. In the remainder of this chapter, I will shift to a discussion of speculative westerns that perform a similar reimagining of the western and of the Indigenous landscapes that have provided the setting for so many mainstream westerns. My focus here will be the desert Southwest generally and, more specifically, the Navajo homeland, Dinétah, as that space is represented in a variety of texts by Native American artists, including the 2012 film *The 6th World: An Origin Story*, by Navajo filmmaker Nanobah Becker, and two novels by Native American and African American writer Rebecca Roanhorse, *Trail of Lightning* and *Storm of Locusts* (part of a series of books, the Sixth World, set in a Dinétah of the future).[21] In so doing, these Native American artists, as does Ramona Emerson in *Opal*, make a "perhaps surprising case for the continued use-value of the Western" for Indigenous filmmakers and writers.[22] Additionally, Indigenous speculative westerns offer an opportunity for intervening in representational practices related to the western landscape, an opportunity for (to amend Hearne's observation for an Indigenous futurist context) "embedding a contemporary *and/or future* Indigenous presence" in that landscape.[23]

RECLAIMING TSE BU NDZISGAI IN *THE 6TH WORLD*

If speculative westerns offer the possibility of critiquing the western from both inside and outside the genre, the hybrid genre also suggests the possibility of a dual critique of each of the conjoined genres. Navajo filmmaker Nanobah Becker does just that, intervening in both science fiction and western genres in her 2012 short film *The 6th World: An Origin Story*. As noted earlier, the colonialist roots shared by westerns and science fiction have been well documented (see, for example, Rieder, *Colonialism and the Emergence of Science Fiction*). Science fiction, like the western, has also used the desert Southwest and Monument Valley as location settings, from Stanley Kubrick's 2001: *A Space Odyssey* to *Transformers: Age of Extinction*.[24] More generally, in the realm of science fiction, "because new planets are often imagined as places of grand vistas and wide-open spaces, the landscape of the West has provided an easy source for sketching the appearance of these new places." Classic science fiction films such as "*When Worlds Collide* (1951) and *Forbidden Planet* (1956) featured the same southwestern locations that so conveniently served western film producers."[25] As Abbott and other historians of science fiction have established, the landscapes of the American West have inspired or served as models for imagined landscapes across science fiction cinema and literature.

The 6th World is the story of Tazbah Redhouse (Jenada Benally, Navajo), a female Navajo astronaut and scientist whose mission is "to safely travel to Mars, with viable corn stock, that can then be used to colonize the planet."[26] If the endeavor is successful, Mars will become

a place of refuge for the people of Earth seeking to escape their eco-
logically damaged planet. Although the story has a science fiction
premise, it also adapts Navajo creation myths, and "it highlights the
Navajo community's links to their homelands through their source
of life—corn is both the basis of Navajo food sustenance, as well as
the heart of their cultural identity and well-being as a people," a gift
from Changing Woman, who also instructed them to use corn pollen
as means of staying in contact with her.[27] Thus, the transplantation
of corn from Earth to Mars symbolizes not just sustenance but also
a shifting of spiritual beliefs and cosmography from one place to
the other.

The 6th World begins with an opening sequence, eventually revealed
to be Redhouse's dream on the night before her flight, showing a
field of corn with Monument Valley in the background. Rather than
signifying the wide-open spaces of the western, the red rocks of
Monument Valley are nearly occluded by this visible indication of
settlement. "Situating The 6th World as a response to the (space)
Western," Monani argues "that through these kinds of Native futurist
imaginings, we re-encounter the frontier as Indigenous home."[28] As
in Emerson's Opal, the western location is represented as home (a
place of settlement and cultivation). And in The 6th World, Monument
Valley is not "empty space" but the site of a scientific knowledge of
cultivation developed over centuries. This opening sequence, Monani
comments, reverses "the typical EuroAmerican frontier tropes that
begin with a sense of the land as uninhabitable, which then move
to possibilities of habitation."[29] Likewise, in centering the story on
Tazbah Redhouse, the film "rejects the classic EuroAmerican image
of the frontier traveler," whether that traveler is in a western (such as
a John Wayne character) or a space western (such as Harrison Ford's
Han Solo of Star Wars).[30] The movement to the frontier of Mars is
also accomplished without the accompanying settler-colonial fantasy
of triumph over savagery, or the displacement and defeat of a people
indigenous to that place.

In The 6th World, the mission to Mars on the spaceship Emergence
is primarily funded by the Navajo Nation, which suggests the positions of power held by the Native Americans among the "people to

come" of the film's future—indicated as well by the rank of General Bahe (Roger Willie), the Navajo leader whose gift of corn ultimately ensures the success of the mission after the corporation's genetically modified corn fails. The group of scientists and military personnel involved in the mission is notably multiracial, including Redhouse's fellow space traveler, Tobias Smith (Louis Lopez Aldana), who combines an English name with Hispanic ancestry (and a slight Spanish accent), as well as an African American company official (Leith M. Burke) who remains on the base and a white guard (Brian Smolensky) who appears briefly at the beginning of the film. White people, although present and participating in the mission, are not central to the film's plot—or to the mission itself.

Even as the film centers Navajo cosmology and tradition as essential to survival, it does not assert an opposition between traditional belief and Western technology. Both are important to that survival, and the future that is imagined is one that involves collaboration between Native and non-Native people, Native and non-Native systems of knowledge and technology. When the corporation's approved and modified corn stock fails during the journey to Mars, Redhouse is able to survive (and ensure the survival of humanity) when she cultivates a sample of Navajo corn instead. As the seeds germinate, Redhouse and her fellow scientist retreat to sleep pods, where she chants a prayer as she slips into suspended animation. Monani argues, "As she sings the Navajo Hoop Song, the film shows her transported to an astral, cosmic plane. Behind her, galaxies rotate, so that she appears to be floating in space. She is dressed in ceremonial clothing and her chants accompany a formalized ritual, involving intonations with yellow and white corn."[31] The ceremonial component is as important to the mission's success as her performance as a scientist, involving an Indigenous knowledge system evoked through prayer and ritual. Redhouse is equally at home in a technologically advanced world capable of planet-to-planet space travel and in a world organized around traditional Navajo practices and cosmology, and the film suggests that it's her ability to draw on the knowledge made possible by familiarity with both of these systems that ensures her own—and humanity's—survival.

If, as Campbell argues, critical regionality emphasizes process, affect, and relationality over fixity, imposed grids, and rigidly drawn lines, *The 6th World* suggests that relationality extends beyond the relationship between individuals and each other and between those individuals and a particular place, to include relations between humans, spiritual beings, other nonhuman beings, the natural world, the entire cosmos. Displaced from her homeland by an ecological crisis, adrift in the emptiness of space in a spaceship, Redhouse, in order "to relocate herself," must "plug in, speak, and listen to the more-than-human community." When the film returns "years later," we are left to infer that the successfully established Martian colony we see has resulted from Redhouse's combination of scientific expertise and spiritual belief and that the actions she took succeeded because of her employment of both of those systems of knowledge: "To ensure her and her humanity's future, she turned to the support of her community—of humans (General Bahe and Dr. Smith) and more-than-humans (the traditional corn, her ancestors and their spirits, as well as the ship itself, and the planet Mars). Each of these acts involved a creative yet respectful acknowledgement of other beings."[32]

The alignment of cosmology, cartography, and place is a crucial element of speculative remappings of the American West. According to Campbell, an affective critical regionality, an understanding of place as felt rather than as imposed through ideological constructions of place, "is embodied, experienced, felt through multiple attunements to the energies of space and place."[33] A region is "a complex and shifting presence of forces, rhythms, and relations that come together and disburse." Place is revealed not through simple representation "but rather by its *presencing* as an affective landscape."[34] We should not, Campbell argues, think of region "as circular, established, rooted . . . but as having lines of connection beyond itself; lines of flight or vectors beyond its geographic and political borders."[35] To extend Campbell's comments to the realm of the speculative, those lines of connection may extend also beyond the geographic, the political, and the social, in order to include the more than human, the spiritual, and the unseen, as well as other forces, energies, and presences. The speculative remapping of the American West involves the attunement of place to the music of culture, the conjoining of cartography and cosmology, a kind of mapping that connects a specific set of spiritual beliefs to a particular landscape.

At the end of the film, we see a Mars landscape in the process of being transformed. In keeping with the traditions of science fiction, Mars is played by Monument Valley, although filmed through a red filter and with roiling red clouds added to the sky. A long shot of the colony shows a CGI encampment, cultivated fields, and domed buildings, inserted into the Monument Valley landscape. That Monument Valley is the shooting location for both the Earth of the film's present and the Mars landscape of the future colony suggests the interrelationship between cosmology and cartography, between systems of belief and the mapping of place. Mars becomes home not only because of the Navajo travelers but also because Navajo spirit beings travel with them and because the Mars landscape, in turn, becomes a sacred landscape through that spiritual presence. The film closes with a view of the planet Mars seen from space, with a thin green strip along its center, as the words "Sa'ah Naghai Bik'eh Hózhó" (which might be translated as "In old age walking the trail of beauty") are superimposed over the image. "Walking the trail of beauty" might be understood as following the path of Navajo philosophy, of which the central concept is *Hózhó*, a word that is difficult to translate directly into English but that is often translated as "beauty," with *beauty* being understood as involving more than just that which is aesthetically pleasing.

Hózhó is "an organizing principle of Diné culture," Cynthia Fowler writes, "and refers to living one's life in order, harmony, and balance."[36] Hózhó, Navajo poet Luci Tapahonso writes, is "the beauty of all things being right and proper."[37] Living one's life in balance also emphasizes complementarity, the ability to see continuity between seeming opposites (male versus female; humans versus holy people), and the necessity of balancing opposites (rather than one overcoming the other). A lack of Hózhó suggests a lack of balance, a dangerous state of disharmony that needs to be set right for the sake of the individual and the community. In *The 6th World*, the state of disharmony is actualized by the ecological crisis that necessitates the mission to Mars. Additionally, according to the Navajo system of spirituality, harmony depends on following the instructions of the holy people, including remaining physically connected to Navajo sacred space as defined by the placement of the four sacred mountains: Blanca Peak, Mountain Taylor, San Francisco Peaks, and Hesperus Peaks. Place, and the individual's relationship to Navajo sacred space, is crucial to one's sense of identity, to the experience of Hózhó. The crisis in *The 6th World* is existential in more ways than one—in the threat to humanity, which requires relocation to be resolved, and also the threat to Navajo identity, as the crisis requires leaving Navajo sacred space.

However, the second crisis is resolved in the narrative in a couple of ways, both of which reference the Navajo value of seeing connection between opposites—between, in this case, home (Dinétah, specifically, and Earth, generally) and elsewhere (outer space, Mars, not Earth, not Dinétah), so that Earth and Mars, by the end of the film, become complementary locations rather than opposing places. The superimposition of Navajo language, in this case the use of a phrase that articulates a central Navajo philosophy, over the changing Martian landscape visually symbolizes the fusion of place and philosophy, the restoration of balance represented by both the survival of humanity and the continuing existence of the Diné as a people. The film also narratively resolves the potential crisis of Navajo identity due to dislocation by connecting the journey to Mars to Navajo sacred stories. The Navajo creation story is a story of emergence (thus, the name of the spaceship in *The 6th World* is *Emergence*) and migration from one world to another, from the First World to the Fifth World (where we currently live). By explicitly connecting the events in the film to the creation story, *The 6th World* suggests that the journey to Mars is another chapter in that story, another emergence and migration to another world, as Mars becomes the Sixth World and, thus, a continuation of the Navajos' ongoing existence as a people.

In her discussion of photographer Hulleah Tsinhnahjinnie (Seminole/Muskogee/Diné), Fowler observes that her work often involves "the appropriation and recontextualization of historical photographs of Native Americans," especially in terms of resituating the landscape and portraiture photography conventions that have paralleled cinematic portrayals of American Indians in the American West. In her

Aboriginal Beauty (1995–98) series, Tsinhnahjinnie poses her Navajo women models in relation to landscapes and rock formations that "locate the subject squarely and unequivocally in the land of the Diné."[38] Tsinhnahjinnie's use of "the visual language of [the] historical image" addresses a "lack of Hózhó," an imbalance, in the field of photography, which has been historically dominated by white viewpoints.[39] By directly referencing within her own images the visual language that has contributed to this imbalance, Tsinhnahjinnie "attempts to correct the imbalances of representation of Native people from the beginnings of photography in America."[40]

Similarly, Nanobah Becker's use of visual language common to both science fiction and the western—her deliberate choice of Monument Valley as a shooting location for the film—both draws our attention to the misuse of Indigenous landscapes in those genres and attempts to correct that imbalance by resituating the imagery and the landscape in a Native American context, one that continues to carry with it the meanings propagated by science fiction and westerns at the same time that it conveys specifically Indigenous meanings. Tse Bu Ndzisgai in *The 6th World* is the Monument Valley of the western and the Martian landscape of science fiction, but while it retains meaningful reference to the visual usage in those two genres, Tse Bu Ndzisgai as represented in *The 6th World* first and foremost identifies the location as Navajo space, whether the diegetic location is on Earth or on Mars. The final shot of *The 6th World* suggests a sense of place defined "by its *presencing* as an affective landscape," a speculative remapping of a specific western place, Dinétah, that reveals "lines of connection" beyond "its geographic," *planetary*, and "political borders."[41]

ALTERNATE CARTOGRAPHIES IN
REBECCA ROANHORSE'S SIXTH WORLD SERIES

Winner of the 2018 Hugo, Nebula, and Campbell Awards for her short story "Welcome to Your Authentic Indian Experience," Rebecca Roanhorse has emerged as an author of Indigenous futurist stories who has also enjoyed recognition and accolades within both Indigenous studies and the field of science fiction.[42] The publication of her 2018 postapocalyptic novel *Trail of Lightning* featuring Navajo monster-slayer Maggie Hoskie further established her as an important new voice with a particular talent for merging multiple genres in a single narrative. As a writer of non-Navajo Native American and African American descent, Roanhorse comes to Navajo culture from a different perspective than do the creators of *Opal* and *The 6th World*, both of which involve Navajo writers and directors. As Lila Shapiro writes in a profile of Roanhorse occasioned by the publication of her 2020 novel *Black Sun*, "Native identity is exceptionally complex. It consists of hundreds of cultures, each of which has its own customs. Further complicating all this is the fact that Roanhorse grew up estranged from Native communities, an outsider through no choice of her own."[43] Adopted and raised by white parents, Roanhorse began investigating her background in her late twenties and, after locating her birth mother, decided to move from New York to New Mexico, where she went to law school, eventually studying federal and tribal law, and ultimately "got a job working for Legal Aid at the Navajo Nation."[44] During her studies, she also met and married Navajo artist Michael Roanhorse. It was also during law school that Roanhorse "met a great aunt and uncle who told her that they'd grown up on the Ohkay Owingeh Pueblo."[45] However, as Shapiro writes, with the publication of *Black Sun*, "in a departure from her earlier works, the author bio that accompanies Roanhorse's most recent book makes no reference to any Ohkay Owingeh origins. This doesn't mean she believes her mother's family didn't descend from Ohkay Owingeh people; she is simply 'trying to be more careful,' she said."[46] The references to her identity here as Native American (and not specifically Ohkay Owingeh) and African American follow that decision on Roanhorse's part.

As a non-Navajo writer, Roanhorse's use of Navajo culture in the Maggie Hoskie novels has received criticism. A statement released in 2018 by a Diné writers' collective (Saad Bee Hózhó), "The *Trail of Lightning* Is an Appropriation of Diné Beliefs," criticized the specific representation of Navajo spiritual beliefs and practices in the novel.[47] Although the Saad Bee Hózhó response focused on *Trail of Lightning* itself and offered a relatively evenhanded criticism of the work, Nick Martin (Sappony Tribe), in "Reckoning with Anti-Blackness in Indian Country," documents a number of vitriolic responses to Roanhorse and her writing that has veered toward more personal attacks in a way that he suggests is indicative of "anti-Black sentiments that colonization baked into Indigenous governing structures [and that] are still being perpetuated by Native communities."[48] In discussing Roanhorse's work in this chapter, I want to acknowledge the criticism of her work (as well as the critiques of that criticism), and I want to draw a distinction between *Trail of Lightning* and the representation of Navajo space in *Opal* and *The 6th World*, in which the primary artists are themselves Navajo.

However, I also want to note that in both speculative literature and in the criticism and theory of speculative art, there is a great deal of cross-cultural borrowing, and part of the energy of the field comes from this border crossing and interaction. As Grace Dillon explicitly observes, the term *Indigenous futurisms* draws from the terminology and field of Afrofuturism.[49] As Catherine Ramírez suggests, Afrofuturism and Chicano/a futurism are "fictive kin."[50] In her discussion of Tananarive Due's African Immortal series (1997–2011), Joy Sanchez-Taylor notes that Due "goes beyond the current conversations of Afrofuturism and uses a variety of references, settings, and characterizations to highlight connections between African American, African, Latinx, and Indigenous cultures."[51] In the geographically expansive series, Due sets the story "in the United States, Africa, and Mexico; these settings and her diverse cast of characters cultivate a non-Eurowestern perspective that combats narratives of white supremacy." Sanchez-Taylor suggests that, as Afrofuturism has influenced other speculative and futurist movements, so have those movements, in turn, informed Due's writing, which merges "Afrofuturist themes with those of other cultures, creating a science fiction that is not merely diverse in appearance, but one which includes non-white and non-Western cultures as integral to its narrative."[52]

In locating Roanhorse's work, we might underscore that she is an Indigenous writer but not a Navajo artist. We might also place her Maggie Hoskie novels in the field of culture-crossing speculative work that is cosmopolitan in its world building and references and that cultivates "a non-Eurowestern perspective that combats narratives of white supremacy."[53] Although my focus in this chapter is the central character Maggie Hoskie, *Trail of Lightning* and *Storm of Locusts* (the second book in the series) are also both stories of the Black West, or stories of the Afrofuturist West, with the African American family the Goodacres important secondary characters. Grace Goodacre's bar, the All-American, located within the wall that surrounds Dinétah, is an important gathering place and sometimes refuge for the often-battle-weary Maggie, and it serves as the key location where interracial alliances are forged. In *Storm of Locusts* Rissa Goodacre emerges as a central character, one of the trio of ass-kicking young women of color (with Maggie in the lead) who head out on a road-trip adventure beyond the walls of Dinétah. Similar to Tananarive Due's African Immortal novels, Roanhorse's Sixth World series combines Indigenous futurist and Afrofuturist themes, thereby creating a science-fictional world in which "non-white and non-Western cultures [are] integral to its narrative."[54]

The future world explored in *Trail of Lightning* and *Storm of Locusts* is one affected by an event called the Big Water. Prior to the Big Water, in response to the ongoing Energy Wars, the Navajo Tribal Council approved building a protective wall around Dinétah, drawing materials for the foundations from each of the four sacred mountains that mark the boundaries of the Navajo homeland. That construction was aided by the Diyin Dine'e, the Navajo holy people, as the rise of the Big Water was accompanied by the return, or the more active presence, of the old gods—and monsters—of Navajo lore. *Trail of Lightning* takes place within Dinétah, while *Storm of Locusts* takes Maggie and the story beyond the walls to explore the world altered by the Big Water.

"The head of the Council," Roanhorse writes in *Trail of Lightning*, "wrote some article for the *Navajo Times* that put the fear in people, especially after the Slaughter on the Plains. Navajo people weren't safe anymore, he said. He invoked the specter of conquest, manifest destiny. And he wasn't wrong."[55] In the context of a "heyday of energy grabs, the oil companies ripping up sacred grounds for their pipelines, the natural gas companies buying up fee land for fracking when they could get it, literally shaking the bedrock with their greed," the funds to build the wall were quickly approved. "They say," Roanhorse writes, "the hataali worked hand in hand with the construction crews, and for every brick that was laid, a song was sung. Every lath, a blessing given. And the Wall took on a life of its own. When the workmen came back the next morning, it was already fifty feet high. In the east it grew as white shell. In the south, turquoise. The west, pearlescent curves of abalone, the north, the blackest jet," with each wall reflecting the materials and colors of the sacred mountain it represents.[56] In her descriptions of the building of the wall, which is brought about by skilled human action combined with religious practice expressed through song and actualized by the power of the holy people, Roanhorse suggests a dynamic understanding of place as "a complex and shifting presence of forces, rhythms, and relations that come together and disburse."[57] As in the film *The 6th World*, those "complex and shifting" presences include both the human and the more than human. The combined power of technology (building skills) and spirituality (the singing of prayers by the hataali) and the actions of the more-than-human beings (the holy people) results in a physical transformation that literally alters the landscape and changes the map.

"I remember the first time I saw the Wall," Maggie comments, her expectation of something "dull and featureless," like "in some apocalyptic movie," countered by the impressive beauty of the council's wall: "I had forgotten that the Diné had already suffered their apocalypse over a century before. This wasn't our end. This was our rebirth." Roanhorse's series takes place in a somewhat near future, with Maggie driving an "ancient" 1972 Chevy truck, in which, at one point, we see old posters on a wall with a 2030 date. This narrative time frame extrapolates from contemporary events (e.g., "ripping up sacred grounds for their pipelines" and references to fracking, Keystone, water protectors, and "Alt-Rangers") a dark possible future brought about, in part, by the activities of the present day and foretold by historical events from a dark past (e.g., "the specter of conquest, manifest destiny"), retelling an Indigenous historical experience of disaster, survival, and rebirth in a speculative form that emphasizes the capacity for survival.[58]

There are troubles within Dinétah but nothing compared to the rest of the world, which has been physically altered by war, earthquakes, and storms:

The Big Water drowned most of the continent, hell most of the world. The coastline these days starts somewhere in West Texas, the island chain of the Appalachians being the only land until somewhere near the Alps. The western half of the continent fared a little better. California was below twenty feet of sea water, but places like New Denver had risen, a chaotic but prosperous place, from what I'd heard. Salt Lake City has extended its influence over most of Utah, Nevada, and what was left of northern Arizona to become the Exalted Mormon Kingdom. Albuquerque was the Burque, a volatile city-state run by Hispanic land-grant families and water barons.[59]

In *The Heirs of Columbus*, Gerald Vizenor (Anishinaabe) imagines a future in which a new tribal nation, Point Assinika, is formed (on the 1992 quincentennial anniversary of Columbus's arrival in the New World) in the Pacific Northwest, after Native activists seize (and rename) Point Roberts, Washington, located between two settler nations on a peninsula just southwest of Vancouver, creating an Indigenous sovereign state between the two colonial powers.[60] As Uzendoski argues, this geopolitical change creates "a speculative space that allows Vizenor to reimagine citizenship criteria and human rights ideals on Indigenous terms."[61] The reconstituted Dinétah of Roanhorse's series similarly creates a speculative space for imagining an autonomous Indigenous geographical and political organization, one that is outside the control of the settler nation of the United States, because that nation has been dissolved as a colonial power by the Big Water—a political dissolution that is rendered physically through the metaphor of geological change. The remapping of the political world that makes possible the Indigenous rebirth of Dinétah is accomplished in the speculative imagining of a literally changing landscape that necessitates a new map of that world. The purpose of this new cartography is "to critique the central, damaging myths of America" in order to "present alternative futures within which the nation, region, and the very land itself is seen as alive and changing," with those changes being brought about both by catastrophic events (the Big Water) and creative ones (the building of the Dinétah wall).[62]

In *Storm of Locusts* Roanhorse draws our attention to the possibilities of mapping and remapping through the frequent inclusion of physical maps in the narrative: "A map catches my eye. Lake Asaayi is clearly marked. . . . Black pencil limns the road back to the main highway and down to the southern Wall. . . . Beyond Lupton, on the other side of the Wall, is the old highway. Route 66, they used to call it, and then Interstate 40."[63] In Tse Bonito, Maggie looks at a "ROAD MAP OF THE NAVAJO NATION in font that's vaguely Indian feeling," a tourist's guide map to Route 66.[64] As Shoshi Parks writes, tourism on Route 66, often guided by kitschy road-trip maps such as the one that Maggie finds, constitutes a story of "erasure, one that conceals the Indigenous history of the land with the expanding White capitalism of early Americana."[65] To counter such maps that have packaged the Route 66 road trip by exploiting "the stereotype of the 'Indian' while simultaneously denying Native peoples (and other non-White groups) self-representation," the American Indian Alaska Native Tourism Association created in 2016 the online travel guide *American Indians and Route 66*, which emphasizes "landmarks and historic places associated with 25 Indigenous tribes and pueblos along the Mother Road" and which Parks describes as "a travel guide decolonizing this most famous of American roads."[66] In *Storm of Locusts* Roanhorse suggests a similar decolonizing remapping, as Maggie's journey down the much-deteriorated Route 66 takes her not to kitschy tourist traps but to encounters with several Navajo gods.

When Maggie's quest to find her friend Kai brings her to the Amangiri Resort and Spa (which the villainous White Locust has taken over for his headquarters), she enters a library filled with maps: "Hung on the walls, even on the floor, like someone had hunched over them, studying their arcane lines. The maps on the wall have been written on, marred by crisscrossing black lines and scribbled numbers in longitude and latitude, others in letters and numbers that look like math equations."[67] The literal remapping here, the physical alteration of the printed maps with "crisscrossing black lines," is another example of the more figurative decolonizing remapping that the novel investigates—although, in this case, the political goal of decolonization is warped by the villain's anger and resentment. The villain of the story, Gideon, or White Locust, is one-quarter Diné, although he grew up in foster care rather than among the Diné. Although Gideon possesses clan powers, he has no knowledge of his ancestry, doesn't know his clan names or lineage ("Foster care took all that away"), and, thus, feels estranged from Dinétah.[68]

Rather than directing his anger at a process of adoption that has consistently and systematically removed Native children from their tribal connections and relocated them to white families, Gideon focuses his anger on Dinétah and seeks vengeance for the sense of rejection he feels: "'Dinétah's days are at an end!' Gideon shouts. 'Once I have cleansed the land, I will challenge the gods themselves. I will take what I was denied, what should have always been mine.'"[69] The cleansing Gideon desires involves destroying dams across the Southwest and releasing the water in a massive flood. Those dams, as much as or more so than Route 66, represent "the expanding White capitalism" of a settler-colonial society and its efforts to realize its sense of manifest destiny. Thus, the destruction of dams could indeed contribute to the goal of decolonization. The altered maps at Amangiri are sketches for a physical transformation of the landscape to be brought about by Kai's clan powers—his ability to alter weather and, thus, to direct water. White Locust's plan, the destruction of dams, is a fantasy genre version of decolonization—the concept of decolonization physically realized by magical means that would literally alter the landscape. However, the ultimate goal of directing the released water to flood and destroy Dinétah is counter to the idea of Indigenous survival.

White Locust is, in a sense, an Indigenous futurist, his remapping and world-altering project taking place in the physical world rather than on the page. Some of his political purposes align with those of the book's author (and with Indigenous futurist writers more generally)—only reflected in the cracked mirror of a genre villain's damaged psyche. As is often the case in a well-thought-out fantasy novel involving a battle of heroes and villains, the goals of the villain parallel those of the hero; or at least, the motivations of the villain are recognizable and potentially sympathetic, even if the means are not. In the case of White Locust, we recognize that his purposes have been warped by the very processes of colonization that his actions seemingly fight against—and thus he directs his vengeance at the victims of colonization rather than at the system that created the conditions of his estrangement.

THE WESTERN AND TRAUMA IN *TRAIL OF LIGHTNING*

The connection to the western in the film *The 6th World* is indirect and structural—the use of locations that evoke the imagery of the cinematic West and the use of a narrative structure (the journey to the frontier) and a character type (the frontier traveler) that are common to both westerns and science fiction. In *Storm of Locusts* we follow Maggie as she leaves Dinétah behind to follow the remnants of Highway 66 westward through the Malpais toward the Glen Canyon Dam. There are clear connections to the western in *Storm of Locusts* (especially as the western has been reinvented by the Mad Max films series, particularly *Mad Max: Fury Road*), but it is in *Trail of Lightning*, the first book in the series, that the engagement with the western is the most direct and concrete.[70]

Roanhorse's critical take on the western is also apparent in her multiple-award-winning short story "Welcome to Your Authentic Indian Experience." In that story, main character Jesse Turnblatt, a Native American man living a more or less contemporary life in a near-future New Mexico, works for a virtual reality company that caters to customers seeking adventure and an "authentic experience" in a fictive Old West world, a virtual western environment where Jesse plays the role of the "Authentic Indian" the customers encounter. By positing two worlds, Roanhorse also suggests the copresence of two genres, the science-fictional present of the story, with its advanced technological achievement of virtual reality, and the fictive Old West world in which the virtual "Authentic Indian Experience" is set.

As the narrator drolly observes, despite the promise of authenticity, the encounters with Native Americans and the virtual western landscape conform primarily to Hollywood western stereotypes. In this virtual world, Native American man Jesse Turnblatt becomes the virtual Indian character Trueblood. "Nobody wants to buy a Vision Quest from Jesse Turnblatt," he explains, "I need to sound more

Indian." The tourists "want what they see in the movies, and who can blame them? Movie Indians are terrific!" In order to become more "authentically" Indian, Jesse memorizes "Johnny Depp's lines from *The Lone Ranger*," hangs "a picture of Iron Eyes Cody" by his locker, and "for a while" gets "really into Dustin Hoffman's *Little Big Man*."[71] Non-Indian actors playing Indian (and western) roles shape Jesse's portrayal of Indian authenticity. The speculative elements of the story aid and enable a critique of the western genre, as the convention of virtual reality is used to dramatize and satirize the way western movies have shaped the image of Indian authenticity.

If Hearne identifies a legacy of Native American responses to cinematic westerns that extends back into the silent film era, Indigenous literary responses suggest a similar long-standing tradition of speaking back to the western, with Okanagan writer Mourning Dove's 1929 novel *Cogewea, the Half-Blood: A Depiction of the Great Montana Cattle Range* being one of the best known.[72] "The popular western appealed to Mourning Dove," Victoria Lamont writes, "because it enabled an Indigenous literary practice that did not equate writing with the assimilation and disappearance of Indigenous culture."[73] The western's dominant nineteenth-century setting enabled Mourning Dove to use the genre as "a vehicle for inscribing a *living* Indigenous culture in print," in contrast to ethnographic narratives' emphasis on contemporary fieldwork, on preserving "supposedly dying oral traditions." Westerns depicted "Indigenous people in active conflict with colonial powers and could be co-opted to resist ethnography's metanarrative of the disappearing 'primitive'" and thus could provide models of active Native resistance to those powers.[74]

"Read as a literary vehicle thoroughly complicit with settler-colonial power, one might expect that American Indians . . . would have avoided the frontier romance like the plague," Kirby Brown (Cherokee) writes, but "this has decidedly not been the case."[75] In addition to Mourning Dove's *Cogewea*, Brown also examines as Indigenous-authored frontier romances *The Life and Adventures of Joaquín Murieta: The Celebrated California Bandit*, by John Rollin Ridge (Cherokee); *Wynema: A Child of the Forest*, by Alice Callahan (Creek); and *Black Jack Davy*, by John Milton Oskison (Cherokee).[76] Writers such as Louise Erdrich (Anishinaabe) and N. Scott Momaday (Kiowa), although not usually identified as genre writers, have been recognized by the Western Writers of America with the Owen Wister Award for lifelong contributions to the field of western literature.[77] Additionally, contemporary authors Robert Conley (Cherokee), whose dozens of novels fit more neatly into current definitions of the genre western and whose work has been recognized on several occasions with Spur Awards from Western Writers of America as well as with the 2014 Wister Award, and Fred Grove (Osage-Lakota), another winner of multiple Spur Awards, have published westerns that center on Native American characters and that emphasize Indigenous points of view and contexts.[78] Most recently, David Heska Wanbli Weiden (Sicangu Lakota) won the 2021 Spur Awards for Best Contemporary Novel and Best First Novel, for *Winter Counts*, a contemporary western thriller and crime novel set on the Rosebud Indian Reservation in South Dakota.[79] As Brown writes, Mourning Dove's *Cogewea* and Oskison's frontier romances (and, I would add, the contemporary works of Robert Conley, Fred Grove, and Rebecca Roanhorse) exist within "American Indian traditions of the genre from the beginnings of American Indian creative writing to the present."[80] Publishing *Trail of Lightning* nearly a century after Mourning Dove and Oskison wrote their westerns, Roanhorse also brings a contemporary approach to the genre, one that, as is the case in "Welcome to Your Authentic Indian Experience," invests the genre with irony and irreverence, creating "a narrative universe defined by impertinent connections" and the deployment of conventions from multiple genres.[81]

In *Trail of Lightning*, apocalyptic climate change has re-created frontier conditions in what used to be New Mexico and Arizona, so we might view the novel as at least metaphorically western in the same way that we might classify numerous fantasy or science fiction works that take place on a frontier—on the edge of or outside civilization. In *Trail of Lightning* there are also multiple direct references to the western genre, including the title, which is part of a long line of trail-oriented western titles in literature and film: *Broken Trail, The Lonely Trail, Sagebrush Trail, The Desert Trail, The Big Trail, The Trail Driver, Crossfire Trail, Oregon Trail*, to name just a few. Through the lens of the western, Maggie is identifiable as a gun for hire. In terms of the novel's belonging to multiple genres, she is simultaneously both a monster hunter and a hired gun. She is also a kind of bounty hunter, tracking monsters rather than outlaws for money, even as the monsters fill, in the structure of the western, the same place of lawlessness and savagery as outlaws (and Indians).

In keeping with *Trail of Lightning* as a twenty-first-century story, there is also a hyperconsciousness about connections to the western, as revealed through a variety of specific references and allusions that draw our attention to western elements of the story. Roanhorse describes the town Tse Bonito as "still more Wild West frontier town than anything else. Bunch of cowboys and Indians, although everyone's pretty much Diné. Last time I came through here looking for a Bad Man, I ended up in a shootout that felt more like the OK Corral than a monster hunt."[82] As Maggie leads a group out of Grace's All-American saloon on the way to the climactic battle, she observes the landscape through a description that would have a place in any classic western: "The western sky is an inky black spot above the open desert. Cloud cover is a blessing that keeps starlight at bay, and the moon is waning to little more than a sliver. The easiest path leads us through Tse Bonita, but we all agree it would be safer to circle well south of town, even if it eats into our time."[83] The strategic circling is a well-worn western tactic, but what is most distinctively western here is the sparse but concrete evocation of the desert landscape at night.

To reach the fighting arena inside the Shalimar, Maggie and Kai pass "through a door that otherwise blended into a detailed painting of the OK Corral," foreshadowing the showdown to come inside the arena.[84] Explicit references to the western often foreshadow moments of danger or violence, as in the case of the Wild West town of Tse Bonito, where only Kai's charm defuses an encounter between Maggie and the Law Dogs. Passing through the painting of the OK Corral at the Shalmar likewise signals the danger that awaits in the arena and foreshadows, as well, the later revelation that Coyote has been pulling the strings to arrange the spectacle of the showdown within the arena between Maggie and her former mentor, Neizghani, the monster slayer of Navajo lore.

In a backroom at Grace's All-American, Kai pulls a western romance book from a shelf: "On the cover is a shirtless, muscled, generic-looking Plains Indian guy with long flowing locks, passionately kissing a white woman whose red hair is caught in the prairie breeze. Wagon trains and buffalo roam in the background."[85] If the western references in "Welcome to Your Authentic Indian Experience" are satirical and ironic, *Trail of Lightning*, with the exception of the western romance cover, offers a more complicated engagement with the genre, one that understands both the cathartic possibilities of the violent western hero and the transgressive possibilities of placing an Indigenous woman in that role, and one that also understands the contradictions inherent in placing a Native American heroine in a genre known for, and in part defined by, celebrating violence against Native Americans.

That ambivalence toward the western is most clearly revealed in a scene early in the novel, shortly after Maggie has met Kai and both have discovered that the trickster Coyote (Ma'ii) has come to visit Maggie. More than any other character in the book, Ma'ii is associated with the western: "He wore a dapper gentlemen's suit right out of the Old West. . . . He was every inch the gentleman scoundrel from some old Hollywood Western."[86] With Kai and Coyote talking in the other room, Maggie has a flashback to the day her grandmother was killed, a memory that begins, "We were sitting on the couch watching an old Western."[87] Westerns conceal the history of settler violence through narratives that invert a history of bloodshed by projecting the savagery of violence onto the victims of it. Thus, what Maggie and her grandmother watch on-screen is a typical western scenario of endangered white womanhood and heroic white masculinity:

On the screen a proper white lady in a bonnet and hoop dress is asking the beleaguered hero with a star pinned to his chest for help against the Comanche Indians. I make some crack about the ridiculous braided wigs the "Indian" actors are wearing, and my grandmother hushes me, not wanting my sixteen-year-old cynicism to ruin her good time.

We both flinch at the unexpected hammering on the door.[88]

As Joanna Hearne observes (quoting Thomas Builds-the-Fire from the movie *Smoke Signals*), scenes of Native American spectatorship of westerns ("Indians watching Indians on TV," as Thomas terms it) are common in Indigenous cinema and literature. Thomas's full comment ("You know, the only thing more pathetic than Indians on TV is Indians watching Indians on TV") draws "our attention to the problematic relationship between the imagined mass audience targeted by television rebroadcasting [of film westerns] and Native viewers' apprehension of mediated images of Indians in the context of home viewing."[89]

Such "images of Native spectatorship—embedded scenes of critical viewing—model ways of looking that are also forms of Indigenous reclaiming," Hearne argues, observing that "traversing a media space structured by damaging representation has involved reappropriating, mocking, and taking political leverage from Hollywood representations through specific strategies" that include "integrating oral storytelling and testimony as compatible modes of transmission and instruction" and "reworking genre conventions."[90] In the scene that Roanhorse describes, in which the western film appears only as a general reference to genre (and not to a specific film), the emphasis is more on the activity of watching than on the text being consumed. The responses of Maggie and her grandmother also suggest two methods of resistant spectatorship. Maggie's mocking of the portrayal of Native American characters clearly suggests a resistance to the western genre's insistence on its own "realism." Maggie's grandmother also models a resistant stance. Not a member of the "imagined mass audience targeted" by television and by Hollywood filmmaking, and, in fact, actively excluded by a genre that represents Native Americans primarily as objects of violence, Maggie's grandmother refuses to have her "good time" ruined, not by her granddaughter's snarky commentary and not by letting herself be excluded from a text that pointedly was not designed for her pleasure.

Hearne writes, "By characterizing its Indigenous audiences in this way, *Smoke Signals* distances itself from the Western—a genre dedicated to representing the erasure of Native nations—and from the idea of a homogenous mass audience."[91] The scene from *Trail of*

Lightning suggests a similar strategy, a means of both including the western in the novel's genre mix and creating distance from it. And the critical, reflective, resistant spectatorship modeled by Maggie and her grandmother suggests, as well, the author's approach to the western—at times mocking and at times horrified by the genre's depiction of violence against Natives and also at times insistent on claiming the genre's tropes and conventions for an audience that is *inclusive* of Native readers, reworking and resituating those conventions to make the pleasure they offer accessible to Native readers. One of the strategies that Roanhorse uses is to acknowledge the potentially traumatizing effect westerns might have on Indigenous readers or spectators and to make ambivalence toward the western a part of the narrative's use of genre conventions.

As Hearne writes, a specific strategy for incorporating westerns into Native texts is through integration with "oral storytelling and testimony."[92] Thus, scenes from westerns are often accompanied by oral commentary from characters, such as Thomas's mocking comments, but also through more extended commentary. In a later Chris Eyre film, *Skins*, the character Mogie, watching a western on television, recognizes one of the actors playing a Native character.[93] Ignoring the story on-screen, Mogie focuses on the presence of his friend Joe Thunderboots, a descendent of American Horse, restoring through his commentary the specific Lakota lineage of the actor erased by the character's function as a generalized Native threat. "Among the Indians coded as enemies in the Western, Mogie sees friends," Hearne writes. "Significantly, Mogie recognizes and appreciates the Western on television not for its myth-making fabrications of frontier history—the function the Western is said to have in much criticism of the genre—but rather in terms of his community networks." The scene from the film is further recontextualized when it prompts Mogie to recount "the events of Wounded Knee and the testimony of Lakota witnesses."[94] The Hollywood western, embedded in the cinematic text *Skins*, is reinterpreted and re-presented through Mogie's oral storytelling, which reveals what the generic western conceals through its celebration of white conquest—the violence of that conquest and the continuing Indigenous pain and anger caused by that violence.

The scene of Maggie and her grandmother watching television similarly integrates (and subordinates) the western to a Native oral-storytelling context. The generic television western is embedded in a story that at times feels like an oral narrative—because of Maggie's first-person and present-tense narration. The scene of television watching is also a prelude to what happens next in that story—an assault by Navajo witches that results in her grandmother's murder. The television western is merely part of a larger story that draws on the Navajo cultural tradition of tales of witches. And as we eventually discover, these events have been orchestrated by Coyote. Thus, the narrative as a whole is built around the oral tradition of the trickster tale, and the western elements of the story are manipulated by the trickster for his own purposes.

The enjoyable ritual of television watching is interrupted when Maggie and her grandmother "both flinch at the unexpected hammering on the door."[95] What happens next replays a clichéd western scene in horrifyingly realistic form. The central traumatic event in Maggie's life is recognizably western—an Indian attack on an isolated homestead, accompanied by "hooting and laughter and the pounding on the walls outside. Somewhere a coyote yips wildly." As is often the case in film westerns, the attacking Indians are heard before they are seen, whether through the sounds of mysterious animallike signals or whooping war cries. The pounding on the walls even suggests the stereotypical-soundtrack sign of Indianness—the beating of drums. Other elements of the description similarly draw our attention to the similarities to western tropes: "Faces glimpsed and then lost through the windows, flickering in and out like firelight. Around and around, and we realize they're circling us. At least half a dozen of them, maybe more, dancing around our trailer like movie Indians circling the wagon, but we're all Diné here."[96]

The "we're all Diné here" shifts the western scenario, with Maggie and her grandmother replacing the "proper white lady" and the "beleaguered hero" in the clichéd western scene, similarly threatened by Native attackers, although in this case, they are not Comanches but Navajo witches dressed in wolfskins. However, even here, the description of the witch "wearing the wolf skin" recalls the description of the costuming of the movie Indians and the "ridiculous braided wigs they're wearing," placed on top of their heads like the witch's wolf head. Of the leader, Roanhorse writes, "He's wearing a wolf's head on top of his own, the jaw gaping at his forehead and the boneless arms hanging down past his ears."[97] The "ridiculous" braids of the movie Indian recur in the form of the wolfskin's "boneless arms hanging down past his ears." In some ways, the sequencing of the scene plays out as if the western itself is the trauma that returns in distorted but recognizable form in the dream that is the attack by the witches.

"I can't say why the memory rushes back with the force it does," Maggie tells us as she prepares dinner for Kai and Ma'ii, but "any time I get the least bit comfortable and let my guard down, it's there, waiting for me, and it always will be."[98] The "why" may also be related to the presence of Coyote in the next room. Traumatic return of the memory here might be a message from her unconscious about what is revealed later—Coyote's role in the murder of her grandmother. The sound of a yipping coyote precedes the attack; although Maggie does not consciously make the connection between that coyote and the supernatural visitor to her house, it's possible that her unconscious does and that the memory is triggered by the presence of Coyote. Whatever the case may be, this scene establishes a close connection between three things: the western, traumatic violence, and Coyote.

As noted earlier, the attack itself also reveals something about the western, a truth about the violence against Native bodies that the western conceals through repeated narratives of threatened whiteness. When the traumatic memory of her grandmother's death returns, it's sometimes accompanied by the memory as well of westerns: "I remember herding sheep with my grandmother, pink pajamas with hearts on the back. Watching Westerns and laughing. But then I remember other things too."[99] "Watching Westerns and laughing" can't be separated from the "other things." The multiple references to the western in *Trail of Lightning* might be interpreted symptomatically. The western itself appears at times like a traumatic memory, a disruption of the narrative, displaced, fragmented, always there, always waiting, but also indicating its presence through incomplete references, allusions, displacement.

The ambivalence toward the western gathers particularly around the character of Coyote, whose western-style clothing suggests the deadly game that he is playing—that through his manipulation of Maggie he is writing a western with her at the center of the story. It is, after all, Coyote who arranges the showdown between Maggie and Neizghani at the Shalimar. It is Coyote who directed the witches to attack Maggie and her grandmother—Coyote who is both the cause of her traumatic experience and the agent of her rebirth as a heroine. Whenever Maggie tries to find a different way of moving forward, Coyote is there, either literally in the scene or working behind the scenes, to nudge events toward western-genre tropes, especially toward violent confrontation. Coyote is not the narrator of *Trail of Lightning*, but he is busily creating a story, one played out for his own entertainment. And he manipulates all the characters toward more spectacles of sex and violence (although he's much more successful in creating scenes of violence than with his matchmaking attempts). Like White Locust in *Storm of Locusts*, Coyote is a creator, one who realizes his imagined stories by altering—or attempting to alter—the world around him. Like White Locust, he does so for selfish reasons—his own entertainment rather than personal revenge—rather than for the good of the community (and even at the expense of that community).

When Maggie arrives at Black Mesa for the final battle, expecting to find her former mentor Neizghani directing the monsters, she finds, instead, Coyote waiting for her atop the slurry tower and its commanding vantage spot. She observes, "He's wearing another Western suit, but this one is done in shades of blacks and grays, a froth of creamy ruffles at his neck, a single blood red rose in his lapel. A black cowboy hat sits atop his head."[100] Although Clive and Rissa Goodacre, in conjunction with the Thirsty Boys, strike the first blows in the battle, Maggie watches "in horror as more monsters pour onto the mesa." "'Ah,' Coyote says, sounding thoroughly entertained. 'The cavalry!'"[101] And thus, the undead cavalry begins to lay siege against the Native American and African American combatants, performing both according to genre conventions and against them. That is, the cavalry attacks their conventional western enemy—the Native Americans and their, somewhat unusual for a western, African American allies (the members of the Goodacres family). However, counter to the western's usual racial configuration of good guys and bad guys, it's the cavalry this time who are the antagonists. The monsters are indeed monsters, and because they have been created as monsters (in contrast to, say, zombies, who were once living humans), they're not clearly connected to any particular living race of people. But they're just as clearly described in terms of whiteness. Indeed, at one point, Maggie sees the Thirsty Boys "go down under a swarm of white bodies."[102]

Coyote, as a player in his own western and as the manipulative director of that western, reveals his villainy at the end by donning a black cowboy hat. However, he seems to forget that no individual author is completely in control of the genre, and the expectations of genre sometimes drive the action, the plot, and the behavior of individual characters. In assigning himself the role of the black-hat-wearing villain, he also preordains his own fate; like many a similar western villain, he ends up with a bullet to the head. But because the western is not the only genre that needs expectations to be satisfied and because Maggie is a badass, she cuts off his head with her knife and tosses it off into the desert: "I watch for a while as the blood runs in rivulets down into the cracks of the parched rooftop. Until the cracks fill and the blood spreads in pools around his headless body. Soaking through the sleeves of his fine Western suit."[103] This scene satisfies the expectations of multiple genres simultaneously and is an exemplary moment of simultaneity. The scene suggests both the desert setting of the western and the gothic setting of the high tower. The bullet to the head, the blood-soaked Western suit, the parched and cracked surface pooled with blood are all identifiably western, but the beheading and the excessiveness of the bloody description suggest horror and fantasy conventions familiar to a battle with a supernatural creature.

The role of the genre western in the novel is complex and ambivalent. The western is a source of parts of the story's stylistic accomplishments, and it is a source as well for the creation of a violent heroine whose badassery we applaud, in part because badass Native American heroines who act violently for the sake of justice itself, a quality of the western hero, are rare. However, Roanhorse is also careful to explore the ambivalence of that portrayal. At least initially, the traumatic experience surrounding her grandmother's death hinges on Maggie's sense of helplessness, her inability to fulfill the role of the cowboy "hero with a star pinned to his chest," as she fails to reach the shotgun in time to prevent the horrifying butchery of her grandmother and her own capture. However, if this moment is the central traumatic event of Maggie's past, it's also her rebirth, her emergence as the avenging hero, the awakening of her power: "I can't say what awakened my clan powers in that moment, before I knew these powers existed, before it was known among the Diné that such a thing could happen. I sometimes wonder if it was the ghostly kiss I felt from the wind, and whether it was that wind that touched me at all. Or something more. Something, or someone, else. That showed me just how terrible I could be."[104] The western genre is bound to the moment of Maggie's originary trauma, the horrifying experience of violence that both devastated her and gave birth to her heroic powers. That Coyote essentially authors her story in *Trail of Lightning* as an entertaining (to him) western, complete with an attack on an innocent woman and child in an isolated western cabin and a cavalry charge, suggests how much of Maggie's heroism is out of her control.

The western has played an ongoing role in settler colonialism, has served as propaganda for the violent dispossession of Native lands, has misrepresented the savagery of colonial violence by projecting the source of that violence onto the victims, and has been responsible for a continuing legacy of damaging stereotyped representations of Native Americans. The placement of a literal western, watched on television, at the scene of her grandmother's death also suggests that the western itself, as a popular genre, is a kind of traumatic event for Native Americans or is at least bound to the trauma of settler-colonial violence. Perhaps situating the western inside a work of speculative fiction creates enough distance from the genre to enable a kind of working through of that trauma. For a Native writer to take on the western form from inside the genre, as it were, is a task fraught with ironies, ambivalences, and dangers. What Roanhorse does in *Trail of Lightning* is to make those ironies and ambivalences part of the narrative itself. Placing the western within the larger context of a science fiction–fantasy narrative also enables Roanhorse to participate in the western genre without necessarily belonging to it, establishing a distance from the genre that opens up a space for reflection, interrogation, and critique.

Speculative Borderlands I

MESTIZAJE, TEMPORALITY, AND HISTORY

Filmmaker Alex Rivera's 2008 science fiction film *Sleep Dealer* takes place in a near-future borderlands where Mexican workers operate machines remotely, performing tasks in the United States while staying on the Mexican side of the border.[1] The new technology the film imagines effects "a neoliberal fantasy of extracting cheap and disposable labor from the Global South without those bodies ever crossing the border physically," extracting needed labor without admitting the individual bodies of the laborers into the larger body politic.[2] In discussing *Sleep Dealer* in conjunction with two other works, John Carlos Frey's film *The Gatekeeper* and the novella *Lunar Braceros* by Beatrice Pita and Rasaura Sánchez, Curtis Marez argues in *Farm Worker Futurism* that all three works "displace farm workers and agribusiness in time space," generating "forms of 'cognitive estrangement,' or a dialectic between historical social realities and another imaginary world, that suggests a critical interpretation of the limits of the actual world."[3] In *Lunar Braceros*, for example, workers are sent to the moon to benefit those on the earth. The gulf of space between the earth and the moon replaces the border between the United States and Mexico, but the exploitive situation remains disturbingly the same. "All three depict future scenarios where capitalists control new high-tech production facilities that reproduce older forms of migrant labor exploitation," Marez writes, speculating a future world in which "technology has not replaced workers but expanded their exploitation." These Chican@-futurist works extrapolate from current systems of exploitation in the United States–Mexico borderlands, using the genres of speculative fiction to critique the speculative practices of capitalism in the present by extending those practices into imagined future worlds.[4]

In his introduction to *Latin@ Rising: An Anthology of Latin@ Science Fiction and Fantasy*, Matthew David Goodwin writes, "Science fiction and fantasy are uniquely able to deal with experiences of migration in that they are generally dependent on the existence of at least two worlds, and it is migration that puts these worlds in contact."[5] As Seo-Young Chu points out, speculative art forms have the "capacity to generate mimetic accounts of aspects of reality that defy straightforward representation."[6] Migration, labor exploitation, the social experience of life on the border—all are "aspects of reality" that receive speculative representation in the work of Latin@ and Chican@ writers and artists. As Lysa Rivera comments in her discussion of Chicano writer Ernest Hogan's *High Aztech*, "Comparable to the ways in which Afrofuturism explores the science fictionality of diaspora—cultural dislocation, marginalization, and alienation—Chicanafuturist texts like Hogan's recast the equally disorienting experiences that attended colonization and migration . . . in the speculative scenarios unique to SF."[7] "Chicanafuturism," Ramírez writes, may explore "the ways that new and everyday technologies, including their detritus, transform Mexican American life and culture." "And like Afrofuturism, which reflects diasporic experience," Ramírez continues, "Chicanafuturism articulates colonial and postcolonial histories of *indigenismo, mestizaje,* hegemony, and survival."[8]

Rivera argues that Hogan speculates in *High Aztech* about future cities, drawing from the convention of "the cyberpunk cityscape," a science fiction setting that "signifies the changing social and cultural landscape of American cities in the wake of globalization." For writers like Hogan, "these 'worlded' cities" also "represent vibrant multicultural heterotopias."[9] In addition to the cyberpunk- and postcyberpunk-genre aesthetics that inform Hogan's work, Rivera also contextualizes *High Aztech* as part of an ethnic tradition of borderlands writing and theory, drawing on the concept of *mestizaje* (racial mixing). She grounds her discussion specifically in the work of Mexican writer

José Vasconcelos's *The Cosmic Race / Las raza cósmica* (1925) and his exploration of the dynamics of identity creation "within systems of asymmetrical power relations . . . as mestizo and mestiza bodies enact new relational subjectivities arising from a history of racial conflict," producing a "race of the future" reflective of the contact zone experience from which it arises.[10]

A work of philosophy, *The Cosmic Race*, as Rivera points out, is also a futurist work, one that theorizes the emergence of a "fifth race" that "is 'cosmic' for two reasons: because Vasconcelos believes it to be the race of the future and because this race, like a galaxy, is a constellation in that it consists of all of the other races to have come before it."[11] Vasconcelos imagines this new race emerging in a fictional city he names Universopolis: "Embracing difference and a more globalized approach to the future, Universopolis does not endorse a cultural politics of homogeneity and identity. Rather than fearing or dreading the idea of multiracial Latin American future cities, Vasconcelos (like Hogan) finds great value in racial hybridity and cultural syncretism."[12] *The Cosmic Race*, with its vision of a future city located in a particular place (the Amazon region of South America), with its emphasis on a sociopolitical environment embracing racial hybridity and cultural syncretism, suggests an early-twentieth-century version of the speculative regionality that I see emerging more broadly in the twenty-first-century texts I examine here. These works, whether fantastic or science-fictional, speculatively reimagine the sociology of living in the borderlands—living in the social space of a contact zone "where cultures meet, clash, and grapple with each other, often in contexts of highly asymmetrical relations of power, such as colonialism, slavery, or their aftermaths as they are lived out in many parts of the world today."[13]

Silvia Moreno-Garcia's *Gods of Jade and Shadow* uses speculative elements to represent the social experience of living in the contact zone of Mexico in the early twentieth century, a place of Spanish, English, French, and American influences and of Indigenous religious cultures nearly buried by the dominance of Christianity but surviving on the margins nonetheless.[14] Indigenous religion—like the bones of the decapitated god Hun-Kame, Lord of Death, locked in a trunk inside a colonial household—is still present, if hidden, waiting to be released and reconstituted. Drawing on Mayan mythology and inspired by the *Popol Vuh*, *Gods of Jade and Shadow* depicts a world where Hun-Kame's reconstitution results, as well, in renewal of contact between the land of the dead and the land of the living. The interactions between the human characters and the Lord of Death suggest the social, political, and geographic history of Mexico. By bringing into contact two worlds, Xibalba, the Mayan land of the dead, and Middleworld, the aboveground physical world we recognize as the land of the living, Moreno-Garcia metaphorically represents the tension between Indigenous cultures and colonizing forces. The 1920s Mexico of the novel is a place with a mixture of Indigenous and European cultures, marked by a history of conquest and colonialism, all of which are reflected in the novel's primary fantasy metaphor—the intersection and interaction of two worlds, humans and deities, the living and the dead.

Hogan's *High Aztech* uses a different speculative metaphor to convey a similar idea, imagining faith (Christian, Aztec, etc.) as a synthetic virus that infects and rewires the brain "to effect new religious beliefs and allegiances," a quite literal (viral) colonization of the individual subject.[15] Hogan's protagonist Xólotl contracts multiple viruses, becoming "a colonized subject whose body functions as host to various (self-replicating) cultural and spiritual ideologies." As Rivera writes, "Xólotl's metaphorical significance is fairly obvious: he is the mestizo about whom Vasconcelos writes, the mixed-race Spanish Indian who is the product of colonial American encounters, alien encounters between two races, two cultures, two religions." Colonized by more than one virus, Xólotl emerges as a new kind of subject, as the viruses mutate and recombine, and he thus "ends up embodying the science fictionalization of Vasconcelos's 'new type' of human who, as a member of the 'fifth race,' is made possible by the fusion of multiple races and cultures."[16] Xólotl's "postvirus mutation" is a similar science-fictionalization of the concept of "transculturation," Fernando Ortiz's word for "'a set of ongoing transmutations,' a process 'full of creativity [that] never ceases' when two or more cultures collide."[17]

In *Gods of Jade and Shadow* the fusion and transculturation takes place in the 1920s rather than in a future Tenochititlán (Mexico City), as in *High Aztech*. In the 1920s setting of the novel, the sense of living in a contact zone is further complicated by a global society that is constantly importing new cultural elements (such as flapper fashions and bobbed haircuts for women). In the city of Porfiratio in Yucatan, where the story begins, everyone "had been all about imitating French customs. Mexico City in the 1920s was all about the United States, reproducing its women, its dances, its fast pace. Charleston! The bob cut! Ford cars!"[18] Even in this fast-paced modern Mexico, the ancient cultures remain, sometimes incorporated into the most modern of imports. In Baja California, the Tierra Blanca resort is described as "a vast complex, recalling the Mayan elements of [Yucatan] but also the Art Deco movement."[19] Although on the surface a fancy hotel, "It seemed . . . it seemed almost like a temple, a place like the ancient ones in Yucatan, although there was nothing that fully imitated the Mayan buildings [Casiopea] was familiar with. Not quite."[20]

Casiopea, the main character of the novel, is a teenager who is looked down on by her mother's family because her father's Indigenous ancestry is visible in her features. She becomes linked to the deposed Lord of Xibalba, Hun-Kame, when she opens the trunk containing his bones—which reconstitutes him in the form of the dark and handsome god of death. In the process of opening the trunk, Casiopea accidentally inserts a piece of his bone into her finger, physically linking her to the god, who can draw on her human vitality as she is able to draw on some of his powers. Decapitated and imprisoned by his twin brother, Vacub-Kame, who then takes possession of the throne as ruler of Xibalba, Hun-Kame leads Casiopea on a quest to recover his missing body parts (removed, dispersed, and hidden by his brother to prevent Hun-Kame from fully restoring his powers). With her mixture of Indigenous and European ancestry, Casiopea in her own person embodies a history of contact. The fantasy metaphor furthers that concept, as carrying Xibalba's bone fragment within her own body links her to the god (and the god to her), the sociological racial mixture of her ancestry metaphorically reflected in this fantastic merging of life and death, the body of a god with a human body, and the sharing of their essences between the two figures.

That the fantasy story reflects and refracts the social reality of life in the contact zone is indicated by the novel's geographic journeys, as well as by its attention to borders, maps, and roads. Casiopea is a map reader: "She had spent enough time contemplating Grandfather's atlas and tracing routes with her fingertips."[21] The quest requires Casiopea to become a navigator and border crosser, as she and Hun-Kame travel from east to west across Mexico, stopping in Mexico City, crossing the border to El Paso. They then follow the border west, crossing again into Baja California, where, in an important moment symbolizing that the Middleworld part of the journey has come to an end, Casiopea and Hun-Kame step into the Pacific Ocean, signaling that they have gone as far west by land as possible. Having reached this final frontier, the next step for Casiopea is to go even further, by crossing the border from the land of the living into Xibalba, the land of the dead. "The borders of Xibalba are ever-changing," Moreno-Garcia writes, "and no cartographer could ever draw an accurate picture of it."[22] As is the case with *Tropic of Orange* by Karen Tei Ymashita, *Gods of Jade and Shadow* "is a story whose geography remains in constant motion," suggesting the "constantly shifting and contested dynamics of social power" in a contact zone, or borderlands, through the literal and physical moving and changing of the border between Xibalba and Middleworld.[23] The rules governing travel back and forth between the land of the living and the land of the dead turn out to be as complicated and byzantine as crossing any political border. And like political borders in Middleworld, the border between the living and the dead is at times rigid, at times porous.

There are various journeys to and from Xibalba, but Casiopea emerges as the novel's central migrant, traversing successfully the ever-changing Black Road of Xibalba and demonstrating a fluidity of identity that enables her to successfully cross one border after another. The social metaphor suggested by Casiopea's journey to the land of the dead is made apparent by linking that journey to her travels and border crossing in the world we know. Although death is the ultimate border crosser ("Death speaks all languages," Hun-Kame tells Casiopea as they wait to cross into the United States at El Paso), Hun-Kame returns to Xibalba at the end of the novel, restored to his throne.[24] Casiopea (who gains the ability to speak all languages, as well, through her physical connection to the god of death) keeps on moving and is last seen driving (for the first time) an automobile: "Casiopea chuckled as the automobile began to move. It was a long road, and she feared the automobile would get away from her and she wouldn't know how to stop, but she smiled."[25] Moving east rather than west, Casiopea is nonetheless a frontier traveler. Learning a new technology, as science-fictional to Casiopea as a spaceship would be to a first-time space traveler, she sets out to explore a world that is unknown to her.

The next two chapters look at a group of texts that speculate about past and present experience in the United States–Mexico borderlands. Rudolfo Anaya's ChupaCabra novel series is set in the twenty-first century and employs such speculative elements as mythical creatures, flying saucers, genetic experimentation, and time travel to imaginatively explore a borderlands experience that mixes together folkloric and science-fictional creatures from different cultural traditions, ultimately collapsing the boundaries between past and present.[26] The Amazon Prime series *Undone*, set in contemporary San Antonio, uses time travel to expand the sociological experience of contact zone existence to include the temporal as well as the social and the geographic. Finally, Alfredo Véa's novel *The Mexican Flyboy* uses its present-day setting of twenty-first-century California as the jumping-off point for a series of time-travel journeys that expand beyond the United States–Mexico borderlands to a wide-ranging exploration of the boundaries of time and space.[27] In both realist and fantastic literature of the borderlands, Micah K. Donohue points out, we can see a "contemporary trend to represent the borderlands as a temporal nexus where past, present, and future all converge." "To move through the borderlands," Donohue continues, "is to move through time," a specific social and cultural experience of temporality that several of the texts studied in these next two chapters will literalize through the device of time travel.[28]

In Rudolfo Anaya's New Mexico–centered time-travel novel *ChupaCabra Meets Billy the Kid*, the title itself is just the first of many signals of the story's playful assemblage of parts from multiple genres, evoking Latin@ folklore (the shape-shifting, goat-eating creature that is the chupacabra), as well as recalling the titles of a series of Abbot and Costello films (e.g., *Abbot and Costello Meet Frankenstein*) in which the comedy duo encounter monsters from Universal's horror-film roster.[29] Anaya's title suggests a similar approach to genre joining, one that is as irreverent and impudent in the genres and genre characters (Billy the Kid and the chupacabra) it brings together as these comedy-horror and comedy–science fiction films from the 1940s. *ChupaCabra Meets Billy the Kid* employs multiple genres, sometimes simultaneously, sometimes changing from one to the other with the speed and ease of a shape-shifting creature.

Although there are humorous moments in *ChupaCabra Meets Billy the Kid*, comedy is not really one of the dominant genres. The novel draws on revisionist history (proposing to tell the real story of William Bonney), ethnography, folklore, oral storytelling, science fiction, horror, and the western. The book builds on two earlier novels, *Curse of the ChupaCabra* and *ChupaCabra and the Roswell UFO*, and it continues a story about the aftermath of a UFO crash in Roswell, New Mexico, in 1947.[30] That crash, in Anaya's version of this long-lasting twentieth-century urban legend, results in the creation of a secret government agency called C-Force and in experimentation with alien DNA, which has been combined with the DNA of the chupacabra to create a new kind of shape-shifting creature called a Himit, of which the most dangerous version is the time-traveling Saytir. The story focuses on Rosa (as do the earlier novels), who has in her possession a thumb drive with the genome information C-Force needs in order to manufacture more chupacabra-alien hybrids. In the present of the story, she is writing a novel about Billy the Kid. To escape the chupacabra and the attempts of C-Force to procure the thumb drive, she travels through a wormhole located at the Pecos River, back into the company of William Bonney, circa 1878, when she rides with Billy until his death at the hands of Pat Garrett in 1881.

In addition to its titular shape-shifter, the central character of Anaya's ChupaCabra series is Cal State assistant professor of English Rosa Medina, whose field might be literature but whose area of fascination is folklore. She is especially interested in the connections between different folkloric traditions, such as between stories of the chupacabra (famed for sucking blood from goats) and legends of vampires and trolls (trolls being, like chupacabra, another forest monster, she argues, that hides in dark places—such as under bridges—and endangers the lives of goats). When an elderly professor scoffs, Rosa's mentor Dr. Cantu responds, "Our Anglo colleagues must acknowledge the myths from the Latino south are penetrating the American consciousness. La frontera between Mexico and the U.S. should be a mirror where we see each other's reflection, not a wall."[31]

Although she has achieved stability as a professor, Rosa, like Casiopea in *Gods of Jade and Shadow*, is the central migrant of the ChupaCabra series. As reflected in her argument with the elderly Anglo professor, Rosa is an intellectual border crosser, one who also values the experience of living in borderlands spaces and who sees the larger American Southwest as a continuous borderland, more so than as a collection of separate states: "The barrios of L.A., she had learned from living in California, represented islands of possibility. Caught between the world of Anglo America and the Latino world of the south, the barrios were a new frontier. . . . The barrios from California to Texas represented a new potential. The border could be bridged, or it could become a wall of separation." For Rosa the ability to see borders as permeable, the willingness to cross borders and make connections with those on the other side, represents the possibility of "understanding, sharing, learning."[32] Throughout the first novel in the series, *The Curse of the ChupaCabra* (which ranges more widely than the two later New Mexico–centered books), Rosa moves easily from place to place, from her university office at Cal State to the East Los Angeles barrio where she tutors a group of students; from Lago Negro, Mexico, where she first encounters the chupacabra, to the Navajo reservation in New Mexico, where she travels to aid her Navajo student, Indio, who has been followed by a skinwalker from East Los Angeles to his home near the Tohatchi area. She moves by plane, car, and even by ocean liner; eventually, she becomes a migrant through time as well as space.

As a literary realization of a speculative borderland, Anaya's ChupaCabra series suggests a supernatural world that mirrors the social world, one in which skinwalkers from Navajo lore as well as goat suckers from more recent Latin@ legend follow the same migrant paths as the people who believe in them. In *ChupaCabra Meets Billy the Kid*, William Bonney escorts Rosa back in time to New Mexico Territory. Staying in Lincoln County with Billy's friends Josef and Martin, Rosa tags along as Martin follows a mysterious set of tracks made by feet that, Rosa realizes, have five toes. The nearby Mescalaro Apaches call it "Kensah, el Patas Grandes," because of the big paws or feet that made the tracks. "Long ago, some natives come from the north, Canada, I think," comments Martin, "come to do ceremony with the Mescalero. They say Sa-quache. Now I think it come with them."[33]

Anaya's novels create a speculative world in which creatures of legend migrate as well. The sociological mixture of languages and cultures in the contact zone is reflected in the expanded supernatural bestiary created through (or reflected by) borderlands oral story-telling: "The Mexicans told stories of creatures that appeared in the night, like El Coco, a kind of boogeyman, and La Llorona, the crying woman. . . . In the village Patas Grandes had become another legend."[34] Whether drawn from the Pacific Northwest by a ceremony (as Rosa later speculates) or arriving with the migrant northwestern Natives on their journey to New Mexico Territory, Sasquatch becomes part of the landscape of New Mexico as he also enters into the language of the area's people as Patas Grandes. His tracks, like a road on a map, create a connection between places in the landscape, as his dwelling place in the wilderness and the routes of his journeys out in search of food become part of a new cartography of the area. His presence is noted in the mental map of the people as a place, perhaps, to avoid, just as children are taught to avoid the riversides where La Llorona lurks. As Patas Grandes becomes part of the everyday life of the village, he also becomes incorporated into the folklore. "Generations later," Anaya writes, "the story would be told about Martin and Billy the Kid chasing Patas Grandes up the mountain." Patas Grandes "entered the people's imagination and became one more story the elders told children when families gathered to tell stories." Those stories, in turn, create a borderlands weird western, one with a displaced mythic creature relocated to a different western landscape than his home, with a Mexicano everyman in Martin, who realizes that the creature is harmless (so "let him take a sheep every now and then"), and a famous western outlaw along for the ride.[35]

The villains of the first novel in the series, *Curse of the ChupaCabra*, both human and supernatural, are also adept border crossers. Their purpose, however, is not to understand, share, or learn but to exploit the permeability of borders for their own selfish gain. In the novel's central metaphor, the blood-thirsty, brain-destroying beast that is the chupacabra (at this point in the series, it is purely chupacabra, unaltered by the genetic experiments of the later books) figures the danger of illegal drugs. If the classic chupacabra of folklore is a goat sucker, "this one doesn't kill goats, it sucks the life out of people."[36] As this young adult novel makes abundantly clear, the danger represented by the chupacabra and by illegal drugs is one and the same: "ChupaCabra was destined for L.A. Like coke and meth, it would be set loose in the streets to destroy people. Crank, crystals, meth, the ChupaCabra, by whatever name, these were the brain suckers of the young and vulnerable."[37] Rosa's fluidity of movement is matched by the novel's villains—the drug traffickers, who use bribery and stealth to move their goods through a global marketplace. A Los Angeles cop named Dill turns out to be Yenaaloshi, a witch from Navajo lore, a skinwalker, who is in league with the drug traffickers. Evil behavior proves particularly adept at negotiating borders and at forming cross-border alliances of drug traffickers, brujos, and skinwalkers.

In adapting the chupacabra as metaphor for the dangerous unfettered capitalism of the drug trade in communities, Anaya builds on a critique already embedded in the folklore associated with the chupacabra, a monster of recent folkloric existence. As William A. Calvo-Quirós writes, the "blood-sucking monster" that is the chupacabra "emerged in the mid-1990s as a sophisticated metaphor for the behavior of late capitalism during that period. As policies of market expansion and global deregulation ravaged rural Latin@ communities, the Chupacabras can be understood as neoliberal ideology turned uncanny flesh." Coinciding with the economic effects created by NAFTA (North American Free Trade Agreement), the actions of chupacabras similarly threatened "members of rural communities," whose livelihoods were already "being sucked away by transnational corporations, international banks, and global markets." The folklore surrounding the chupacabra represents "a sophisticated epistemic product rendering visible the invisible economic policies whose deadly effects were being felt in vulnerable communities."[38]

Although not as explicit in critiquing global capitalism as *Sleep Dealer* and *Lunar Braceros*, *The Curse of the ChupaCabra* demonstrates how the drug traffickers use the infrastructure and technology of legitimate capitalist exchange to move and distribute their product. Through bribery and co-option, the drug traffickers bring dockworkers, cruise line employees, and policemen into their schemes. In both *Tropic of Orange* and *Sleep Dealer*, Bahng argues, "transborder and cross-ethnic collaborations among characters . . . facilitate the undoing of global capital's border speculations."[39] To counter the transborder and cross-ethnic collaboration of drug traffickers, brujos, and a red-eyed chupacabra, Anaya suggests a counter set of collaborations, emphasizing the potential power of alliances between different social and cultural groups and suggests, as well, the power of a coalition of traditional folkloric defenses against evil to combat the technically sophisticated drug trade. The Chicana professor Rosa is protected by the Navajo healing ceremony performed by Indio and his uncle Billy, which pulls Rosa from a nightmare about the chupacabra into the protected space of the hogan, where Uncle Billie "performed his ceremony [and where] the evil of the ChupaCabra could not enter."[40] The speculative elements of the novel dramatize and figure the political argument that Anaya makes—that turning back to the wisdom of traditional cultures and joining those traditions together can serve as a defense against the exploitation in the present of communities of color.

"Proximate to the U.S.-Mexico border," Bahng writes, "U.S. Southwest locations like New Mexico constitute what Alex Lubin has called a 'transnational crossroads,' entangled in 'multiple legacies of colonialism.' One of these crossroads is that of military science and science fiction at sites like Los Alamos and Area 51."[41] In the second book in the series, *ChupaCabra and the Roswell UFO*, Rosa leaves California behind to travel back to her home state of New Mexico, drawn by a call for help from a high school classmate named Ed, to investigate the strange goings on near Roswell, New Mexico. What Rosa discovers in New Mexico is not just a "transnational crossroads" but an interstellar one, a contact zone where nationalistic military interests, mythic creatures, and alien explorers meet.

If the mestizo or mestiza is the multiethnic, racially mixed human figure produced by life in the contact zone, Anaya's novel reflects that reality in the dark mirror of science fiction and horror. C-Force (Clone Force), a secret government agency, is revealed to be involved in genetic experimentation, initially cloning aliens, using the alien recovered from the 1947 Roswell crash as the DNA source. Additionally, Ed reveals that similar experiments have been taking place with chupacabra, with the clandestine scientific activity centered in Puerto Rico (home of the original sightings of the chupacabra). At the center of *ChupaCabra and the Roswell UFO* is a further development of the experiment: "C-Force used ChupaCabra DNA to mix with alien DNA."[42] Genetic experimentation is the horrific parallel to the mixing of cultures and peoples that the series elsewhere celebrates: "Synthetic biology gone wild. Monsters far more frightening than Frankenstein walked the earth."[43]

As Anaya makes clear, however, it is not the mixing itself that is problematic but the purpose behind that mixing. As librarian Marcy observes, "The aliens that landed are not evil. And neither are ChupaCabras. It's the way that men use these creatures that's evil."[44] "The original aliens," Rosa thinks, "might have been a group of space wayfarers just looking for a place to have dinner. The Argonauts of space. Harmless. And the ChupaCabra was a creature in many world legends."[45] Rosa even recalls that Marcy refers to the aliens as the brethren: "What did brethren mean in Spanish? *Familia*. Did Marcy mean the extraterrestrials were family from outer space? Primos, cousins."[46] The contact zone of New Mexico expands upward into the heavens when Rosa observes an alien ship, lights shining "like a gigantic stained-glass window," landing in the desert to pick up the waiting Marcy to carry her off to the stars.[47]

The Curse of the ChupaCabra and *The Chupacabra and the Roswell UFO* take place in the present, but the third book in the series, *Billy the Kid Meets the ChupaCabra*, takes us back into the past, to the Lincoln County War in New Mexico Territory and to Billy the Kid's role in that conflict from 1878 (the year of time traveler Rosa's arrival in the past) until July 14, 1881 (the day of Billy's death). Time travel serves as a metaphor for historical research, as English professor Rosa takes on the role of historian—her time travel into the past being part of her research for a novel she's writing on the life of Billy the Kid. Ultimately, Rosa's novel may center on Billy the Kid, but the borderlands history she excavates points to the Lincoln Country War as part of a larger history of American empire building, exploitation, and genocide.

In his discussion of the John Sayles film *Lone Star*, Neil Campbell argues that Sayles offers a Deleuzean "'archeology of the present' digging into the 'deserted layers of our time which bury our own phantoms.'" The archeological metaphor that Campbell uses here (drawing on Deleuze) can easily be transposed to a temporal one. If we consider a similar excavation of the past and uncovering of the tangled history of border communities taking place in a different genre than a mimetic film such as *Lone Star*, the time travel of science fiction fulfills a similar function to that of Deleuze's "archeology of the present." The time traveler indeed understands that "if we want to grasp an event, we must not pass along the event, but plunge into it," literally journeying into the "deserted layers of our own time which bury our own phantoms," investigating "what is remembered, who is remembered, how these memories are constructed."[48]

Part of what Rosa discovers through plunging into the past is the difference between reading history and the affective experience of witnessing traumatic events directly. Not only is written history "shaded by all the prejudices, whims, values, and motives of the historian," but historical writing was also "distanced from the real event.

Being there, hearing the barrage of gunfire, smelling the gunsmoke, seeing the sheriff fall dead . . . that was real."⁴⁹ As with other time-travel stories that involve traumatic events, the time-travel device is a strategy for conveying not just the story of what happened but also the emotional and psychological impact of violent trauma. The fear that keeps Rosa awake after witnessing the death of Sheriff Brady becomes part of the telling of the history of that moment. In another gun battle, the wounded Buckshot Roberts "limped toward Rosa and pointed his pistol at her. 'You're next!' he shouted. Just then Dick Brewer rushed him. Buckshot took aim and fired, and Brewer took a bullet that blew away half of his skull."⁵⁰ In that moment, Rosa escapes and is protected by Billy, but her experience of this historical moment involves direct witness of horrific violence and the fear of becoming a target of violence herself.

With a western outlaw made famous as much by twentieth-century westerns as by his own exploits at its center, the novel simultaneously critiques the genre western (particularly by taking jabs at Hollywood films) and utilizes its conventions. There are exciting shoot-outs, sublime landscapes, outlaws and lawmen (and it is sometimes hard to distinguish between them), chases on horseback, ambushes. As a hybrid genre story, there is also a monstrous shape-shifting creature; a point-of-view character (Rosa) who uses a laptop to take notes on nineteenth-century events and to communicate with her parents in the future and with her friend Marcy, who is located aboard a UFO; and, of course, wormholes and time travel.

Hyperconsciousness about the genre western is revealed most clearly through explicit references to western films. The chupacabra first appears in the novel in the guise of Pat Garrett: "I love role-playing. I get it from watching western movies. John Wayne and others."⁵¹ Chupacabra's explicit commentary on his "role-playing" ironizes the genre tropes, as does his flamboyant embrace of western costuming:

Not even the city dudes in the movie *Blazing Saddles* had looked this out of place. Saytir wore purple bell bottom pants with silver rosettes sewed down the sides of the legs, a bright red shirt, and a dazzling blue satin vest. His neckerchief was pink, his hat a poor excuse for a large mariachi sombrero. . . .

"Rosa," he whispered in his best imitation of Gary Cooper in the movie *High Noon*. "We meet again."[52]

Like Marty McFly wearing a western hat (and little else) and whispering lines from *Taxi Driver* while he practices his fast draw in a mirror, Saytir's western cosplay often involves multiple layers of references. And just like when we see a flash of Marty's bare bottom as he does an "air draw," his cool pose and costuming are not nearly as cool (or convincing) as he thinks they are.

If chupacabra's role-playing satirizes the western, sometimes historical events themselves appear cinematically in the novel—as if the western genre can sometimes convey the truth of history (at least the emotional and mythic truth) more effectively than objective description. When Billy and the Regulators set up an ambush (an event, Rosa observes, that must take place in order for "history to be history"), Sheriff Brady and his deputies walking down a dusty Lincoln street is described as "a scene straight out of a western movie."[53] Billy's life, however, Rosa observes, "was not as romantic as the western movies portrayed it."[54] As is the case with the western time-travel episodes of *Timeless* and *Legends of Tomorrow*, Anaya's novel revises the western's version of history as a myth of white nation building. Billy the Kid's violent life is played out in the larger context of American conquest of Mexican and Native American lands—and the novel presents Billy (or el Bilito, as he is named in Spanish) as being sympathetic with the plight of Mexicans, joining them in resisting "the Americanos from los Estados Unidos [who] were moving in to claim Hispanic and Indian land."[55] The novel also comments on the way western films have contributed to erasing the Mexican presence from Billy's history: "Except for one dark cowboy with a Spanish accent, the Mexicanos were kept in the background. Movie extras."[56] As with other twenty-first-century time-travel westerns, central to the story is a critique of the western's history of racial representation.

Rosa herself is also an unlikely hero for a western, as a woman, an English professor, a writer. She is nonetheless a frontier hero in both the western and science fiction sense, as she rides on horseback along with Billy and his men, experiences gun battles, and lives for three years in the frontier space of New Mexico. In the science fiction sense, like protagonist Valentine Smith of Robert Heinlein's *Stranger in a Strange Land*, Rosa also feels like "an alien in a foreign land." Whereas Smith is a Martian who journeys to Earth, Rosa's sense of alienation is temporal rather than geographic (she remains on the land that is her home in the present), a time traveler whose "new frontier" is a different moment in time rather than a different place.[57] She is both a "tenderfoot" western character who has a transformative frontier experience and the time traveler of science fiction whose temporal journey into a new territory parallels the geographic traveler of the conventional western. Again, the time traveler is a particularly apt figure of generic hybridity, as the traveler's split identity of the future existing in the present of the past suggests the narrative's own generic simultaneity—science fiction, western, revisionist history.

TIME TRAVEL, HISTORY, AND THE SOCIAL CONSTRUCTION OF TIME

History is "clouded," Rosa observes, by self-serving accounts of events (such as Pat Garrett's memoir of his killing of Billy), by later retellings (such as the cinematic versions of Billy's life and death), and by official histories that celebrate westward expansion and manifest destiny.[58] "In 1848," Anaya writes, "U.S. Imperialism took all of Mexico's northern territories in an unjust war," and the novel places the Lincoln County War in the context of the westward expansion of American nationalist interests that followed.[59] "Whatever was happening in Lincoln County was a microcosm of what was happening in the western territories"—the removal and genocide of Native Americans; the wave of Texans migrating into the Pecos Valley after the Civil War; and the arrival of ranchers with thousands of cattle, as "Mexicanos and Indians were pushed aside as a new wave of migrants began to homestead the fertile cattle country."[60]

In *In the Mean Time: Temporal Colonization and the Mexican American Literary Tradition* Erin Murrah-Mandril argues that time, or the imposition of a particular way of experiencing time, "is a mode of colonial domination." "Just as the U.S.-Mexico borderlands have come to signify a site of spatial dislocation," Murrah-Mandril writes, "the mean time is a site of temporal dislocation. U.S. colonization fractured the temporal structure of the U.S. Southwest by disrupting and disavowing the ways that Mexican Americans had experienced time."[61] Drawing on "Chicano/a studies' examination of space, especially in its iteration as borderland studies, which argues that something seemingly fixed and natural—space—is, in fact, a socially constructed medium imbued with ideological power," Murrah-Mandril points out that "time, too, is a social and ideological formation."[62]

The colonization of both time and space are central to the history of westward expansion and to the narrative retellings of that history. In the essay "The Great Nation of Futurity," John O'Sullivan, who coined the phrase *manifest destiny*, envisioned U.S. territorial expansion in speculative terms, describing a U.S. history that had not yet happened as if it was the only possible future: "The expansive future is our arena, and for our history. . . . We are entering on its untrodden space. . . . The far-reaching, the boundless future will be the era of American greatness."[63] Time (the "future") is described in terms of space ("our arena"), with American history understood as an inevitable "expansion" of both. The "untrodden space" of the future is, as Murrah-Mandril comments, "much like the imagined virgin wilderness of the U.S. frontier," an empty space on which the United States could "chart its own history as a smooth processual narrative of progress."[64] Manifest destiny "constructed the future as having already happened by projecting U.S. domination of the present onto a future of perpetual growth and expansion and foreclosing all other historical possibilities."[65]

"The United States lies like a huge page in the history of society," writes Frederick Jackson Turner in his 1893 frontier thesis, offering his own version of "history as a smooth processual narrative of progress," proceeding "line by line, as we read this continental page from West to East."[66] In contrast to such progressive nonfiction histories, Murrah-Mandril turns to the genre of realist historical fiction by Mexican American authors, which she posits as a kind of counter-genre to nonfiction histories. Historical fiction, written in a present moment and looking back at the past, "transforms history into a reading present with the potential to be historicized in new ways," depicting the other "historical possibilities" (and sometimes historical realities) that narratives of progress foreclose.[67] Historical fiction positions the reader in two moments of time: the "has happened" past represented in the narrative and the reader's own present, in which what "has happened" is experienced by the reader for the first time.

Historical fiction unravels "the temporal ideology of Manifest Destiny by reopening the past to the phenomenology and hermeneutics of the reading present."[68] And I would amend Murrah-Mandril's statement to note that historical fiction "transforms history into a reading present" whether in realist or speculative (e.g., featuring time travel or an alternate history) modes. Time-travel narratives, in particular, depict history both in the "reading present" and in the narrative present, as the time traveler's experience of the past (which takes place in the present tense as the traveler experiences that past for the first time) reflects that of the reader's. Time-travel narratives that return us to key moments in the history of westward expansion similarly "unravel the temporal ideology of Manifest Destiny" by unraveling time itself, with time travel figuring the practice of resistant reading by literally reopening the past and retelling the story of the past from the perspective of another present—that of the time traveler.

The introduction of standardized time was a cognitively estranging event (or series of events) for many groups of people who heretofore measured their experience of the passing of time by ways other than clock time. *In the Mean Time* documents how in the process of western expansion, spatial domination (as symbolized by the growth of the railway system) preceded and was reinforced by temporal standardization, as "railroad time" replaced local time: "Building on its colonized past, the United States also colonized the present through increasingly uniform systems of timekeeping to facilitate its capitalist production and exchange. In the 1880s U.S. railroads instituted the nation's time zones. By 1918 the Standard Time Act codified these time zones and created daylight savings time. This revolution in timekeeping effectively homogenized U.S. time, making it a mechanized tool of science, capitalism, progress. These changes coincided with the systemization and institutionalization of Mexican American disenfranchisement in the U.S. Southwest."[69]

In westerns, the railroad's arrival in a settlement signals the end of the frontier, and individual train arrival in westerns is often linked with clock time (with characters checking to see if the train is on time or late or asking clerks for the schedule, which is even referenced in titles, e.g., *3:10 to Yuma*). In a sense, when the train arrives on time in *High Noon*, the very fact of its on-time arrival renders the outcome of the battle between the sheriff and the outlaws moot—like a battle that takes place after an armistice has been signed because the news is late in arriving to the front lines.[70] Whoever wins the gun battle, the time of Wild West shoot-outs between outlaws and lawmen has already passed. Will Kane's tossing his badge into the dirt at the end of the film is just a more dramatic repetition of the gesture he makes at the beginning of the film, removing the badge before his wedding ceremony, as the film essentially loops backward in time to complete the action disrupted by a kind of time travel (the sudden arrival in the present of enemies from the past)—as Will and Amy Kane finally complete the departure for their honeymoon.

As do the late nineteenth- and early twentieth-century Mexican American narratives that Murrah-Mandril examines, *ChupaCabra Meets Billy the Kid* demonstrates the connection between colonialism generally and the "colonial practice of subordinating local forms of time to national and capitalist time."[71] The tension and resistance in those narratives, Murrah-Mandril argues, is apparent in the way they bring "together a number of situated and often contradictory forms of time," thereby revealing "the disjointed, conflicting forms of time that undergird national attempts to form a hegemonic narrative of progressive historical development."[72] "These temporal practices place Mexican Americans not outside of U.S. modernity," Murrah-Mandril writes, "but always moving across multiple forms of time in a way that exposes time's ideological implications."[73] Anaya follows Mexican American realist writers by using similar techniques of juxtaposition, pointedly contrasting, for example, Rosa's chronological observations of Billy the Kid's history (carefully noting the calendar dates of significant events as they happen or are about to happen) with Mexican American people's observation of celestial, seasonal, religious, festive, and ceremonial forms of time.

ChupaCabra Meets Billy the Kid is a story of temporal dislocation on several levels, most obviously through Rosa's time-travel adventure (her individual dislocation in time); more generally, the novel also documents U.S. standard time as it is imposed and mapped onto the space of Lincoln County. The visible manifestation of settler-colonial time is the steady influx of businessmen, entrepreneurs, land grabbers, ranchers, cattle drivers, a "new wave of migrants" who pushed aside "Mexicanos and Indians" and "began to homestead the fertile cattle country," their actions a physical implementation of the abstract linear idea of manifest destiny.[74] The waves of migrants that Anaya describes suggests a simultaneous measurement in time and space. The spatial displacement also disrupts the way time is experienced, beginning with the imposition of a newly significant calendar date, 1848, which marks the starting point of a sequence of measurable waves. The violence of the Lincoln County War, Anaya suggests, is just a symptom of the disruption caused by the larger incursion and occupation by waves of migrants, part of a series of events (including the slow violence of increased homesteading and cattle grazing) expanding in time and over space that interrupts sacred, seasonal, and localized ways of marking the passage of time (such as regular dances and celebrations). Anaya, through Rosa's eyes, shows us the alternate forms of time disrupted by this influx—the cycle of planting and harvesting, the religious calendar of celebration and commemoration—as they are interrupted by the violent events of the Lincoln County War. However, in keeping with the general argument of the ChupaCabra novels, Rosa finds in folk experience of time the possibility of resistance to the linear colonized time of ideological narratives of progress and development.

In part, that comes from Rosa's encounter in the past with practices that she recognizes as still ongoing in the future—her observation, for example, of "*La Pastorela*, a traditional nativity play, [that] has been reenacted for generations in New Mexico," a representation of a kind of sacred, ceremonial, or spiritual time that continues to exist alongside settler-colonial time. Rather than staying in the past as a ritual associated with a primitive culture, *La Pastorela* endures and continues to mark the passage of ceremonial and seasonal time. Natural time, Rosa observes, continues to endure, the steady march of seasons from one to the other, the movement of the sun across the sky marking night and day—"the Milky Way and the winter moon [that] were guiding lights," providing another linkage between the precolonial past and the colonized present and future.[75] "Few calendars marked the passing of time on the llano," Rosa thinks. "Seasons told the time. It was either blazing hot, stone cold, or windy."[76] The violence of the Lincoln County War may disrupt these natural ways of experiencing time, but it does not completely displace them.

Rosa's journey into the past, literally "moving across multiple forms of time," ultimately enables a counterhistory to the popular version of Billy the Kid as constructed by nonfiction history, memoir, and western films. "For the struggling Mexicano farmers of Lincoln County, the war wages on," Anaya writes, and "the violent times attracted outlaws to the area, and the poor and honest people were caught in the middle."[77] Ultimately, this is the counterhistory that Anaya tells, a history from the ground up, one that features a bilingual Bilito, who sings and speaks in Spanish, one who is not a generic western outlaw famed for his gunfights with lawmen but who is known for his alliances with and protection of the Mexicanos of Lincoln County. Part of that history is Rosa's story of those farmers and, particularly, of the women in those communities, including Josefita Chavez, "an appointed deputy in the Regulators' posse," a leader of the Mexicanos in fighting back "to protect the land that was being encroached on by the Americanos."[78] Josefita gives Rosa a small derringer that she eventually uses to fend off the menacing chupacabra Saytir. Later in the story, Rosa "found safe haven with Abrana Garcia," the querida of Billy whose romance with the outlaw has been ignored by film westerns but whose story becomes part of Rosa's Billy the Kid narrative, which becomes "a detailed history not just of Abrana, but of all the women who in this windswept land boiled in summer and froze in winter."[79] By associating the women in the narrative with seasonal time (e.g., "boiled in summer and froze in winter"), she also posits their survival and endurance as an ongoing resistant mode of timekeeping.

The death of the outlaw Billy the Kid is part of manifest destiny's narrative of linear time and progress, a marker of civilization's march through the untamed West. By complicating that image, by placing Billy in a context that frames his actions as part of a resistance to colonial incursions, and by telling that story from the perspective of a time traveler, Anaya also suggests a resistant experience of time. Or to put it another way, Rosa's time travel is a figure for that resistance—a literal plunge into history that creates not another time line (events continue to play out as they do in the history we know) but an alternate perspective on those events. "Linear, progressive time allows colonizers to narrowly define and control the past," Murrah-Mandril writes, to control the story of "what really happened."[80] The figure of time travel literalizes the revisionist historian's disruption of settler-colonial narratives of "what really happened" by taking us back into the past and showing us what narrowly progressive versions of history exclude or ignore.

Building on Chela Sandoval's observation that colonized people "survive and contest domination" through developing "the ability to shift between divergent ideologies," an ability Sandoval terms "differential consciousness," Murrah-Mandril argues that "Early Mexican American literature performs a differential time consciousness that reads and deploys multiple conflicting, ideologically imbued forms of time to survive and contest U.S. domination."[81] A "differential time consciousness" suggests the ability to shift between different temporal formations, the ability both to navigate dominant discourses of time and to experience time in alternate or resistant ways. Rosa's time travel literalizes this ability. Anaya (as does Alfredo Véa, as will be discussed in the next chapter) takes a thematic and stylistic concern of Mexican American realist writers and reformulates it through the high-intensity realism of science fiction, utilizing the trope of time travel to figure the "temporal adroitness" and "differential time consciousness" that Murrah-Mandril posits as a "constitutive feature of Mexican American writing."[82]

After the death of Billy, Rosa returns to the present by following the Pecos River, realizing that the river is a nexus where the map of time and the map of space are one and the same, not the location of a wormhole but the wormhole itself. "The river was a bridge from time present to time past," she observes, connecting "separate points in space-time," the route that she travels becoming part of the new cartography the novel suggests, one that maps history as well as place: "The river was history, ancestors, family, home, fields of corn and chile, patches of squash, apple orchards, fiestas, stories, neighbors sharing, giving, loving, community, and community as village."[83] Not just a means of traveling through time, the river is also a container of different forms of time: chronological (history), familial (lines of descent to ancestors), natural (seasons of planting and harvesting), and communal.

Anaya constructs the Pecos River valley and the village of Puerto de Luna as what Michel Foucault calls a heterotopia, "a kind of effectively enacted utopia" that is "at once absolutely real" and "absolutely unreal," a countersite that models for Rosa a past, present, and future resistance based in the ideal of community as village, an alternate sociality in contrast to nationalizing narratives and formations.[84] Museums (and libraries) are "heterotopias of indefinitely accumulating time," Foucault writes, "a sort of perpetual and indefinite accumulation of time in an immobile place." Anaya offers a different sort of heterotopia (rather than a museum) in the figuration of the Pecos River. The Pecos River valley is a physical and material location for gathering multiple forms of time. The river itself connects separate points in space-time both figuratively (metaphorically linking all members of the community, past and present, who have existed in proximity to the river) and literally (as the wormhole that takes Rosa back and forth between the twenty-first century and the nineteenth). Rather than a museum or library, the river is more in keeping with Foucault's type of heterotopia that is linked not to the accumulation of time but "to time in its most flowing, transitory, precarious aspect, to time in the mode of the festival." Or perhaps more accurately, the river as Anaya describes it brings together two types of temporal heterotopia, the mode and the place, "the heterotopia of the festival and that of the eternity of accumulating time . . . as if the entire history of humanity reaching back to its origins were accessible in a sort of immediate knowledge," which, for time traveler Rosa, it is.[85]

In *ChupaCabra Meets Billy the Kid*, the time-travel motif is also connected to the borderlands political perspective of the ChupaCabra series as a whole, its preference for building and using bridges (and rivers) to navigate between cultures and times, a preference that is explicitly brought to bear on contemporary politics and contrasted with the (in the novel) unnamed U.S. president's desire to build walls. Already a connection seeker, Rosa returns from the past with an expanded sense of empathy and a renewed sense of willingness to fight against "a mad president who murders the soul of our village," who "turns people against people," and who "does not see that the children are drowning. La Llorona, this wounded mother, will not be silenced. Her cry echoes across the country: Build bridges, not walls." Rosa returns from the past determined to "make new resolutions for the future. With others she would cry out protest, cry with La Llorona and awaken the people, march with the sisters of the Crying Woman."[86]

Linear notions of time distinctively separate past and present, a separation essential to narratives of progress (like manifest destiny), which posit the past as inferior (primitive) and the future (the transformation of the primitive into civilization) as superior. The separation of past and present also enables progressive narratives to disavow responsibility for past injustices (such as land theft) by relegating them to the past tense rather than as ongoing—present—injustices in need of being addressed. By traveling back to the nineteenth century, Rosa makes the colonial injustices of the past part of the present of the narrative, as we as readers experience them as they are happening. When she returns to the present, she reflects back on her past experiences, discovering new linkages between the injustices of the nineteenth century and those of the twenty-first.

Speculative Borderlands II

TIME TRAVEL AND CARTOGRAPHIES OF TRAUMA

Trauma and traumatic experience, broadly reflective of the legacies of violence in American history, continue to provide an important thread of investigation for the chapters in this book, as the subject of trauma is one that has been taken up by writers working in a variety of generic and ethnic traditions. As explored in chapter 2, time travel, likewise, provides a useful science fiction device for exploring the historical experience of trauma (by literally going back in time to investigate traumatic historical events) and for experimenting with narrative form as a means of conveying the psychological effect of trauma on individuals and groups. In this chapter, I look at two time-travel narratives that explore trauma and post-traumatic stress disorder through the broader geographical concept of the borderlands. The Amazon series *Undone* plays out in the specific place of San Antonio, Texas, located in the area of the United States and Mexico border region (and site of the Alamo, which plays only a minor role in the series).[1] Although (in contrast to the *Watchmen* series discussed in chapter 2) its exploration of time travel and trauma is personal rather than collective, a family tragedy rather than an act of violence affecting a whole community, *Undone* uses its geographical location to suggest main character Alma's (Rosa Salazar) larger connection to the sociology of living in the borderlands—living in the social space of a contact zone, "where cultures meet, clash, and grapple with each other, often in contexts of highly asymmetrical relations of power, such as colonialism, slavery, or their aftermaths as they are lived out in many parts of the world today."[2]

The geography of Alfredo Véa's *The Mexican Flyboy* is extensive and complicated, reflective of a main character, Simon Vegas, whose background as a migrant worker carried him through a wide swath of California agricultural fields and whose experiences include a childhood in Arizona, a wartime experience as a soldier in Vietnam, and a present-day life in San Francisco.[3] As a time traveler (enabled by a device he wears strapped to his chest) intent on rescuing victims of violence throughout history, Simon Vegas journeys widely in space and time.

Undone and *The Mexican Flyboy* extend the concept of the borderlands as a contact zone by connecting it to the science fiction trope of time travel, reimagining a cartography of the borderlands that emphasizes the dimension of temporality, the exploration of the frontiers and crossroads of time as well as space. The necessary fluidity of living in the social, political, and geographical place of the borderlands is reflected in the time traveler's ability to move temporally. Or we might say that both *Undone* and *The Mexican Flyboy* use the device of time travel to actualize the lived experience of borderlands temporality. The "differential time consciousness" and "temporal adroitness" that Murrah-Mandril claims as typical of Mexican American realist writing find their speculative counterpart in these time-travel stories, a representation of "aspects of reality" (lived experiences in the contact zone of the United States–Mexico borderlands) that "defy straightforward representation" via the "high-intensity variety realism" offered by the conventions of science fiction.[4]

UNDONE IN TIME: TRAUMA, TIME TRAVEL, AND THE BORDERLANDS

In contrast to the time-travel narratives discussed in chapter 2 that involve temporal journeys to the Alamo and its famous battle, *Undone* does not actively reinforce or reiterate the national and racial mythologies associated with the site. Although at one point Alma shouts disparaging comments at reenactors at the Alamo site, neither does *Undone* actively interrogate the colonial and racial history of the city in which it's set. Contemporary San Antonio as depicted in *Undone*, how-ever, is suggestive of the "borderlands West" that Lutenski describes, a place of "complicated networks of race and ethnicity."[5] In the San Antonio of *Undone*, Indigenous religions continue to rub against the borders of the dominant Christianity. The history of colonialism is made present in multiple ways: through Alma's mixed ancestry, through her identification as "mestiza," through her Mexican-born mother's assimilationist insistence on identifying as Spanish and rejecting a familial connection to Indigenous ancestors. We also see the presence of contemporary cross-racial networks, as members of different migrant and immigrant communities meet and inter-act: Alma's boyfriend Sam (Siddharth Dhananjay), who immigrated from India as a child; her African American coworker Tunde (Daveed Diggs); her Jewish father, Jacob (Bob Odenkirk); her bilingual mother, Camilia Diaz (Constance Marie); and various Indigenous characters who exist on the edges of Alma's community. Alma's time travel ultimately becomes a way for her to negotiate these networks of dif-ference, as she comes to know different members of her community through visiting moments in their pasts that encourage empathetic understanding of the choices that have made them the individuals they are in Alma's present.

Time travel in *Undone* is slipstream rather than device driven. The science fiction element comes from Alma's father, Jacob, a scien-tist whose research focuses on a combination of scientific study (of enlarged ventricles in the brain) and mysticism (the ways of shamans, who Jacob believes are able to experience time differently because of their brain structure). Time travel in *Undone* ultimately ventures toward stereotyped notions of Native mysticism—time-traveling Native American shamans having been a feature of comic books and weird westerns for decades. The Indigenous characters in *Undone* (particularly in season 1) always appear in traditional dress; at times, when we see them in the present, it's uncertain whether they are ghosts, time travelers, or (as it usually turns out) dressed traditionally because they are performers. Likewise, the series' emphasis on genetic connection rather than mutual relations and responsibilities—the suggestion that there is something in the blood (or in this case, in the physical structures of Alma's brain), which connects Alma to an Indigenous legacy of supernatural ability—suggests settler-colonial definitions of Indigeneity.

As in other speculative stories of trauma, time travel in *Undone* is presented as symptomatic. One moment Alma is in a hospital bed, and the next, she has been pulled out of the hospital and into a car as she reexperiences the traumatic injury, a car crash, that landed her in the hospital. That is, in the present, something happens that triggers the traumatic memory, and Alma experiences the insistent and involuntary reenactment of the traumatic past. Only, in this science-fictionalized version of PTSD, the involuntary return to the past happens literally through time travel. The first episode of the series begins with the accident, as Alma speeds through a stoplight.[6] The story then takes us back several days earlier, before returning to the crash at the end of the episode—revealing for the first time the cause (or one of the causes) of the crash, the sudden appearance of her dead father by the side of the road. The second episode, "The Hospital," follows Alma's recovery as she becomes, like Billy Pilgrim in *Slaughterhouse Five*, "unstuck in time" ("I feel like I'm caught in a weird loop," she comments).[7] The same moments recur over and over again but from slightly different perspectives and with slightly different outcomes. In keeping with other narratives of time travel and trauma, Alma, at any moment, can be propelled from the present back to the car crash. That return to the moment of trauma is sometimes signaled aurally before it happens physically—the sound of car horns blaring as she sits in her hospital bed or a rumbling noise in the cafeteria where she sits. The hospital room, the cafeteria, or wherever she might be starts to shake, sometimes shattering like a glass or mirror, the shards reforming as the interior of the car.

The sudden abrupt movements from one point in time to another suggest the disruptive symptoms of PTSD. But as Alma gains more control over her ability to move through time, the border crossing from one moment in time to another occurs more fluidly, and time travel becomes a therapeutic means for Alma to investigate the traumatic losses in her life—particularly the trauma of her father's death. Jacob is an ambiguous character in the story. His ghostly appearance at the side of the highway distracts Alma and contributes to her crash, and he reveals to her that his appearance was meant to cause the accident and thus jump start her time-travel abilities. Although initially apparitional in his encounters with Alma, he is a time traveler more than (or perhaps in addition to) a spirit from the world of the dead, and he sets about teaching Alma how to control her abilities—a therapist of sorts who helps transform her time travel from involuntary symptomatic event to intentional therapeutic effort, although he also has his own agenda.

Jacob's traumatic death in a car crash during her childhood (a trauma that Alma repeats through her own car accident) is a traumatic loss that affects Alma's present. The physical trauma of her own car crash is in some ways secondary to the psychological trauma caused by the loss of her father. After receiving a phone call from his lab assistant while her father was out trick-or-treating on Halloween with Alma, he leaves her alone on the street to go to his lab—and never returns. While Alma waits on the sidewalk, her father and his assistant die together in a car crash. The continued traumatizing effect on Alma more than a decade later is visible in her lack of affect in the present (especially as seen in the first episode), her tamping down of emotion, her focus on completing a daily series of repetitive tasks, her resistance to committing to her relationship with Sam. As with *Watchmen*, *Undone* addresses the generational transmission of trauma, as the task that Jacob leaves unfinished becomes Alma's mission: to find out who killed him and to prevent his death from taking place—thus both changing his personal history and erasing the traumatic loss of her father from Alma's childhood.

The geographical setting of the story is important to its play with time travel. The San Antonio that we travel through—the River Walk, the Alamo, the churches, cathedrals, childcare centers, hospitals, bars, restaurants, houses, and apartments—is a physical representation of the multiple borders and boundaries that cross Alma's life, as well as being a physical representation of the different areas associated with her mestiza identity. Alma's transformation in *Undone* also suggests formulations of borderlands identity in Gloria Anzaldúa's later work, which shift from the focus on the "new mestiza" of *Bor-*

derlands / *La Frontera* to an exploration of "Nepantla" and "Nepantleras."[8] "Anzaldúa's nepantlera offers a more fluid subjectivity" than that of the "new mestiza," Susana Ramírez writes, suggesting an understanding that "boundaries are more malleable."[9] The spatial or geographical metaphor of the new mestiza gains a more explicitly temporal element, as "Anzalduan nepantleras are agents constantly moving between time and space and beyond the material body."[10] The transformation of consciousness that Anzaldúa theorizes as *nepantla* is figured in *Undone* through the trope of time travel, which literally enables Alma to cross the boundaries between the different selves she has developed in the various communities she has inhabited throughout her lifetime, her border crossing taking place not only geographically but across a chronology of selfhood. The experience of being dislocated in time that is initially a sign of psychological disturbance is ultimately replaced by a sense of "temporal adroitness," as Alma's movement through time becomes more intentional and controlled.

Alma's ancestry is Jewish and Catholic; American and Mexican; and through a distant relative on her mother's side (a great-great-great-grandmother), Indigenous; and perhaps, the narrative suggests, Nahuatal. At the hotel where Becca's wedding is taking place, we see several Nahuatal characters moving through the hallway. We wonder if this is a moment of time slipping or if ghostly figures from the past are moving through Alma's present, but they are revealed to be performers at (in keeping with the borderlands mix of the story) a bar mitzvah. Alma later shares a cigarette with one of the dancers, Tonatzin (Tonatzin Carmelo), and reveals that she felt connected to their dance performance.[11] "You're mestiza, right?" Tonatzin replies. "So, it's in you." Tonatzin's smoke break is one of the few moments when the Nahuatal characters are fully in the present, a contemporary Native individual and not a somewhat ghostly representation (or symbolic present-day incarnation) of a mystical Indigenous past. The moment also reinforces *Undone*'s repetition of a familiar trope of Indigeneity as a kind of racial (and spiritual) inheritance received by a non-Native character—an appropriation of Indigenous identity that has a long history in American culture.

Undone is at its most effective when it interrogates the borders demarcated by disability. Perhaps the most significant marker of difference is Alma's hearing impairment, caused by pneumonia when she was three. Her crossing over from the world of the deaf to the world of hearing (via a cochlear implant) is one of the story's most significant moments of border crossing, one that is linked metaphorically to Alma's temporal abilities and one that parallels the narrative's exploration of the losses caused by abandoning belonging to a minority group in favor of assimilation. "Remember when you got your implant, and you could hear for the first time," her father reminds her, "but your brain couldn't process it, make sense of it? . . . This is kind of a new way of 'hearing.'"[12] The episode "Alone in This (You Have Me)" focuses on this element of Alma's identity, suggesting a parallel between ethnicity and disability through drawing connections to Sam's personal story—his migrant journey from a childhood in India to a life in America, his sense of difference and exclusion from his English-speaking classmates, and his efforts to assimilate into his new world. The episode also erects a barrier between Sam and Alma, as Alma discovers that Sam has been lying to her. Before her accident, she broke up with Sam, but as a result of Alma's brain injury, she does not remember the breakup and assumes they're still together. Sam lets her go on thinking they're a couple and still living together.

"Alone in This (You Have Me)" is the most geographically and temporally wide-ranging episode, as Alma travels in time to significant moments in both her life and Sam's. The episode takes us to Mexico (to a ceremonial pool at the site of an ancient ruins that her family visited together on vacation), to India (where she witnesses Sam saying goodbye to his childhood friends on the day before he leaves the country), and to Chicago (where Sam went to elementary school). The borders in the episode are personal as well as geographic and temporal. Alma and Sam spend most of the episode in separate rooms, as Alma repeatedly shuts doors to keep Sam out, and their conversations take place through these barriers. At one point, Alma removes the exterior device that connects to her implant, closing the border to the world of sound and hearing and shutting Sam out not only physically but aurally.

In one scene, Alma and her father travel back to observe her arrival at a school for the hearing impaired. She takes her place in a circle of children playing various instruments, their teacher signing to them as they play, "Feel the vibrations of the music. Imagine it's moving through your neighbor's body. It's moving through all our bodies, connecting us." The sound waves become a medium of connection, traversing the borders of individual bodies, as Alma joins in, playing the other half of a set of bongo drums with another girl who will become her closest friend at the school. When her father moves them elsewhere (to the site of the ruins, where Alma stands in the empty ceremonial pool), she protests, speaking to him in sign language (one of the few moments when the adult Alma uses sign), "Wait, Dad, I want to stay here. . . . Dad, don't change it yet. I was happy here."

All of this is happening as the argument between Sam and Alma is taking place in the present, as Sam, on the other side of one door or another, tries to explain and tries to apologize. While listening to Sam, Alma is transported to moments in his childhood. She observes Sam's childhood struggles with American bullies who make fun of his accent and of his response to the bullying—a disciplined, solitary effort to erase his accent by repeatedly imitating a recorded voice telling a children's story, echoing her own difficult experience with speech therapy after the installation of her implant. There are several traumas in the narrative—the trauma of her father's death, the physical trauma of her own car accident, as well as the trauma of border crossings, the loss that occurs when moving across a fixed border. Alma's time travel contrasts with the lack of fluidity in her life elsewhere, the difficulty of crossing the multiple borders that divide her life and identity into segments. The Alma who finds a home in the deaf community is not the same Alma who negotiates the world of the hearing, but through time travel or, in Anzaldúan terms, as a nepantlera, she can experience both those selves simultaneously.

From the perspective of the psychology of traumatic experience, time travel also provides her with an opportunity to visit the past and, by so doing, to leave it behind, an opportunity to mourn the losses but also to move forward. She signals her willingness to do so at the end of the episode by leaving the bathroom where her father has been trying to convince her to focus on developing her time-travel skills rather than her boyfriend problems. For the first time, as well, she willingly separates herself from her father. Her conversation with Sam (revealing the truth about her time travel and her conversations with her dead father) for the first time puts into language traumatic experiences that have been heretofore unspeakable. Although Alma (with Sam's help) will continue to aid her father's search for the truth about his death, her time travel in this episode serves a therapeutic purpose—it enables her to confront her losses; to put those losses into language and begin the process of mourning; and, finally, to begin to move forward into the future.

THE ANTIKYTHERA DEVICE AND "SPECULATIVE RASQUACHISMO"

The Mexican Flyboy further explores the concept of the borderlands as a geographic and temporal contact zone, as Simon Vegas travels through both time and space to rescue the marginalized and the powerless. "La máquina, the machine," the time-travel device in *The Mexican Flyboy*, is fashioned by Simon with the aid of the former professor Roberto Cantú, who drove off to teach a class on Octavio Paz one morning and just kept going, dropping out of academia and adopting the name Hephaestus Segundo, naming himself after a mythic "blacksmith to the gods" and alchemist, two professions that he takes up himself, both of which prove useful in reconstructing la máquina.[13] At the core of the machine is "the original Antikythera device," recovered from an ancient shipwreck near Crete in 1901, which had been "designed and constructed in 100 BC, probably by the great Archimedes himself," made up of a complex system of "finely tuned wheels and gears, shafts, bearings, splines, and sprockets."[14] For years the newly discovered Antikythera device had been misused as a doorstop and, eventually, was misused again in the 1960s as a weapon by the U.S. Army in Vietnam, where "the machine somehow fell into the hands of a lowly private first class named Simon Vegas," who "had hidden the device in his duffel bag and carried it out of the country when his miserable tour of duty in Vietnam came to an end."[15] In contrast to the U.S. Army, Simon realized that the device "had been built by Archimedes to bring comfort, not pain," to provide "a tiny morsel of solace" in "a world of hurt."[16]

Simon then spent years undoing the changes made by the military, "carefully, painstakingly, prying it apart, piece by infinitesimal piece," and reconstructing the mechanism in as close to its original form as possible. Once restored, Simon commissioned Hephaestus Segundo to fabricate "new gears, springs, and wheels" for the device.[17] Working for months, Hephaestus fashioned "replacements for the modern components" the military scientists had "ham-fistedly crammed into the small box," using instead "miniature vacuum tubes, antique oil-filled capacitors, and hand-formed wire-wound resisters and coils" and, "his proudest achievement," an addition of "two bearings and a tiny spigot made of purest gold."[18] For the final ingredient, after discovering that "expensive turbine lubricants wouldn't work," Hephaestus finds at "the auto parts store on San Pablo Avenue" a can of "Marvel Mystery Oil," which the "Antikythera device seems to love." With that final addition, an engine additive of the type beloved by street and shade tree mechanics on both sides of the border, the "two desperate alchemists" manage "to coax a miraculous liquid from a jumble of metal and wires," which dripped from the gold spigot to a clay container—"just a few crystalline drops of the ever-elusive *aurum potable*, the only known antidote to human cruelty."[19]

As Cathryn Josefina Merla-Watson observes about the work of Chican@ futurist visual artists, we can see here, as well, in the descriptions of the scientific artistry of "the two desperate alchemists," the mobilization of "the defamiliarizing power of science fiction in tandem with the disordering 'underdog perspective' . . . of a speculative rasquachismo that stems from a working-class Chicana/o sensibility of creative recycling or 'making do.'"[20] Although "rasquachismo" has "traditionally noted the tacky or funky," the term was reappropriated by Tomás Ybarro-Frausto "to describe a unique working-class 'Chicano sensibility' of utilizing and recycling what is available in one's immediate material surroundings to create aesthetic beauty or pleasure, as demonstrated in everyday barrio practices such as yard art, lowriders, or self-presentation."[21] What Merla-Watson in turn repurposes and renames as "speculative rasquachismo" retains the original term's "aspects of hope and 'making do,'" as it also suggests the "explicitly visionary praxis of reusing, melding, and refunctioning of images, icons, or significations associated with the primitive and the modern."[22] The Antikythera time-travel device, with its combination of ancient and modern parts, its jumble of repurposed metal and wire, its use of Mystery Oil as a "making do" lubricant, seems an exemplary symbol of "speculative rasquachismo." Playfully evoking the street-level "making do" technological bricolage of everyday Chican@ life (batteries are connected to the device by "that most ubiquitous of Mexican tools: a set of jumper cables"), combining the mechanical genius of the two Mexican American collaborators with their appreciation of their Greek predecessor Archimedes, the device exemplifies life in a global contact zone.[23]

An omnium gatherum, la máquina, like other devices in narratives of the speculative West, also suggests metaphorically through its hotchpotch conglomeration of parts the novel's multigeneric combination: ancient science (the Antikythera device is an actual mechanical device, the history of which the novel mostly reports accurately), ancient mythology, contemporary urban folklore (the magical efficacy of engine additives such as Marvel Mystery Oil), comic books, science fiction, and even the western—especially the western's evocation of Mexican characters. Véa describes Simon with the machine in place: "[Simon] lifted the jerry-rigged machine from the workbench and strapped it around his upper body, using a pair of antique leather bandoliers that formed an X across his chest. He looked just like the Mexican bandido Pancho Villa. Three motorcycle batteries had been taped together and were in a small pack that he slung over his left shoulder. A folded map was stuffed beneath one of the bandoliers."[24]

As Conway observes in *Heroes of the Borderlands: The Western in Mexican Film, Comics, and Music*, the outlaw heroes of Mexican westerns contrast sharply with the bandido stereotype prevalent in American films.[25] For example, the outlaw heroes of corridos, the folk-song-ballad tradition of Mexico and the borderlands, "constitute a borderlands type who stood for la raza against Anglo-American racism and injustice."[26] By linking Simon's bandoliers to Pancho Villa (rather than to generic bandidos), Véa suggests a connection to the "borderlands corrido tradition of celebrated Mexican shootists," a western outlaw tradition associated more with Mexican nationalism than with the bandido character type found in "every racist Hollywood Western that cast Mexicans as murderous bandits."[27] Although Simon might be connected to this corrido tradition, as he is an outlaw hero of sorts, one who certainly stands against racism and injustice, his actions are internationalist rather than nationalist, and his real weapon is the "folded map" held in place by the bandoliers rather than guns and bullets. Part Pancho Villa, part comic book character (Simon is directly influenced by stories of Doctor Strange and of Mandrake the Magician), part science fiction adventurer, and assisted by an equally outlandish artist-blacksmith-alchemist, Simon in the guise of the Mexican Flyboy is an ethnic and generic bricolage appropriately representative of the expansive borderlands experience he represents.

In la máquina, we can also see a technological incarnation of "differential consciousness," as Chela Sandoval describes it: "a mobile, flexible, diasporic force that migrates between contending ideological systems . . . [that] operates as does a technology—a weapon of consciousness that functions like a compass."[28] Differential consciousness, an ability attributed to colonized subjects, is certainly an ability demonstrated by individual characters in *Mexican Flyboy*, but it also appears in the mechanical form of la máquina, which has indeed been converted by Simon into a "weapon of consciousness" and conscience that "functions like a compass" and a chronograph—a mobile, flexible force that enables Simon to migrate within and between "contending ideological systems," adroitly maneuvering through time and space in order to rescue individuals damaged by those systems.

The narrative of *The Mexican Flyboy* ultimately creates a cartography of trauma that is global in scope. Traumatic experience in the novel is both personal and collective; it is both individual and generational, inherited and transmitted from one generation to another. Simon's wife, Elena, observes that he "suffered from every symptom listed" in books on PTSD except for depression and that "in every other way he resembled other men who suffered from *melancholia de querre*, shell-shock, nostalgia."[29] Elena associates his disorder with his experience in Vietnam, visibly present in the scar on the back of his hand left by a bullet wound, but she also realizes that "there was almost certainly a deep-seated reason, a ground zero, for Simon's malaise, his case of walking, high-functioning lunacy—perhaps more than one ground zero."[30] The wound in his hand was caused by a bullet that had previously passed through the neck (and killed) his friend Fulgencio. Simon and Fulgencio also shared another trauma—they had been ordered to shoot and kill a Vietnamese boy suspected of being laden with explosives (when, in fact, his shirt had been stuffed with candy bars). "Every day," Simon comments, "I land on a scarred and pocked hill that I've landed on a million times. When I get there, I see, for the millionth time, a young boy who is lying on his back," and every day, Simon finds his own face in a group of men looking at the body: "Once I pulled a trigger and a little boy died. . . . I followed orders."[31] Even more deeply in Simon's past, as a child working in grape cultivation fields, he observed an accident (or suicide) involving a woman skydiver who plunged from the sky without opening her parachute and hit the ground in front of him. And there is an even earlier trauma, a mass accidental death in his childhood that left Simon orphaned.

In a helicopter in Vietnam heading toward "Landing Zone Cherokee," Simon and Fulgencio "had been ravaged by the same unspeakable memory as it played through their minds over and over again."[32] Véa writes,

He had been trying so hard to suppress the awful memory. He had shoved at it and choked it with every positive thought that he could cull from his recollections, but the only thought that had the momentum and the gravity to shove the vision of the dying boy aside was the all too familiar image of a woman with red hair streaking downward to the ground. Private Simon Vegas was trapped at that place, caught between two awful memories and hovering above a landing zone filled with North Vietnamese troops. He felt like his body and soul were being torn into three pieces.[33]

The psychological experience of traumatic memory takes on physical form in Véa's description of the helicopter flight, as Simon is both hovering in physical fact and in memory, neither in one place nor another and in more than one place simultaneously. Simon's experience of PTSD is also reproduced during his time-travel experiences, which are described in similar terms, as he hovers above another "landing zone," the final violent moments of the individual he hopes to save. Likewise, his repeated time travel to traumatic moments in the past literalizes his psychological experience of going back "a million times" to the moment of violence that he himself committed. The time travel in that sense might be interpreted as symptomatic, repeated reenactments of a traumatic event that he isn't able to access fully except in the displaced form of someone else's trauma. Time travel as traumatic symptom seems to be the case especially when he repeatedly (and unsuccessfully) tries to stop acts of violence similar to the one he himself committed.

In an effort to save Amadou Diallo from being shot by police on February 14, 1999, "the Mexican Flyboy lifted off unnoticed and shot over the Sierras" and increased his speed until "his first glimpse of the Hudson River and the dark ocean beyond," where he dropped down and "found himself hovering over Soundview in the Bronx."[34] However, "it had happened again. He had arrived too late." Rather than saving the man, Simon "heard the crack of guns firing, and he witnessed the body of Amadou Diallo collapsing downward," Simon moaning "as he watched the last of nineteen rounds entering Amadou's shaking, jerking body." As in every case when Simon arrives too late, the damage done to the body is described in vivid detail. Late arrival means that he must adjust the time machine and turn time backward, a process that causes Simon to witness the horrific trauma a body has experienced yet again in reverse motion. In the case of Amadou Diallo, as Simon watches the shooting in reverse, "he suddenly heard another noise emanating from a time in the future and from a place three thousand miles away." Hovering above the "landing zone" in the Bronx in 1999, suspended between the past and the present, Simon is called back west to San Francisco, whispering as he leaves, "But I'll be back before I've left. I promise. I promise. No mistakes next time."[35] As in other traumatic time-travel narratives, the time travel literalizes the therapeutic process of returning repeatedly to—and sometimes being forced away from—the traumatic memory as part of the working through of trauma.

To rescue the victims of violence, Simon must repeatedly visit those scenes of violence: "No matter how precise his calculations had been, no matter how many times the machine was recalibrated and readjusted, for some unknown reason the Antikythera devices always forced him to be a witness to the suffering."[36] To even locate these moments in time, he must first immerse himself in the details of the trauma through careful study of what happened (and thus he knows exactly what damage each bullet does to Amadou's body); then if his calculations are off, he must witness the horrors of the scene of violence, often repeatedly, as he continues to adjust his machine to arrive at the right moment. As with traumatic memory, Simon is repeatedly drawn to the scene of violence, where the traumatic event is repeatedly and vividly reenacted. The closer the scenes he visits are to his own trauma(s)—in their resemblance to his own traumatic memories or in their connection to his family history—the harder they are for him to reach. In the novel's metaphorical rendering of resistance to therapeutic return to traumatic events, he cannot reach one key traumatic moment in his life, because despite his years of searching, he is unable to determine the precise place where the event occurred.

REGIONALITY AND CARTOGRAPHIES OF TRAUMA

The concept naming the connection between place, person, and history that Campbell describes as regionality is "expressed as a layered or entangled sense of time and space, of memory and event, history and story, affect and emotion, and from which assembles a critical regional presence/present, always already inflected by the past, haunted by memories, myths, and everyday realities." *The Mexican Flyboy* renders that concept objectively through its time-travel trope, which actualizes a "layered or entangled sense of time and space," as Simon quite literally travels through layers of time to explore the connections between "memory and event, history and story," between the haunted present and the traumatic past, reached in every case through a specific place.[37] Those specific places are then connected to one another via the routes of Simon's journeys, which create lines and trajectories joining region to a global network of traumatic experience. That "layered or entangled sense of time and space" is also objectively rendered through Véa's descriptions of the cartographic assemblages Simon creates from maps and various physical objects, which quite literally juxtapose different regions and different moments of time in what might seem like a random collage but ultimately reveal an entanglement of connections waiting to be understood.

As in Roanhorse's *Storm of Locusts*, Véa draws our attention to the possibilities of mapping and remapping through the frequent inclusion of physical maps in the narrative. In keeping with the book's attention to maps, Elena's father is revealed to have been "a professor of ancient cartography."[38] Searching through the garage, Elena and her friend Zeke "found themselves wading ankle deep in maps—grid maps, topographical maps, military and street maps. There were maps of Germany, Cambodia, and France. There were maps that her own father had loved: the Hereford Mappa Mundi, the Pirit Reis map, and the *Fragmenta tabulae antiquae*."[39] Elena observes that "each time Hephaestus came to the house to work, the bag of comics, the maps, and the ledgers would be spread out across the floor as though the two men were using them as some sort of template or diagram."[40] Simon's map collection is an assemblage creating a larger single map with multiple dimensions, a layered archeology of maps charting an extensive cartography of trauma: "pre-Civil War Atlanta and haunted Goree Island, a diagram of Sing Sing Prison lying on top of a map of Auschwitz and one of the Bastille."[41]

In her investigation of her husband's odd activities in their garage, Elena discovers copies of comic books about Mandrake the Magician, Doctor Strange, and the Phantom. As a child Simon carried his comic books in an "indestructible map pouch" given to him by a cook at a migrant work camp—the cook had been using the pouch to protect maps he had been carrying since the Second World War.[42] That "map pouch" was an appropriate storage place, as the comic books become part of the larger map of a temporal and geographic borderland that Simon navigates with the aid of la máquina. Additionally, the garage is home to "hundreds of maps and countless ledgers filled with incomprehensible codes—page after page of scribbled and scrawled numbers," which, we eventually discover, are also maps of Simon's own making—ledgers full of latitude and longitude, map coordinates to guide him to scenes of trauma.[43] The maps range from the ancient to the contemporary, from ones created by the most famous cartographers in history to Simon's self-made maps, including one imprinted on his own body, "a fading, spreading tattoo on Simon's belly, a line of numbers written above the next," coordinates like the ones scribbled in his ledgers.[44]

Like Campbell's *Affective Critical Regionality*, *The Mexican Flyboy* "is a book about different forms and processes of mapping that explore the complex territories of 'regionalism' by moving beyond conventional mapping or its objects," a book that explores "what lines, grids, circles, trajectories, and complex geometries intersect as places, people, spaces, histories, memories, energies, forces, and affects; and how . . . they entangle and disentangle with each other to build networks, meshworks, cities, neighbourhoods, regions, nations, and worlds."[45] Specifically located in several western regions—southern Texas, southeastern Arizona, the grape cultivation region of California, and California's Bay Area encompassing San Francisco and Oakland—*The Mexican Flyboy* constructs a complex map of Simon's regional belonging, through the migration of his Irish ancestors to Mexico; his grandfather's sojourn in Waco, Texas; Simon's family's life in Arizona; his personal journey from Arizona to California; and his international travel during and around the time of the Vietnam War.

However, the most complex geometries and intersections of "places, people, spaces, histories, memories, energies, forces, and affects" occur through his time-travel adventures, an unconventional mode of travel that the novel reflects through its equally unconventional understanding of cartography—its attention not only to traditional maps but also to Simon's cartographic bricolage, complex assemblages constructed of historical maps, scribbled numbers, photographs, tragic family stories, snatches of song, emotional trajectories, names of people as well as places, and histories. Simon must use concrete temporal and geographical coordinates to time travel accurately to the correct time and place, but the maps he builds to guide his journeys require more than traditional cartography in order to be effective. Those maps are mixed-media constructions, comic books combined with coordinates, history woven intricately with understanding of place, and inclusive of an emotional element that is crucial to the project: a sense of empathy. Simon's maps are never stable, finished, singular objects. The improvisational and ever-changing quality (continually altered and amended by Simon's scribbled notations, lines of direction, X-marked spots, handwritten names and initials) of the maps also suggests the kind of provisional and constantly evolving regional mapping that Campbell describes: "nested, knotted and gnarled, woven and entangled," "always weaving, always in process and—like social life itself—never finished to form."[46]

As Campbell writes, "*Affect* affects the meanings of places, too, for it alters our angles of sensibility. . . . Region in these terms is always more-than-representational precisely because it engages with intensities of affect."[47] *The Mexican Flyboy* dramatizes this element of regionality through its attention to the relationship between place and trauma, which amplifies "intensities of affect." Simon must literally return to the place of trauma in order to experience that intensity of affect, and he must then transform traumatic memory to narrative memory through action (time travel and rescue) and through representation (the naming of person, place, and time). Of the skydiver's death, Simon comments, "I have witnessed her death through the eyes of a child ten times a day, every day of my life, since then."[48] Simon is thwarted by not knowing her name or the exact location of the death. Although the event took place in California, someplace "where Pinot noir is grown on a large scale," his vineyard labor during his childhood was so extensive "that I don't know where she was geographically, and that means that I can't get to her. I can only get near her—in proximity, and that's all. I need to know her exact longitude and latitude and the precise moment it happened—Greenwich Mean Time. If I don't know her full name, I can't lift her."[49] Simon needs an accurate map of the past to work his rescues, but in this crucial case, his memory of geography is obscured by the reality of migrant labor. Thus, the violent death remains unspeakable, cannot be brought into representation, until Simon can honor and memorialize the victim, which he cannot do properly until he is able to speak her name.

And even if he knows the location, coordinates by themselves are just numbers; they do not become a map until they're connected to a history. Scrolling through a ledger, Zeke reads out entries at random, a series of numbers that only become meaningful when interpreted by Simon: "Before he could finish reading the coordinates, Simon whispered, 'Wounded Knee. The slaughter of Hunkpapa and Miniconjou families by American cavalry.'" The "dizzying array of numbers, dates, and times written on page after page after page" are an extensive map of slaughter, but those numbers only become meaningful—only become a map—when Simon connects them to history, when he remembers and, by remembering, pays tribute to the past.[50] The time machine, Simon explains, "helps me look for lines and for the intersection of lines."[51] With the Antikythera device, Simon locates borders and frontiers, temporal and geographic lines designating when and where. In *The Mexican Flyboy*, locations disconnected by time and place are brought together by a cartography that maps locations by the violence and cruelty they birthed, so that Waco, Texas; Le Havre, France; early twentieth-century Manhattan; and seventeenth-century Azores are mapped together, thus creating a new map of the borderlands West and of the West Coast, by making visible their "multiple relations with the world."[52]

Simon tries to turn traumatic memory into narrative memory by creating a story of rescue and survival in place of the story of trauma and death. When his friend Zeke asks him why he does it and who it helps, Simon responds, "It's for me. . . . It helps me. . . . Every time I do it, I'm sane for another minute, another hour. Brick by brick, I build my own world—one that I can live with—even if it only exists for a microsecond in a single synapse."[53] By helping others, he helps himself, at least for a moment. But because these therapeutic rescues don't resolve the underlying problems, he has to repeatedly enact them, and it's certainly possible that his rescues are symptomatic, a displacement of his individual trauma, as he travels to traumatic moments other than his own as a substitute for working through his own trauma. Viewed as a response, however, to a collective sense of trauma, Simon's time travel suggests a confrontation with an inherited human history of violence, as deliberate acts of remembrance. An accurate mapping—one that ties together place and history, one that charts the manifold connections between a particular place and the rest of the world, one that also marks the points of connection between different moments in time—becomes the novel's dominant metaphor for recovery from trauma, and particularly for recovery from collective trauma. In discussing generational transmission of trauma, Fromm writes, "There seems to be an almost inevitable outcome to trauma cut out of social discourse; the next generation must deal with it and sometimes represent it."[54] Simon travels through time in order to create both a map and a memorial, tying together place and history, returning to moments "cut out of social discourse" in order to represent the full story, a representation that only takes place when trauma, place, and history are brought together through an act of narrative remembering that is simultaneously an act of speculative cartography.

To return to Campbell's discussion of the film *Lone Star*, we might argue that Véa's approach, like that of *Lone Star* director John Sayles, "is 'an archeology of the present' digging into the 'deserted layers of our time which bury our own phantoms.'" Again, the time traveler of science fiction fulfills a similar function to that of Deleuze's archeologist of the present, understanding that "if we want to grasp an event, we must not pass along the event, but plunge into it," in order to investigate "what is remembered, who is remembered, how these memories are constructed and recycled to form a particular new form of history."[55] Although the border community that Simon investigates is ultimately a global community connected through a shared experience of trauma, Simon is also grounded by his connection to a specific regional community, and it is from his experiences within that regional western community that he forms connections to the larger world.

With his brown skin and red hair, Simon is a character whose visibly mixed-racial history is reflected by his equally mixed sources of

PTSD—his troubled psychology as much a product of the violent history of the United States–Mexico borderlands as it is by his individual experiences. Simon's great-great-grandfather "had been an Irishman, a member of the famous Batallón de San Patricio—the Saint Patrick's Battalion, which had helped to defend Mexico against the onslaught of Zachary Taylor and the gringo armies from El Norte."[56] In addition to the familial trait of red hair, that ancestry is reflected in a pattern of naming—his great-grandfather Ciarón; his mother, Siobhan; and Simon himself, whose Irish-descended name, Simónn, is spelled as the Spanish Simón and pronounced as the English Simon and whose full name is Simón Ó Floinn Vegas. Captured by the American army, Bardán Ó Floinn was then hanged in 1847, refusing a final meal but demanding the right to sing a final song (the Irish folk song "Molly Malone"). In the novel's metaphor for the transmission of trauma, the melody is then passed down from generation to generation: "[Simon's mother's] grandfather Ciarón had always hummed his father's haunting gallows tune and had handed it down to his own son, Éamonn, her papa." Simon's father, Augusto, observes to his wife, "Whenever you hum that tune, it means that something is troubling you."[57] The "gallows tune" becomes part of Simon's psyche as well—connected not only with his great-great-grandfather's execution but with another traumatic moment in his family history, another hanging, a lynching in Waco, Texas, a moment in which the trauma is an experience not of being the victim of violence but the victimizer.

In terms of generational transmission of trauma, there are two moments central to Simon's psychology, two moments of western violence, both of which involve a hanging and which, taken together, point to another mestizo element of Simon's borderland identity, his dual legacy as both victim and victimizer. If the first involves an Irish ancestral victim (his great-great-grandfather), the second involves an Irish ancestral victimizer, his grandfather Éamonn, who participated (even though somewhat by happenstance) in the Waco, Texas, lynching of an African American man, Jesse Washington, in 1916—a spectacularly gruesome historical act of violence, one preserved by a Waco photographer. The existence of those images, photographs of the crowd of thousands gathered for the lynching, photographs of

Washington's burned and charred body, became central to the National Association for the Advancement of Colored People's antilynching campaign, and they were subsequently published in the NAACP's journal *Crisis* as well as in other African American newspapers.

The photographs are also at the center of a radio show that Simon broadcasts on location at San Quentin prison, as he describes each image to his (literally) captive audience. This is in keeping with the book's general approach to traumatic events, especially the ones that are most affecting to Simon. We circle around them, seeing them first from a distance. The first mention of the Waco tragedy is a map that Elena discovers in Simon's workspace in the garage, with an X and initials J.W. written next to the X, "a very old map of Waco, Texas."[58] That old map is as close as Simon can get—and as close as we can get—to the traumatic event, at that early point in the story. Likewise, before Simon travels back in time to Waco, we are introduced to the event through representations, the photographs, which Simon describes in horrific detail, also observing, in the corner of one of the photos, "a young red-haired Irish boy" lighting a cigarette. Of the boy, Simon observes, "You can't see it in his freckled face or his white skin, but he is half Mexican, and he is about to do something awful."[59]

Unlike most of the time travel in the book, Simon's journey to Waco occurs before an audience, during the nine minutes and thirty-four seconds that it takes to play the Thelonious Monk Quartet's "Sweet and Lovely" on the radio show: "In those nine minutes I'm going to Waco, Texas," he tells his listeners, "back to 1916 and carry him away from all that cruelty."[60] As the song starts to play, Simon mumbles and murmurs his usual "string of odd, mystical words," his lips buzzing "with the vowels of a thousand comic book obscurities all shrouded by an Irish tune."[61] In keeping with the book's general contact-zone aesthetic, his listeners hear an odd concatenation of sounds, Simon's "eerie flow of words superimposed" over "Sweet and Lovely," combined with snatches of "Molly Malone" ("In Dublin's fair city where the girls are so pretty"), and Simon's particular incantatory combination of Latin, Spanish, German, and comic book ("Brimborium. Brimborium. Through the eye of Agamotto as written in the Book of Vishanti. Tontus Talantus and Muchos Milagros").[62] And because

Simon has left the microphone open as the record plays, his listeners hear "Sweet and Lovely," including "John Coltrane's sweet solo," simultaneously with Simon's voice, crowd noises, barking dogs, and whinnying horses.[63]

Not knowing the exact time of Jesse Washington's death, Simon arrives in Waco ten minutes too late, which means that not only must he directly witness the sight of the burned body (and just as disturbing for Simon, the sound of the cheering crowd) but he is forced once again to watch the process of the body's destruction in reverse. Afterward, as he flies through the air with Jesse on the way to Boca Raton, Simon confesses that he knows the man who provided the match that lit Jesse's body on fire: "He is mi abuelito—my grandfather. Fifty years after what happened down there, he would tell me stories in bed. Every night when the stories ended and the lights went out, I saw him bury his face in his pillow, and I heard him scream your name into it. Every night."[64] Simon returns to that memory later on, recalling Éomann's recounting of that day: "I was wandering in Texas a long time ago and stopped in a little town. In the town center a black boy was hanging from a pole. A boy and his papa threw gas on him. . . . And someone in the crowd shouted out for a match. I reached into my pocket for a match. I did that. I did that."[65]

Éomann's confession does not bring him solace, although it does pass along the burden of responsibility to Simon, a transmission of guilt from one generation to another, a mission of reparation that Simon acts out through time travel. Zeke, who has been commissioned by Simon to help him locate the name of the skydiver and who takes it upon himself to track down the deepest trauma in Simon's life (the mass death of family members and friends that left Simon an orphan), reports back to Simon that Éomann also "taught you songs in Spanish and Gaelic. He taught you the song that Bardán Ó Floinn sang from the gallows. It was always on your mother's lips, and then it found new life on yours."[66] Transmitted from one generation to the next, "Molly Malone" mostly exists in the novel as a submerged melody or occasional fragment of lyric: "Zeke thought that he could hear a faint tune, a hauntingly familiar melody modulating every word that came from his friend's mouth."[67] During his first time-travel adventure with

Simon, Zeke heard "nothing in his ears but the wind and that familiar Irish tune on Simon's breath."[68] When Zeke questions him about
his family, Simon responds, "Don't ever ask me about them!" and
falls into a period of paralysis during which "he began humming the
familiar tune, but at a level that anyone within ten feet could hear."
Although Zeke recognizes the melody, "he couldn't remember its name
or its lyrics."[69] Simon's symptomatic response to the reference to his
family suggests how deeply the song is connected to Simon emotion-
ally and psychologically. The melody of "Molly Malone," unspoken
but insistent, drives Simon's actions through the book. The song is
"a little refrain" that is part of the larger project of a cartography
of the borderlands that Simon creates, one that is joined together
with multiple "local histories" as part of the larger telling of familial,
regional, national, and international history that *The Mexican Flyboy*
creates.[70] If, as Campbell writes, "region in these terms is always more-
than-representational precisely because it engages with intensities of
affect," then the "Irish tune," in its manifold connections to individual,
family, region, and nation, conveys that intensity of affect.[71]

In keeping with the novel's metaphorical rendering of trauma
and recovery from trauma, it is only at the end of the novel that the
song emerges in full, that the name of the song and its lyrics are fully
remembered. Zeke takes over Simon's time-travel responsibilities,
observing, "Simon Magus Vegas, the Mexican Flyboy was right, and
Frederich Nietzsche was wrong. We *can* bear remembrance. We *can*
bear it."[72] The novel's argument is that we *must* bear remembrance,
for the sake of witness, for the sake of history. And ultimately, la
máquina is a technology of memory, as it enables Simon to recover
histories that might otherwise vanish and enhances the deliberate
acts of remembrance that are the novel's ethical imperative. At the
end of the novel, Zeke uncovers Simon's deepest past trauma—that
only he among his childhood family and friends remained alive after
a heating malfunction resulted in the death of everyone gathered for
a celebration at his mother's house. Simultaneously, as that unspoken event is brought into representation, Elena gives birth, as Simon
attends and, for the first time, sings the entirety of "Molly Malone" to
welcome his daughter into the world. The naming and remembering

of the past makes possible for the first time Simon's consideration of the future, as he both completes what is ultimately a song of mourning ("that was the end of sweet Molly Malone") and turns it into something new: "The fluid lyrics were interspersed with tribal names and historic locations, abruptly tapped out on Simon's lips and tongue like the staccato rhythm of a flamenco dancer's hands and feet."[73] Simon's performance, with its Irish tune, its Mexican rhythm, its lyrical additions global in scope, is a song of both celebration and mourning, an act of remembrance and a welcome to new life, one that encompasses all Simon's traumas, the personal, the familial, the collective human losses that he names, mourns, and remembers.

The Jewish detective Zeke, who ultimately becomes part of Simon's multiethnic time-travel team, has his own legacy of inherited trauma. He relates a story to Simon, a memory from his childhood:

My grandmother Goldie would be sitting alone after dinner. After the plates were cleared, she would turn her chair away from the dining table and keep turning it until she was facing the wall. She would stare at that wall for hours. I knew that the projector in her brain was starting up again and the reels were spinning. I could see the lights of a horror film flickering in her eyes. She spent three years in the concentration camp at Treblinka. Funny thing was she seemed to get a little happier with every day that passed.[74]

Simon, whose time-travel excursions represent a similar form of self-therapy, recognizes what she is doing, not only reliving the past but also imagining an alternate past, as she mentally is rescuing "one person at time," as Simon comments.[75] For mass deaths, Simon at times also has to limit himself to one person at a time. Carrying away more than one person requires more energy, which is why Hephaestus sometimes follows along with extra batteries; in some cases, Simon must make repeated trips into the same moment in the past to rescue all the victims of violence and cruelty. The story of Zeke's grandmother and her self-therapy makes clear that Simon's time travel is the objective equivalent—the acting out in time and space—of the internal psychological process of recovery from trauma.

Van der Kolk and van der Hart discuss several examples of thera-
pists guiding patients through memory-altering scenarios to aid their
recovery from trauma. One patient finds comfort in imagining flowers
growing in Auschwitz. However, "the question arises whether it is
not a sacrilege of the traumatic experience to play with the reality of
the past?"[76] As Caruth summarizes the dilemma, trauma "requires
integration both for the sake of testimony and for the sake of cure.
But on the other hand, the transformation into a narrative memory that allows the story to be verbalized and communicated, to be
integrated into one's own, and others', knowledge of the past, may
lose both the precision of and the force that characterizes traumatic
recall."[77] According to this theory of trauma, testimony to trauma
that is ethical must paradoxically both speak that trauma and convey the unspeakable force of the event that makes it traumatic in
the first place.

As noted in earlier discussions, contemporary narratives about
traumatic events have developed various formal strategies for addressing that paradox, one of which is to make paradox itself a formal element of the narration. In *The Mexican Flyboy*, as in other time-travel
narratives, Simon's actions, his repeated travel to scenes of trauma,
are both symptomatic and therapeutic. Like Zeke's grandmother,
like the patient visualizing naked corpses clothed, Simon alters the
past to lessen the trauma, but he does so in a way that suggests the
paradoxical ethical imperative of trauma narratives to both speak the
trauma and convey the force of its unspeakability. Simon both does
and does not change the past. "Jessie Washington died a horrible
death," Zeke states, "but he didn't."[78] In the world of the novel, both
of those things are true. Simon carries away the victims of violence,
or perhaps, he removes them from their bodies before they experience the pain of that violence, or perhaps again, he removes them
bodily from the scene while also leaving their bodies behind to live
out their historical destinies. Consciously, anyway, the victims whom
he rescues live out the rest of their days in what Simon refers to as
"Mexican heaven," a version of Boca Raton, Florida, where everyone
wears Hawaiian shirts and beachwear, a community of survivors living
in a place that is both real and imaginary: "I think they just live out

their lives—the lives they would have had if people had left them alone. . . . I learn about them. I study and honor them. Then I go get them. I collect them and bring them to Mexican heaven. . . . Does an eccentric have to think things through, Zeke? Is a shell-shocked weirdo like me really supposed to be consistent?"[79] Véa's formal innovation in the genre of traumatic time-travel narratives is his particular realization of paradox: time-travel interventions that both change the past and don't change the past, which for the sake of witness, for the sake of testimony, for the sake of history and remembrance remains the same; for the sake of recovery, such interventions imagine the possibility of alleviating individual suffering.

El cielo mexicano, Mexican heaven, also memorializes Simon's mother (Mi Cielo Mexicano is the name with which she humorously dubs her newly built indoor bathroom, celebrated with a Hawaiian-shirt-wearing party—one that ultimately ends in tragedy) and her dream of one day moving from the desert to live in Boca Raton and to "wear luau clothes and watch the sea as the sun went down. We would still be there drinking funny drinks and laughing when the sun came up."[80] The celebration of the arrival of Mexican heaven (in the form of the new indoor bathroom) is also the cause of the traumatic tragedy that sets the orphaned Simon on his itinerant journey. Again, paradoxically, Simon makes the site of tragedy into its opposite—a haven for the traumatized, a final destination for a large group of time-travel migrants and refugees.

In Simon's version of Boca Raton, we can see an idea similar to Foucault's descriptions of heterotopias, "real places—places that do exist and that are formed in the very founding of society—which are something like counter-sites, a kind of effectively enacted utopia."[81] Boca Raton is "at once absolutely real" (Boca Raton is indeed an actual place) and "absolutely unreal" (this version of Boca Raton somehow exists in addition to the real Boca Raton). Because Simon populates it with the thousands of people he has gathered from throughout time, Boca Raton is also a heterochronia, "a sort of perpetual and indefinite accumulation of time in an immobile place."[82] Rather than objects collected in a museum or library, the "accumulation of time" in the living archive that Boca Raton becomes is realized by the creation of a community of people, all brought together in one place from different moments in time, a migration that is both geographic and temporal.

"Black migrations," Jones writes, "were spatial movements, bodies creating new paths to selfhood and enfranchisement"; their activities in the places where they arrived were "assertions of space—cultural or political, as land or property—that create place, whether actual sites in the world or positions in the global imagination."[83] If we extend Jones's observation to include migrations of the disenfranchised more generally, that concept is objectively rendered in *The Mexican Flyboy* through the imagined time-travel-aided migration to a fantastically transformed version of Boca Raton, Florida. His mother's concept of Mexican heaven is an assertion of space, an imagined insertion of her impoverished Mexican family into a life of ease and enjoyment, one that Simon realizes with an additional twist—imagining a version of Boca Rotan as Mexican heaven as a kind of refugee resort, an afterlife (or the fantastic continuation of a life interrupted) imagined as a contact zone. "I'll put Hank Williams in an apartment with Paul Robeson, Sam Cooke, and Sappho," Simon whispers. "He'll be next door to Susannah McCorkle, Janis Joplin, and Aida. The music in that section of Boca Raton will be amazing!"[84] "That portion of the complex," Simon enthuses, "is filled with Hussites, Sethians, and Gnostics, Japanese from Hiroshima, and two million Cambodians, all dressed for a day at the beach."[85] Boca Raton becomes its own borderlands space, consisting entirely of migrants from other places and times, a Mexican heaven that is not in Mexico but that is nonetheless reflective of borderlands culture. Boca Raton is a speculative borderlands space—a mirror image of the global borderlands that Simon traverses but one that reflects peace and survival rather than violence and death.

The Mexican Flyboy provides what is perhaps the most extensively realized example of speculative regionality examined here in its imagining of Boca Raton as el cielo mexicano, a society comprised of a complex network of newly created relationships, a product of millions of temporal and geographic migrations, both an actual site in the world and an imagined possibility, a specific site in the borderlands Southwest (a newly installed bathroom in an Arizona house) that is reimagined and relocated to Florida, where it becomes an exemplar of "contemporary globalization," a piece of "the region-West" that enacts "multiple relations with the world," encompassing the "multiple experiences and stories of diverse peoples, moving across borders and frontiers."[86] In *The Mexican Flyboy* Véa provides a real history of bodies and spatial movements, a real history of trauma and recovery, of remembering and memorializing, as well as an exploration of possible histories, places, and futures existing outside the limitations of the here and now and the here and then.

Speculative Slave Narrative Westerns

African American writers have been involved with science fiction (and proto–science fiction) for much of its existence as a genre. They have done so with a particular sense of collectively intervening in the world of science fiction since the 1990s, as indicated by the emergence of Afrofuturism, a term coined by Mark Dery "to refer to African American artists (musicians, filmmakers, writers, visual artists, among others) who 'have stories to tell about culture, technology, and things to come'" and who do so while specifically treating African American themes and concerns.[1] As Isiah Lavender observes in *Afrofuturism Rising: The Literary Prehistory of a Movement*, Afrofuturism as a "historical phenomenon" (and not necessarily as a self-conscious creative movement) begins with the earliest African American texts, because "African American literature perpetually reflects the science-fictional reality of blacks in America."[2] Lavender writes, "As Greg Tate perceived about a quarter-century ago, 'Black people live the estrangement that science fiction writers imagine' (qtd. in Dery, 'Black to the Future,' 768). Abducted, chained, and transported to the far side of the world by white people. Cultures stripped away, languages stripped away, and autonomy stripped away by white people. . . . And now afrofuturism has emerged to understand the science-fictional existence that blacks have always experienced living in the New World—an unreality driven by economic demands, would-be science, and skin color."[3]

If African American existence is already science-fictional and if that existence has already been given literary form in nineteenth-century slave narratives, parallels between historical slave narratives and contemporary Afrofuturist stories are not surprising. As

Lavender writes, Afrofuturism emerges in the form of early African American writing "in parallel with its sister genre, science fiction, at the dawn of modernity, specifically in the period of American chattel slavery," a period coinciding with both colonialism and westward expansion.[4] Thus, it is probably also not surprising to see a variety of parallels among the literary forms that emerge in this historical moment: captivity narratives, slave narratives, science fiction, and westerns.

Alondra Nelson suggests that Afrofuturism "looks backwards and forward."[5] "The historical legacies of slavery and colonization," Lavender observes in *Race in American Science Fiction*, "which have shaped black cultures in the Americas, are easily taken up within SF motifs to explore the dynamics of race and power." The "peculiar institution" of slavery "can be made even more peculiar when imagined in terms of technological forms of bondage or captivity."[6] As distinct from nineteenth-century nonfiction narratives written by fugitive or former slaves and as distinct from later realist fictional narratives of slavery, science-fictional narratives of slavery and bondage use "technology or science to distance and defamiliarize the institution and practice of slavery, resulting in constructions of slavery as neo–slave narratives or *meta–slavery narratives*," the latter being Lavender's preferred term for science-fictional narratives that involve the exploration of the experience of slavery.[7] "The prefix *meta-* calls attention to the distancing and analytical dimensions that SF provides in shedding light on representations of *slavery*," Lavender explains, enabling "writers to transcend the narrative arc between historical and literary accounts of captivity and take us into a space where the interplay of past, present, and future allows readers to experience slavery and examine the painful social divisions it has created in our culture."[8]

The potential affinity between the western and the slave narrative (both of which share a predecessor in the captivity narrative) has certainly been visible from the earliest versions of each. As Joshua Smith points out in "*Uncle Tom's Cabin* Showdown: Stowe, Tarantino, and the Minstrelsy of the Weird West," connections to notions of the West and westernness are present in Harriet Beecher Stowe's *Uncle Tom's Cabin*, long before Quentin Tarantino's more self-consciously-hybrid slave narrative western *Django Unchained* was ever conceived.[9] As Eric Gardner observed in his chapter "Gateways and Borders," abolitionist writing of the era played on the notion of St. Louis as the "gateway to the West" by pointedly representing it as the opposite, as "a gateway to the heart of slavery" for enslaved people whose route was down the river rather than westward across the country.[10] In the 1840s and 1850s, southward of St. Louis was also considered heading west, a journey toward recently acquired territories in Louisiana and Texas. For Stowe, Smith writes, "the frontier energies of *Uncle Tom's Cabin* are inherent in its protest of the Fugitive Slave Law, which Stowe understands to be a piece of legislation turning 'the broad land between the Mississippi and the Pacific' into 'one great market for bodies . . . souls and human property.'"[11] References to the American West, to notions of the West as a place of freedom and mobility, are not exterior to abolitionist writing or to the slave narrative or even the neo–slave narrative but have been part of the genre for a very long time. The slave narrative western (from *Uncle Tom's Cabin* to *Django Unchained* and beyond), as a hybrid genre, juxtaposes the western's promise of unfettered freedom on the frontier with the slave narrative's threat of the opposite.[12] The two genres work so well together, in part, because of that inherent tension.

In the author's note at the end of *Deathless Divide*—the sequel to *Dread Nation*, an earlier slave narrative, zombie apocalypse, alternate history, and western novel—Justina Ireland remembers asking herself "what new adventures made sense" in the world she had created, finally coming to a central goal: "The more I thought about it, the more I knew I had to visit the narrative of the Old West. I love Westerns, but they have long been the province of steely-eyed cowboys and plucky frontierswomen, always white."[13] As both *Dread Nation* and *Deathless Divide* suggest, if the stories of Black westerners are less visible in more conventional stories of the American West, there is a place for those stories within the framework of the speculative western. And even if the stories of the Black West are not well known, African American artists have been joining together stories of enslavement with narratives of frontier freedom for a very long time, with one of the earliest examples being Pauline Hopkins's *Winona: A Tale of Negro*

Life in the South and the Southwest, set on the pre–Civil War border between free territory Kansas and slave state Missouri.[14]

Captured illegally by slave catchers, Winona and her brother, Judah, are taken into slavery in Missouri, eventually escaping to join John Brown in Kansas. The western's racially marked division of civilization and savagery undergoes a revision in *Winona*. Hopkins shows that civilization is the place of savagery, as represented by the "civilized"—that is, legally sanctioned—slavery of Missouri. Truly civilized behavior, the extension of liberty and freedom to all no matter their race, is found in unsettled Kansas, in the wilderness encampment of John Brown. African American–centered film westerns that touch on slavery, from *The Skin Game* and *Buck and the Preacher* to *Blazing Saddles* and *Django Unchained*, have appeared periodically since the 1960s.[15] Speculative western slave narratives have been around at least since Ishmael Reed's *Yellow Back Radio Broke-Down* (1969), which featured a Hoo-Doo cowboy, the Loop Garu Kid, whose practice of the vodun religion brought a supernatural element to Reed's wild western.[16] Whether weird or straightforward, African American westerns have generally followed Hopkins's revision of the western's eastern-civilization versus western-savagery binary in order to overturn the genre's racial assumptions, disrupting the association of whiteness with civilization and the centrality of whiteness to the quest for western freedom and displacing the western's villainizing of Native Americans by placing white characters (such as slaveholders or vigilante groups such as the Ku Klux Klan) in the role of "savage other."

Following the distinctions among subgenres of the hybrid western (SF western, space western, weird western) that Paul Green draws in *The Encyclopedia of the Weird Western*, Melanie A. Marotta writes, "The difference between the SF Western and the space Western is an environmental one: while the SF Western is set on land, the space Western occurs, logically, in outer space." The SF western subgenre "contains attributes of both the science fiction and Western genres set in a space representative of the frontier" and retains an essential element of the western, "namely humanity's journey into the new—the frontier."[17] Speculative westerns that feature Black characters, especially considered in terms of the general definition offered by Marotta (set "in a space representative of the frontier"), is a potentially broad topic.[18] Thus, my focus for this chapter will be speculative western narratives that explicitly engage slavery or the slave narrative tradition as they also reimagine the American West of western tradition through a science-fictional or fantastic frontier setting.

Those works fall into several categories in their relationship to the western: SF westerns, as in the film *The Brother from Another Planet*, where the reimagined setting is Earth itself, which is experienced as a new frontier by a new arrival (the titular "Brother" from another planet); fantasy westerns, stories that are set in a fantastic other world that is identifiably and explicitly built on the model of the Old West (as in Charlotte Nicole Davis's *The Good Luck Girls*); and SF-horror westerns, as in Justine Ireland's *Dread Nation* and *Deathless Divide*, which take place in the traditional setting of a nineteenth-century American West that has been speculatively altered by the presence of monsters (i.e., zombies, or "shamblers," as the walking dead are named in the books).[19] As Victoria Lamont points out in *Westerns: A Women's History*, "The popular western, widely considered a male-authored tradition, was founded as much by women writers as by men and played a significant role in American women's literary history at the turn of the twentieth century."[20] This chapter also argues that Davis and Ireland draw on this specifically female literary history, particularly in centering stories of heroines who are agents of western violence and justice. By discussing these contemporary speculative slave narrative westerns in dialogue with Pauline Hopkins's 1902 serial novel *Winona*, I demonstrate that Davis and Ireland draw on a history of the literary western that is both female and African American.

NEW YORK AS FRONTIER

Two touchstone films in Afrofuturist cinema, *Space Is the Place* (directed by John Coney and starring Sun Ra, who is also one of the credited screenwriters) and *The Brother from Another Planet* (directed and written by John Sayles and starring Joe Morton), are also both notable as films that we might consider as SF westerns.[21] As Nama comments in *Black Space*, these are "two of the most self-consciously black SF films in American cinema," even as both were also "directed and for the most part produced by white men."[22] We might think of the films, however, not so much as the product of white auteurs but as collaborative projects that succeed, in part, because of the African American contributors—namely, Sun Ra's contribution to the script of *Space Is the Place* and his central role as actor, musician, and composer, as well as Joe Morton's central performance in *The Brother from Another Planet*, since he is in almost every scene of the film, along with the ensemble work of a variety of Black actors. Nama continues, "Both SF films are ideologically robust in directly confronting white supremacy and the politics of racial inequality in its historical and contemporary guises by exploring the interior social dynamics of the black community and the politics of the resistance that resides there."[23]

Although both films are widely recognized as important and influential Afrofuturist works, I want to underscore here how, as early as the 1970s and 1980s, the western and the American West are important elements of Afrofuturist art. *Space Is the Place* is particularly attentive to African American western history, with its Oakland, California, filming location and setting and its direct evocation of the city's Black activism and its historical importance as birthplace of the Black Panthers organization. *Space Is the Place* begins with Sun Ra returning to Earth from a newly discovered planet, with the goal of leading a Black exodus to the new planet. At the end of the film, with the planet Earth exploding in the background, Ra transports all of the planet's Black people to his spaceship, as they head out to explore this new frontier. As Fawaz comments, "Doubly indebted to Marcus Garvey's 'back to Africa' movement in the early twentieth century, and the colonial vision of national expansion into space promulgated by American *astrofuturism*, the tale of planetary exile narrates the possibilities that lie in the willful relocation of African Americans . . . to outer space."[24] The "trope of planetary exile" that Fawaz observes in several Afrofuturist and science fiction films also suggests parallels with another Black migratory movement, the Exodusters of the late nineteenth century, who traveled westward out of the American South, sometimes establishing all-Black townships in Texas, Oklahoma, and Kansas. *Space Is the Place* is western in location (with much of the action taking place in Oakland) and western in its references (evoking the history of the Exodusters movement), and it suggests the SF western in the genre elements it evokes (i.e., a journey across space to a new frontier on another planet).

The Brother from Another Planet is a frontier narrative of first contact that references multiple western themes and conventions, even with its alien-from-another-planet protagonist and New York City setting. As a hybrid genre film, *The Brother from Another Planet* effectively illustrates the "playful assembly" of the three genres (speculative, slave narrative, and western) that are definitive elements of the texts examined in this chapter.[25] *Brother* also adds at least one more genre to the assemblage, the immigration narrative. As Guerrero writes, "The Brother's construction is multivalent, as an alien from outer space, a runaway slave, and a West Indian immigrant," and, we might add, a frontier adventurer.[26] The film begins with the unnamed alien arriving via a spacecraft, which plunges into New York Harbor just offshore of Ellis Island. Like many an immigrant before him, the alien enters the United States through Ellis Island, moving through the empty immigration station at night before hopping into a passing boat and moving deeper into the city, eventually finding his way to Harlem, where he makes friends at Odell's bar and ultimately becomes part of the community.

Like the majority of people he encounters in Harlem, Brother is Black, which aids his assimilation into the community, even as he is also clearly marked as different from them. He is mute, and although he communicates with people who speak both English and Spanish, he seems to interpret intuitively, through context and body language as much as linguistic understanding. When he first arrives, his movements are noticeably unusual, although they later conform more closely to human locomotion. As viewers learn, he also has unusual feet (with three large toes) and demonstrates numerous skills, such as an ability to self-heal (he regrows a foot severed in the crash) and to heal others and an ability to remove an eye (which he uses as a recording device). And as he reveals to his new friends, he has a way with electronics, which he demonstrates by fixing video game machines.

"The figure of the alien" in the science fiction genre, Janani Subramanian writes, is "a powerful metaphor for different kinds of disfranchisement," making science fiction "a testing ground for issues of identity." "In most sf films," Subramanian continues, "the alien represents a threat to and/or the displacement of racial difference onto species difference." That an African American actor plays the alien in *The Brother from Another Planet* draws our attention to the science fiction convention of using "species difference" as racial allegory by, as it were, doubling down on the conventional signification—as Brother represents both racial difference *and* species difference. By speaking what is usually unspoken (the relationship between race and the sf alien), *Brother* "reverses the direction of displacement: its alien *is* a black man, whose alienation is compounded by Harlem's unfamiliar landscape."[27] That "unfamiliar landscape," a genre trope of both science fiction and westerns, becomes more familiar as the narrative progresses, as Brother assimilates or acclimates to his new surroundings.

Harlem, as depicted in *The Brother from Another Planet*, is a contact zone, in the way that any large urban area might be, but because we share Brother's perspective, it is also a frontier, a place of first contact between Brother and the others who already reside in this place. Fawaz writes that as the film progresses, Brother "meets a host of characters with different ethno-racial backgrounds—including Bernice, the white, single mother with whom he boards and whose mixed race son he develops a telepathic bond."[28] Brother absorbs "the cultural environment in which a combination of racial and ethnic communities live in close, but uneasy association," including "the second and third-generation descendants" of the immigrants whose voices "flood the brother's mind at the beginning of the film" as he makes his way through Ellis Island. "By virtue of his entry into their diverse communities," Fawaz writes, "the brother literally lives up to his name, becoming a cultural sibling to those he comes in contact with."[29] The Harlem of *Brother* is constituted as a multicultural borderland comprised of complex networks of relationships among different ethnic groups.

As the arrival at Ellis Island suggests, *The Brother from Another Planet* is also an immigration allegory, and we eventually realize that the movie is a meta–slavery narrative. He is tracked by two white bounty hunters, listed in the credits as Men in Black, played by director Sayles and David Straithairn. Brother takes little Earl (Bernice's son) to a *Road to Freedom* exhibit at the Schomburg Center for Research in Black Culture. As a tour guide tells the story of Harriet Tubman (foreshadowing the eventual revelation of a similar underground railroad of fugitive aliens operating in Harlem), her narration suggests elements of both the western and the slave narrative. Harriet Tubman would lead escapees "through hostile territory," a description evocative of the western's wilderness landscape, "going from station to station" on "the underground railroad." (Traveling through hostile territory going from station to station would also be a fair description of the narrative arc of *Stagecoach*.) In front of an image of a Black man with broken chains running from dogs and pursued by slave catchers, Brother stops and points to the picture and then points to himself, indicating that this is his situation as well. "Sometimes," the guide continues, "bounty hunters would trap them up north and kidnap them back to slavery. Now, New York was the promised land." The image (and the guide's narration) further links the Men in Black (a character type often featured in UFO stories) to the slave catcher of the slave narrative. Having the guide also directly name the slave catchers specifically as bounty hunters provides a textual connection to the western.

The Brother from Another Planet makes clear the functional similarity between the bounty hunter of the western and the slave catcher of the slave narrative. Both operate somewhere on the border between official law and the vigilante, between tracking lawbreakers and acting criminally themselves. The Sayles and Straithorn characters simultaneously belong to all three genres (science fiction, slave narrative, western), and elements of each genre are evoked at various times— the strange behaviors often attributed to the Men in Black in science fiction, the predatory for-profit activities of the bounty hunter and the slave catcher, the fuzzy legality of all three.

One of the images in the *Road to Freedom* exhibit is of Henry Box Brown, famous for escaping slavery by mailing himself north (from Richmond to Philadelphia).[30] The image shows Brown, the top of the crate having just been removed by several men, starting to emerge from the box. That Brother's gaze lingers on this image suggests a particular moment of identification—a recognition of the metaphorical similarity to his own mode of escape, encased in the close-fitting box of a small spacecraft, traversing the "hostile territory" above on his way to what turns out to be the "promised land" of New York. Although Lavender doesn't discuss *The Brother from Another Planet* in *Afrofuturism Rising*, Brother's moment of recognition provides further evidence in support of his argument that the *Narrative of Henry Box Brown* (1849) is important as an Afrofuturist text—at least, that certainly seems to be the way Brother interprets the image, as illustrative of his own escape from slavery similarly enclosed in a (technologically sophisticated) box.[31]

The story of the "good bad man," the outlaw tracked by a posse or by bounty hunters who represent not so much law as a corrupt civilization, is a familiar enough western narrative. Considered as a western, *The Brother from Another Planet* roughly follows what Will Wright names as one of the four primary western plots, "the classic plot of a stranger arriving in town and restoring order."[32] As in the classic western *Shane*, the hero's arrival is mysterious, his background unknown. Like many a western hero, Brother is tight-lipped and even does the terse cowboy one better by not speaking at all. Brother is also a man without a name, aligning him with other roles played by Clint Eastwood—in Sergio Leone's films, for example, as well as in his own *High Plains Drifter*.[33] A subplot in *Brother* involves heroin sales, and our stranger, if he doesn't exactly clean up the town, traces the heroin back to its source and takes care of at least that particular problem—through a showdown of sorts with the wealthy white man who is profiting from the heroin trade.

The 1980s is not the Old West, but to the technologically advanced Brother, it is as much a step back in time as it would be for a twentieth-century time traveler landing in the 1880s. For Brother, who arrives from the east (from offshore), New York is the West, or at least, New

York is the frontier, the location of a first encounter between the traveler and the indigenous inhabitants of this new place. The city itself is also significantly divided. When Brother is entertained by a card-playing street magician (or perhaps con artist) traveling the subway, the cardplayer smiles up at the traveler and says, "Watch me make all the white people disappear," as they approach the last stop before the West 125th Street station. The subway takes Brother uptown and downtown, back and forth across the frontier that separates the mostly Black residents of Harlem from the wealthy whites who, for example, exploit them for profit from the safety of a downtown office building. The subway train is an important element of the film, one that suggests both the slave narrative (as it is a literal underground railroad) and the western, in which trains are often key locations.

The most identifiably western setting in the film may be Odell's bar, which is a central location for much of the film's action. Cynthia Miller observes that "the saloon stands as a quintessential icon of the Old West," and it has traditionally served as a stage for encounters, between East and West, hero and villain, good and evil, as well as a meeting place for allies. The various scenes that take place inside the bar play out in familiar ways, including a climactic bar fight between the bar patrons and the alien bounty hunters. "When horror was introduced to the western," Miller writes, "the saloon also became the stage for encounters of a different kind—between the living and the undead."[34] Adapting Miller's statement for the SF western, we might state that the saloon also becomes the stage for encounters between humans and aliens.

Odell's is both a neighborhood bar (the filming location was an actual bar in Harlem) and a figurative western saloon. The bar's swinging doors are full-length rather than classic batwing style, but the westernness of the entryway is made clear with the first appearance of the Men in Black, who stand framed in the doorway as they look around the bar, a camera setup that recalls the saloon entry of Clint Eastwood's bounty hunter character at the beginning of *For a Few Dollars More*.[35] There is no piano or piano player in the bar to fall suddenly silent with the arrival of the two strangers, but there is a video game that provides constant background noise in the bar scenes, which abruptly drops out of the soundtrack as the bounty hunters enter and as all the patrons in the bar turn to look at the strangers. As is the case with Eastwood's bounty hunter, the initial appearance of the Men and Black is made all the uncannier by their initial silence and by odd movements that clearly unnerve the bar's patrons.

Rather than unrolling a wanted poster (as happens repeatedly in *For a Few Dollars More*), the bounty hunters have a photo they show to Odell, Smokey, and Walter. When Odell asks to see identification or a badge, the Men in Black reply,

BOUNTY HUNTER ONE: Badges?
BOUNTY HUNTER TWO: What badges?
BOUNTY HUNTER ONE: We don't have to show you any badges.

The dialogue references *The Treasure of the Sierra Madre*, rendering a more polite version of the famous and often-quoted line "I don't have to show you any stinking badges."[36] This quotation (or almost quotation) is the most direct reference in *Brother* to the western genre, and putting these western words in the mouths of the Men in Black makes sure that we have an intertextual connection joining them to the western.

There are other moments in the film that reference westerns. A shot of Brother standing at the top of the subway stairs shows him framed by the entranceway like John Wayne standing in a doorway in a John Ford film. In the video arcade where Brother works repairing machines (using his ability to affect electronics with a touch of his hand), he encounters a woman named Ace whose game-playing skills have outpaced the games themselves. In her conversation with Brother, she talks like a weary gunfighter, disappointed by the lack of competition, complaining that the games are "not fast enough," telling Brother that she will wear them out faster than he can repair them. There's "no way you can beat me," she tells Brother as he moves toward the back of the machine and turns to face her. What follows, as Brother touches the machine and steadily increases the speed of the game play, is filmed like a showdown, a contest between gunfighters to see who's the fastest. The camera cuts back and forth between the two combatants, intercut with close-ups of Ace's hand operating the trigger on the joystick. The scene plays out specifically like the lead-up to a Sergio Leone gunfight, with a series of increasingly tight close-ups of the two fighters—with the framing of Brother eventually just extreme close-up shots of his nose and eyes. In contrast to a western shootout, Ace responds when she loses, "That was fantastic," the result of this battle being not death but pleasure.

Although the bounty hunters eventually capture Brother, he manages to slip away from them. As they give chase, they suddenly come upon a group of Black men and women (many of whom we have seen throughout the film in the background), dressed as they would be for their day jobs, who array themselves protectively around Brother. Considered in terms of western conventions, the final defeat of the two bounty hunters, accomplished by a kind of underground railroad of former aliens, suggests the restoration of order and provides another significant showdown, one that takes place, appropriately, on the city streets. After Brother's rescue, he questioningly points his thumb upward: Am I going back up there? The response is a thumb pointed down—to Earth but also to the underground, literal and metaphorical, as the thumbs-down gesture has also been used to indicate the subway. The gesture suggests that Brother will become part of this underground railroad group posing as humans living in Harlem, acting to aid others who are escaping enslavement.

The film ends with Brother taking the A train to Harlem, which the soundtrack tells us is "the promised land," no longer an alien but a member of the community. The penultimate shot of Brother on the back of the train suggests the final image of the western, of the cowboy hero riding out into the distance, moving away from a stationary camera. In this case, rather than riding into the sunset, Brother is going back to Harlem. However, doubling often takes place in hybrid genre films, and as Brother has two showdowns (each of which resolves a different element of the plot—the town-protector plot involving heroin use, on the one hand, and the conflict between the bounty hunters and their quarry, on the other), the film also has two final shots. In the actual last shot of the film, we see Brother back in Harlem looking at a basketball court, and when he turns toward the camera, we also see that there's a smile on his face, content in the knowledge that he has found not only freedom but home. Thus, we have two endings, each appropriate to different genres—the moving-on final shot of the western and the finally at home (or finally free) ending typical of both immigration stories and the slave narrative.

Considering the western elements of *The Brother from Another Planet* points to the instability of the categories that have defined the western (and the West). It also expands the (still-too-sparse) archive of the Black West. To not consider the western elements of *Brother* risks foreclosing too quickly the signifying possibilities of a richly intertextual film. We might also, therefore, miss the film's implied critiques of the western: the suggestion that in the 1980s a western with a Black actor in the lead role could appear only through multiple layers of generic disguise; the rejection of the western hero who continues on west at the end of the film; the critique of the bounty hunter character type as a western hero, one whose close connection to the slave catcher the film makes explicit.[37] It would not take a particularly creative act of adaptation to reset the plot of *The Brother from Another Planet* in the nineteenth-century West, perhaps in a setting such as Indian Territory, in what is now Oklahoma. *The Brother from Another Planet* makes visible the affinities between genres as disparate as science fiction, the western, the immigrant story, and the slave narrative, joining together in one narrative several genres that we often separate into discrete fields of study. Within the study of the western in particular, a greater critical awareness and inclusion of such hybrid narratives will contribute to diversifying and expanding our understanding of a genre that greatly needs such diversification and expansion—or that greatly needs a better critical understanding of the diversity within the genre that already exists.

The Brother from Another Planet is a film that *makes use* of the western, incorporating it into the generic mix of the film in a way that sticks out, that makes itself known. Although director John Sayles, in his DVD commentary on the film, describes *The Brother from Another Planet* as a story of assimilation, it might be more accurately described as a story of mixing, hybridization, and syncretic combination, of "playful assemblage." *The Brother from Another Planet* is definitely not a melting-pot allegory. The alien Brother may become more human as the story progresses or become more adept at passing as human, but he does so without losing his sense of difference. His Blackness makes it easier for him to find a home in Harlem, but as the various encounters with whites demonstrate, he does not disappear into the mainstream, does not assimilate (culturally or physically) into whiteness. By the end of the story, his muteness remains a sign of his difference from those around him, even as he continues to learn to communicate effectively with his fellows. That the film mixes together several genres—the immigration story, science fiction, the slave narrative, and the western, to name four of the more visible genres—actualizes the theme of social hybridization at the level of form and style. *The Brother from Another Planet* is the story of the making of an American, the making of an African American, the making of a New Yorker, the making of a Harlemite. As such, the film draws on such distinctively American genres as the western and the slave narrative, mixing them in a way that reflects the coming together of the complicated combination of identities that transforms the Brother from another planet into a Brother of this world—a Brother if not from then certainly *of* Harlem.

WESTERN WOMEN

As Victoria Lamont points out in *Westerns: A Women's History*, the popular western "was founded as much by women writers as by men." From Emma Ghent Curtis's 1889 *The Administratrix*, "the first known cowboy novel outside of the dime novel tradition" (published "thirteen years before the popular west was supposed to have been invented by Owen Wister" with *The Virginian* in 1902), "women were active at every turn" while the genre was being established.[38] Although women writers were particularly active during the early twentieth-century period when the "quality" popular western was forming as a genre, "women authors of popular westerns remain virtually invisible" in scholarship about the West, partly because "gendered categories of popular fiction invented by marketers in the 1920s became so deeply entrenched that the 'women's western' eventually became a contradiction in terms." Even when studies of western women writers began to appear in the 1980s, they emphasized a "focus on domestic writing, memoir, and other 'private' genres," helpfully recovering the work of literary writers like Willa Cather but also contributing to the "explicit denial of the possibility that women *could* write westerns in the popular tradition."[39]

Because the western is a genre associated with violence, cultural attitudes about gender and violence have also contributed to the invisibility of westerns by and about women. As Kerry Fine observes in her discussion of two television shows set in the contemporary American West, *In Plain Sight* and *Sons of Anarchy*, "Traditional depictions of heroic power in western literature and film suggest that heroic power is inherently masculine, a 'natural' attribute of men."[40] Drawing on developmental psychologist Kaj Bjorkqvist's analysis of different types of aggression, Fine notes the distinction between "expressive aggression" (which is impulsive, emotional, marked especially by anger, and also encompassing self-defense) and "instrumental aggression" (which is more calculated, "cool," and "formulated with forethought and carried out purposefully").[41] These types of aggression have also been culturally gendered, with expressive aggression being associated with the feminine and instrumental aggression being associated with the masculine. Because instrumental aggression is proactive (and not reactive, as in the case of defensive action), "it fits neatly into the active/passive gender binary, solidifying its association with the masculine."[42]

Although it's tempting to claim that contemporary speculative westerns like *Trail of Lightning*, *The Good Luck Girls*, and *Dread Nation*, with their violent heroines, mark a departure from the limitations of the gendered roles in the classic western, it would be more accurate to state that these speculative westerns extend and contribute to an already-established tradition of women's westerns written in the realist mode. As Lamont points out, "Rather than melt into the cowboy's arms, . . . most of the fictional women I discuss play an active and independent role in the narrative."[43] Additionally, Curtis's *The Administratrix*, the novel that Lamont places at the beginning of this tradition, posits a heroine who enacts a bloody and violent justice on the group of men who killed her husband: "Now stand still while

I pass sentence on you, and do not disturb me. Your father was the head of the ring that made me a widow . . . and for it, *you shall die*."[44] Although revenge is a motive here, Mary arrives at this moment through calculation and planning (by disguising herself as a man and joining the gang), and the coolness of Mary's speech as she passes sentence and of her execution of the men one by one contributes to the portrayal of a character whose heroic power is exercised through instrumental aggression.

As a woman's western and, specifically, an African American woman's western, the primary ancestor for *The Good Luck Girls* and Ireland's duology is Pauline Hopkins's 1902 novel *Winona: A Tale of Negro Life in the South and Southwest*. Published in serial form in *Colored American Magazine*, *Winona* appeared in print in the same year as Owen Wister's *The Virginian*.[45] The existence of a novel like *Winona*, written by an African American woman and distributed to a predominantly African American readership, reinforces Lamont's observation that the western was "a complex cultural field in which both men and women participated, although not always on equal footing." "The fact that these women did not always reach vast readerships" or the fact that African American authors like Hopkins wrote specifically for Black readers "should not exclude them from discussion of the genre: To do so would be to reconstitute the power relations that marginalized them in the first place."[46] "When we cordon off women writers in a feminized subcategory" or when we dismiss texts because of the size or demographics of their readership, "we tacitly endorse their continued exclusions from discussions of the genre when we should be rethinking our understanding of the genre in order to account for them."[47]

Winona was one of a trio of novels, also including *Hagar's Daughter: A Story of Southern Caste Prejudice* and *Of One Blood, or, the Hidden Self*, that Hopkins wrote for publication in *Colored American Magazine* (for which Hopkins served as the literary editor for a number of years), all of which are included in *The Magazine Novels of Pauline Hopkins*.[48] As Rachel Ihara writes, *Colored American Magazine* itself was "a unique endeavor to create a popular magazine that was, to a large extent, written by and for African Americans."[49] As Hazel Carby notes in her introduction to *The Magazine Novels of Pauline Hopkins*, Hopkins's serial novels "represent a sustained attempt to develop an Afro-American popular fiction," one that "utilizes the strategies and formulas of nineteenth-century dime novels and story papers."[50] The success of that endeavor, in Ihara's estimation, was the result of Hopkins's "shrewd attentiveness to audience and keen understanding of the potential for popular periodical literature" to "function as a source of pleasure and psychological uplift for an audience of black magazine readers."[51] That is, Hopkins reimagined popular genre formulas and conventions as a strategy for providing African American readers access to the pleasures provided by a type of reading experience that generally did not address Black readers or represent them, their experiences, or their desires.

Regarding *Of One Blood*, Nisi Shawl writes in the introduction to the novel's 2021 Haunted Library of Horror Classics edition (the latest of multiple editions of the novel currently in print) that it is not surprising that Hopkins has emerged in the twenty-first century as "the foremother of Octavia Butler and Tananarive Due, and many of today's leading science fiction, fantasy, and horror authors." Particularly within the world of speculative fiction, Hopkins's work (especially *Of One Blood*) has become increasingly celebrated, "primarily because she's another African-descended woman using a popular genre to write speculatively about hard philosophical questions, surprising truths, and the wonders of the occult."[52] "Many," Jalondra A. Davis writes, "in tracing a genealogy of Afrofuturism, have identified this novel as a precursor to the contemporary form."[53]

Despite the twenty-first-century success of *Of One Blood*, Hopkins's nonspeculative western *Winona* remains, Colleen O'Brien writes in a 2014 article, her "least-known book."[54] Four years later, in a 2018 article, not much had changed, as Lisa McGunigal similarly describes *Winona* as "her least-known serial novel."[55] Contemporary Black westerns like *The Good Luck Girls* and *Dread Nation* encourage us to look back at Hopkins's *Winona*, with the continuities among the works suggesting that these novels are not aberrations or singular examples of an unusual thing but part of something like a tradition of women's—and specifically Black women's—western writing.

"'Tradition,'" Lamont writes, may be "too strong a word, for it implies the existence of woman-centered cultural networks capable of its transmission. The women in this study wrote in relative isolation from each other and from the male-centered frontier club that dominated western cultural production at the turn of the twentieth century."[56] Whether or not *Winona* is a conscious influence on either of these contemporary African American women writers, we might note, as does Lamont about the women writers she discusses, "their westerns are linked by certain themes, tropes, and motifs, suggesting that women writers put the western to different uses than did their male counterparts."[57] From *Winona* to *The Deathless Divide*, we likewise see the deployment of shared elements, which might be accounted for by the logic of adapting and blending western and African American forms as much as (or rather than) by direct influence.

THE GOOD LUCK GIRLS

The web page for *The Good Luck Girls* on the McMillan Press website describes the book as "*Westworld* meets *The Handmaid's Tale* in this stunning fantasy adventure from debut author Charlotte Nicole Davis."[58] As there are no cyborgs or other *Westworld*-like science fiction elements in *The Good Luck Girls*, the novel might be more accurately described as a version of the film *Unforgiven*, one that adds supernatural elements to the western's frontier setting and one that centers its story of abuse, revenge, and retribution on the sex workers from the brothel rather than on Clint Eastwood's Bill Munny.[59] Central character Aster; her sister, Clementine; friends Tansy and Mallow; and frenemy Violet all escape from the Green Creek welcome house after Clementine accidentally kills a "brag" (a client at the brothel) while defending herself from his violent behavior. The five young women in the story (all in their teens) have been bound into slavery at Green Creek. Violet, as the daughter of a former sex worker (her mother deceased by the time the story begins), was born into servitude, but the other women were sold to the house by their desperate families.

Just as science fiction stories use alienness as an allegory for race, this fantasy novel reconfigures notions of racial difference. Aster, Clementine, Tansy, and Mallow are all described in terms that suggest that they are Black, and the cover image of the dark-skinned Aster in a battered leather coat with a "dustkerchief" around her neck against a backdrop of a desert landscape of red rock and scrub brush reinforces the narrative descriptions that suggest race. But the more significant marker of difference in this imagined world is a shadow: "Dustbloods, they were called. They looked just the same as ordinary, fairblood folks, except that they couldn't cast a shadow. The first dustbloods had had their shadows ripped away as part of their punishment [for rebelling against the Empire], and their children had been born without them."[60] To be a dustblood is to live a life not as a slave exactly but as a kind of perpetual debtor, resigned to working in mines in the Scab (a wild mountain range).

Drawing on the world-building conventions of fantasy (rather than of science fiction) "to distance and defamiliarize the institution and practice of slavery" (and other forms of social oppression, such as peonage), *The Good Luck Girls* is a meta–slavery narrative that allows the reader to experience a real-world racial hierarchy via the distancing technique of metaphor—the difference between the shadowed and the shadowless that determines one's place in the world.[61] Although dustbloods are not enslaved as such, the Good Luck Girls, the sex workers in the welcome houses, most definitely are, their status as property indicated by the novel's defamiliarized version of branding, a tattooed flower (a "favor") on the neck that grows as the girl ages, fully blooming into the flower that is the girl's slave name (Aster, Violet, etc.) as she reaches sexual maturity, which is celebrated by the Lucky Night ceremony and experience—the night when the young woman takes her first brag to her bed. This magical favor burns and glows if covered up for longer periods of time (even just a few minutes), making it difficult to conceal the mark of enslavement. Like *The Brother from Another Planet*, *The Good Luck Girls* is a story of fugitives being tracked by bounty hunters, being befriended along the way by unexpected allies, and ultimately finding "freedom" not in individual escape but in collective endeavor, or finding "home" in the form of an underground railroad–like organization that aids others seeking to escape bondage.

The story of fugitive slaves on the run also plays out in an identifiably "western" frontier landscape in a narrative that features such
western genre staples as outlaws, bank robberies, coach holdups,
horses, gunfights, saloons, ghost towns, abandoned mines, and a
duster-wearing cowboy outlaw hero who joins the cause of the five
women. The technique that creates the cognitive estrangement from
both the slave narrative and the western is not technology or science
but the creation of a fantastic world that is similar to our own. The
Scab is a reimagined frontier landscape that recognizably evokes the
American West, with "the ragged line of mountains that cut through
the middle of the country"—a "wind-torn wilderness" with deadly
snakes ("rattletails") where "condors climbed through blank blue skies
and gather in trees stripped bare by wind"; a place with "red dust
swirling up in the air" and sublime size with "towering mountains";
and a place of dangerous and savage inhabitants, both natural (cat-
amounts and snakes) and supernatural (home of "the restless dead,"
particularly "vengeants," "spirits born of the raw anger and anguish
of a tortured soul, released at last upon death").[62]

As both *Westworld* and *Unforgiven* (and hundreds of other westerns)
suggest, the prostitute is one of the most common roles westerns
offer for female characters, a practice that continues in SF westerns.[63]
However, the prostitutes in *The Good Luck Girls* are the subjects rather
than the objects of the narrative, the point-of-view characters who
continually criticize and deeroticize their relationships with the brags.
And ultimately, the primary western role that the young women play
in *The Good Luck Girls* is that of outlaws. The story may begin in the
Green Creek welcome house, but by the end of chapter 4, the setting
of the welcome house has been left behind, as we follow the characters while they ride on horseback through the Wild West of the Scab.

There are multiple moments that evoke the western. The women
discover their images on posters, "WANTED ALIVE" for "*the vicious
murder of Baxter McClennon*."[64] Partially out of revenge against the
brags, who have taken from Good Luck Girls for years, they become an
outlaw gang, robbing brags on their way to or from welcome houses.
In a town with a distinctively western name, Scarcliff, they set in

motion a plan to rob the (distinctively western-named) Red Rock Bank. The name of Aster's sister, Clementine, suggests a nod to the film *My Darling Clementine*.[65] The most identifiably "typical" western character in *The Good Luck Girls* is Zee, short for Ezekiel, the good-looking Black cowboy whom Aster meets on the trail, when they have to join together to fight off a catamount attack. Zee is "a rangeman—a Scab guide. . . . He wore a long brown duster coat over a simple work vest. Dark denims. . . . Riding boots. A wide-brimmed hat." Dressed head to toe in cowboy clothes, he was also, "of course," "seemingly traveling the Scab alone. That's what rangemen did: they tamed the wilderness, they explored the unknown, they protected the weak and helpless from all the wicked things in the mountains."[66] Additionally, this cowboy (or rangeman) uses his wilderness craft, tracking, and weaponry skills to aid the five women in their escape and in their quest to find the mysterious Lady Ghost, whom they hope will have the skill and magic to remove their favors, a necessity if they wish to escape from their old identities. In the speculative western that is *The Good Luck Girls*, Zee represents that part of Black western history that has been for too long a minor element of the western genre, and he does so with appropriate derring-do, dusty wisdom, and an attractively tragic back story that also makes him an appealing love interest (in this young adult novel) for Clementine.

As in *The Brother from Another Planet*, in the town of Scarcliff there's a scene that evokes the classic western moment of the stranger entering the saloon: "Aster stopped and nodded imperceptibly to the others. They walked in through the double doors." The description of the saloon is particularly evocative of this familiar western location: "The inside of the saloon was stifling, cherry-wood floors scuffed from the soles of a hundred shoes and half-lit gasoliers hanging from a tin tile ceiling. The smell of alcohol and smoke and sweat hit Aster like a wall as soon as she walked in. The men's voices around them were magnified tenfold. Talking, laughing, joking, cursing. Hands slamming down on tables. Glasses clinking together."[67]

The scene is not simply a repetition of a western staple but a significant variation. When the women enter in their riding clothes with their dustkerchiefs pulled up to cover their favors, the men in the saloon do not pause to observe the incursion. They do not, like Clint Eastwood in *For a Few Dollars More* or the bounty hunters in *The Brother from Another Planet*, enter and dominate the space. The stranger's entry into the saloon in the western is an assertion of his power, as the other men recognize him as a potential threat. Empowered by her days on the run, by her robberies of the sort of men who previously exploited her, Aster in this scene, instead, flashes back to a sense of powerlessness: "She had not been in a room like this, utterly surrounded, since Green Creek. She stopped short in the doorway, panic rising up in her belly, filling her lungs until her chest threatened to burst."[68] Davis rewrites and revises the western's saloon entry scene here. It is Aster, not the men inside, who "stops short," Aster, not the men, who feels threatened. For male western characters like Clint Eastwood's bounty hunter, the saloon is the place where they exercise their power, demonstrating their dominance over others. But for Aster this all-male space is a place of traumatic experience, and she is, for a moment, brought back to a former identity. Davis's version of the saloon scene underscores the female difference in this women-centered western.

The saloon scene does not play out as western genre conventions would suggest, because however many wanted posters may carry Aster's image, she is not the typical outlaw hero of the western. Aster may look like a cowboy ("like you stepped off the cover of a penny novel") with her dustkerchief pulled up over her nose and mouth, but it only conceals her favor from the eyes of others.[69] The favor is still there, and the pain it causes her when covered is a fantasy genre literalization of the psychological pain caused by a traumatic past. The panic she feels entering the saloon is only a more extreme version of the pain she experiences every time she raises her kerchief to play the part of the cowboy outlaw. Moments such as this one, which evoke western conventions to go against genre expectations, are part of the way a speculative western such as *The Good Luck Girls* reinvigorates the western genre, using familiar conventions in unfamiliar ways in order to depict experiences different from the usual run of western plots. The entry into an all-male space is not the same for a character who experiences such places as sites of trauma rather than as opportunities for pleasure, community, commerce, or adventure.

The Good Luck Girls may be a western with a difference, but it also offers its readers the pleasure of the expected western thrills as experienced through the exploits of its Black female gang of outlaws. Cornered during the bank robbery, they shoot their way out: "*Bam!* Mallow fired a shot above the heads of the three lawmen in the back doorway. . . . *Bam!* Another warning shot and the air swirled with gun smoke and panic."[70] Chased by a posse, they make their way across a dilapidated wooden suspension bridge. Aster and Clementine "were a little over halfway across when [their horse's] hoof punched through a plank of wood."[71] They manage to make it across without plunging to the river below, and then as bullets fly around her, Aster cuts the ropes of the bridge and strands the chasing posse on the other side. And ultimately, like many a western outlaw before them, the five women are headed for the border, to cross over out of "Arketta and into Ferron, where dustblood debts don't exist."[72] Or we might say instead, their escape to the border simultaneously suggests the western and the slave narrative, evoking both the journey of the western outlaw escaping imprisonment or execution and the fugitive slave's journey north to freedom.

The titular character of Hopkins's *Winona* is described as having "the pluck of a man," and she is given plenty of opportunity in the narrative to demonstrate as much courage and bravery as any of the women in *The Good Luck Girls*.[73] Building on a western convention as old as Calamity Jane in the Deadwood Dick dime novels or Mary in *The Administratrix*, Winona at one point dresses herself as a man, an act of western cross-dressing that enables her to infiltrate a prison where the injured Warren Maxwell, the white British man who befriends Winona and ultimately joins up with John Brown, is held captive. Although her activities (nursing Maxwell back to health) while in disguise fulfill female gender expectations, her time spent in an all-male prison is a decidedly dangerous subterfuge, especially as it brings her back in range of the southern captors from whom she has so recently escaped. However, in other ways, Winona is very much a novel of its time. In contrast to the former prostitutes at the center of *The Good Luck Girls*, Winona's sexual purity is a point of emphasis, in part because Hopkins is intent on undoing the era's prevalent "stereotype of the hypersexual African American female."[74] And although Winona carries a rifle to protect the camp when Brown and his men go on a raid, she doesn't join them in battle, and she does not fire her rifle. As part of laying claim to dominant notions of femininity for her heroine, Hopkins separates her from the violence, even the violence represented as necessary in a just cause. Winona may have "the pluck of a man," but there are no scenes in the novel that would connect her either to expressive aggression or instrumental aggression.

Although each of the Good Luck Girls has opportunities to act heroically, heroic power, particularly when exercised through instrumental aggression, is primarily associated with Aster. Clementine's killing of the brag is a clear example of expressive aggression—impulsive and committed in an act of self-defense. During the bank robbery, the young women take a couple of brags hostage. As part of controlling a hostage, Aster "whipped around and slammed his jaw with a back fist." Her violence is purposeful, to achieve a particular goal, which it does: "They all shut up then, walking in silence." Looking at the other women, "she saw flashes of doubt in the others' eyes as they exchanged glances. They wouldn't be able to pull the trigger if the time came." Aster, however, "was becoming more sure of herself by the second."[75] In a later incident with a ravener (a kind of overseer figure with supernatural powers), Aster similarly acts with purposeful aggression: "She had known the second she saw this ravener that she would kill him if she got the chance. Had known, since her first night at the welcome house, when the raveners had tortured her into submission, that they would never show mercy and would never deserve the same."[76] This particular ravener, having recognized the women as the wanted escapees that they are, is even more of a danger, and Aster stabs him in the throat with her knife, "leaving the ravener behind in a spreading pool of his own cursed blood."[77] Although there are elements of revenge here and the violence takes place during a fight (so her own life is in danger), the killing is purposeful, with the intention to do so established beforehand, and the goal is ultimately tactical. Their escape depends on Aster's ability and willingness to act violently, to kill if necessary, in order to protect herself and, importantly, to protect the other women.

As does Brother in *The Brother from Another Planet*, as do Judah and Winona in their incorporation into John Brown's camp, the group of Good Luck Girls discover a network of abolitionists operating on the frontier. There are actually two such organizations in *The Good Luck Girls*, both of which are literally underground: the Scorpions, a group of men hidden in abandoned mines (and working to connect the mines to create a route under the border), and the Hotfoots (who are helped by the Scorpions), runaways seeking to escape the Reckoning. Lady Ghost, they discover later, is not a particular person but the identity adopted by a group of women, former Good Luck Girls, who operate their own version (also hidden in an abandoned mine) of an underground railroad over the border: "There has never been just one woman named Lady Ghost. It's all of us, working together. . . . We help girls borderjump to Ferron and start new lives."[78] For Winona, the final border jump to freedom involves migration to England and marriage to Maxwell. In both *Winona* and *Of One Blood*, Ihara writes, there is "an increased sense that the solution to racial strife is to be found beyond U.S. borders."[79] As Ihara points out, commentary on the books has been critical of that resolution, suggesting that the "decision to transport her protagonists to locations outside the U.S. suggests an abdication of civic responsibility" and a "decisive rejection of the African American community as a site for justice."[80] Ihara suggests an alternate interpretation—the migrations in *Winona* and *Of One Blood* "held out the promise of someplace better" for African American readers of the magazine, "an 'imagined community' beyond the reach of U.S. racism," at a time when "U.S. citizenship seemed to offer little hope of fair treatment under the law."[81] The duality of these responses (the criticism of the ending as an "abdication of civic responsibility" versus the praise for an ending that imagines equality in a future place) suggests an enduring double consciousness in African American studies.

One of the guiding concepts in Afrofuturism that Lavender identifies is what he calls "the hope impulse," a "charged impulse representing the desire for life, liberty, and knowledge," which "reverberates across time and space, linking past, present, and future."[82] The hope impulse links multiple Black migrations to various geographies: the Exodusters' movement westward, imagined returns to Africa in the folklore of flying Africans, the journey to another planet in *Space Is the Place*, as well as Winona's quest for freedom outside the borders of the United States. The countering impulse, the embrace of the African American community of the present as a site for justice and the exercise of civic responsibility, is equally a guiding concept in African American literature generally. The ending of *The Good Luck Girls* suggests that Davis understands the appeal of both of those choices, and she offers readers the "promise of someplace better" in the successful escape of Clementine, Tansy, and Mallow across the border. However, like Brother in *The Brother from Another Planet*, Aster realizes that her destiny is down, not up, as she stays behind and becomes part of the underground railroad of Lady Ghosts. "Green Creek would always be a part of her whether she wore its favor or not," she realizes. "She couldn't change the past. But neither did she have to let it decide her future."[83] The novel resolves the dilemma of double consciousness by imagining a scenario other than the existential choice made by a single character as representative of the "best" political action, in favor of one that understands the appeal and viability of multiple possibilities as revealed through the choices made by several characters.

Aster's final gesture in the novel, in keeping with Afrofuturist principles, both acknowledges the past and looks to the future. Her favor cannot be removed, but it can be altered. As the flower tattoo represents the new name and identity given to her by the welcome house, her redesigned tattoo represents a new beginning and a new name—or rather, an old name, as she becomes once again Dawn, the name given to her by her parents: "Dawn, the girl she'd been, and the woman she hoped to be." True to that name, "there on the side of her face, stretching down into her neck, tracing rays of light around the petals of her cheek: her favor transformed into a spreading sun."[84] The rising sun symbolizes the new beginning, but it also evokes and reverses the conventional ending of the western—the image of the cowboy hero riding into the sunset. Dawn similarly merges with the sun at the end of *The Good Luck Girls*, as the sun becomes (once more) her name and as the image of the sun becomes a physical part of her body. Like the final shot of *The Brother from Another Planet*, the final image of the novel tells us that, unlike the hero of the western, she is not riding off alone and leaving behind the community of which she has become part. She, like Brother, has found a home, has concluded this part of her western adventure as she embarks on a new one, an adventure linked to building a community that will help others as it helped the young woman formerly known as Aster.

THE ZOMBIE FRONTIER

As Miller and Van Riper observe in their introduction to *Undead in the West*, the frontier—the classic western's traditional dividing line between civilization and wilderness, savagery, and lawlessness—is replicated in the "undead western" by the boundary between "the worlds of the undead and the living."[85] Justina Ireland's *Dread Nation* imagines a nineteenth-century alternate-history America, the nation's trajectory altered by an event during the Civil War's Battle of Gettysburg (a not infrequent alternate-history trope). The key event is not some actual historical element of the battle itself (e.g., What if Pickett's Charge had been successful?) but the moment when the dead suddenly rise and start trying to eat their comrades and enemies alike. General Sherman's March to the Sea in this version of history involved "burning and putting down the dead," although the military maneuver "wasn't much more than a temporary setback for the shamblers."[86] "The Lost States of the South are called that for a reason," comments narrator and central character Jane McKeene.[87] Surviving humans have fallen back to northeastern cities (such as Baltimore, where the first part of the story takes place), which (at least according to the propaganda of the ruling party) provide sanctuary from the dead.

Based in part on the history of boarding or industrial schools for Native American children (and a similar system of vocational training schools for African Americans), *Dread Nation* imagines a system of combat training schools for African Americans and Native Americans, who, according to the racist logic of the era, are closer to animals than humans and, thus, are less likely to be turned into zombies if bitten by the dead they are trained to fight (this turns out not to be the case). When we first meet Jane, she is enrolled at Miss Preston's School for Negro Girls, where the girls are trained as Attendants for wealthy white women: "An Attendant's job is simple: keep her charge from being killed by the dead, and her virtue from being compromised by potential suitors."[88] Despite the inspiration of Native American history, the book focuses primarily on its African American characters, with a fairly minor role assigned to the primary Native character, a Lenape man educated at the Carlisle Indian Industrial School, the enigmatic Daniel Redfern, who is sometimes an enemy, sometimes an ally to main characters Jane McKeene and Katherine Devereaux.[89]

Dread Nation is divided into two sections, or books, with the first, "The Civilized East," taking place in Baltimore and the second, "The Cruel West," in the frontier town of Summerland, Kansas. As it turns out, the civilized East is not particularly so, despite the desperate efforts of politicians to pretend that everything is fine. The ascendency of a white supremacist party (the Survivalists) over their rivals (the Egalitarians) contributes to the cruelty of the "civilized" East. The frontier town of Summerland, established by members of the Survivalist party, also turns out to replicate the social divisions of the East and, more disturbingly, of the "lost South." Once Jane and Katherine arrive in Summerland, the first half's novel of manners and boarding school adventures (Miss Preston's offers both "close combat" classes and "tea serving lessons") becomes a full-fledged western, one that ends with the characters moving farther west in search of the town of Nicodemus, one of the most famous of the all-Black townships established on the western plains.[90]

Deathless Divide, the second book in the series, begins with Jane and Katherine on the run from Summerland. Part 1 of the novel, "In the Garden of Good and Evil," takes place primarily in Nicodemus, which, like Summerland before, eventually falls to the zombie horde. Part 2, "The Road to Perdition," takes up the story about a year and a half later, with both Katherine and Jane arriving in California, each having made her own way out west after their separation during the fall of Nicodemus, and with Katherine believing that Jane is dead. Although elements of the slave narrative remain in "The Road to Perdition," for the most part, when Katherine and Jane reach California, the story becomes a traditional western (well, a traditional western with zombies), with the two joining back together to offer protection to a wagon train of African American migrants seeking a new frontier in interior California, somewhere away from the segregated living conditions in San Francisco.

As a meta–slavery narrative, *Dread Nation* differs in several ways from the other meta–slavery narratives discussed here. The history of slavery it evokes is the real history of American slavery, not a reimagined version thereof. However, as a slave narrative, *Dread Nation* is a bit of an oddity in that it takes place after the abolition of slavery (known in the books as the "Great Concession") or, at least, after "the kind [of slavery] that ended with the War between the States."[91] Elements of enslavement remain: "The Negro and Native Reeducation Act mandates that at twelve years old all Negroes, and any Indians living in a protectorate, must enroll in a combat school 'for the betterment of themselves and of society.'"[92] Although Jane is in training to earn wages as an Attendant, her education is compulsory. At the end of book 1, Jane and Katherine are kidnapped, tossed aboard a train heading west, and unloaded in Summerland to fight off zombies and protect the white citizens. "You ain't slaves," the sheriff of Summerland tells Jane and Katherine, "because as far as I know that's still illegal, more's the pity."[93] Although Jane is paid for her services (defending Summerland from zombies), her presence in Summerland is due to abduction, her job is forced labor, and she has little freedom of movement (she can't leave Summerland, and she must follow a curfew).

And as a woman they befriend, Ida, comments, "They got loopholes in that there Thirteenth Amendment." For example, anyone bitten by a shambler is considered no longer human (and thus not protected from enslavement); given the (false) cultural belief of Black immunity to zombie bites, Ida claims that she's "seen folks testify Negroes have been bit and then those Negroes get sold off by the compound. Same if you're a criminal."[94] False testimony, as it sometimes did for free

Blacks during slavery, results in enslavement. Through its fantasy-horror metaphor (anyone bitten by a shambler being considered no longer human and thus not protected under law), the duology addresses the real-life constitutional failures of postbellum America. The Thirteenth Amendment abolished slavery, but Black Americans nonetheless find themselves in situations approximating the conditions of enslavement.

Whether or not slavery has been abolished in the novel's world, *Dread Nation*, generically speaking, is a slave narrative, one that pulls multiple tropes from and makes many references to the tradition. Although Jane is literate, she has to pretend at times that she can't read, because prohibitions on Black literacy remain in the postbellum period of the novel. Jane, likewise, at times, plays the dissembling slave, pretending a lack of knowledge and intelligence as a subterfuge to disarm white enemies. *Dread Nation* also evokes western conventions. Although Jane's weapons of choice are a specially designed pair of sickles, she also carries a "six-shooter" that she loves, observing, "According to the newspapers, the Remington single-action is the gunslinger's pistol of choice, which makes it even more ace."[95] After she kills the corrupt sheriff of the frontier town of Summerland, she takes his revolver and his cowboy hat, "adjusting it so that it sits at a jaunty angle," all part of her transformation from her role as an Attendant in *Dread Nation* to her emergence as a full-fledged western gunslinger in *Deathless Divide*.[96] A series of epigraphs at the head of chapters in *Deathless Divide*, taken from multiple volumes of the fictional *Western Tales*, playfully evokes the western in both its "tales of the true west" and dime novel forms through its pastiche of the breathless prose of such narratives.

As slave narrative westerns, there are multiple points of contact between Ireland's novels and Pauline Hopkins's *Winona*, including a prominent Kansas setting and the centrality of a pair of mixed race characters, Winona and her brother Judah in *Winona* and Jane and Katherine in *Dread Nation*. Ireland's examination of a shared history of exploitation between African Americans and Native Americans provides another point of contact with Hopkins's *Winona*, which draws parallels between slavery and the U.S. project of Indian removal, examined from the specific viewpoint of Seneca history. As O'Brien writes, "Hopkins's literary engagement with Seneca history and culture, though limited and at times problematic, offers an early example of an African American activist writer attempting to represent Native American people and the issues they faced."[97] African American westerns have with some frequency explored interactions between African Americans and Native Americans, a feature as well of Rebecca Roanhorse's speculative westerns. If, as Sanchez-Taylor suggests, contemporary Black writers fuse "Afrofuturist themes with those of other cultures, creating a science fiction that is not merely diverse in appearance, but one which includes non-white and non-Western cultures as integral to its narrative," there is already a history of such fusion in African American westerns, one that may begin with Hopkins and one that Ireland extends.[98]

Although Hopkins's story illustrates Winona's brave and heroic action, her heroism does not extend to acts of violence, which the novel genders as a masculine capacity. The debate in the novel, as is typical of the western, revolves around the justness of male violence—the necessity of that violence in a dangerous world, the risk that participating in such violence will result in becoming like the savage other being fought against. Consistent with the era's understanding of gender roles, *Winona* explores through its male and female characters the balancing of restraint and passion deemed necessary for civil life, with Winona's femininity providing a check on the masculine anger and violence to which her brother is (and other men, white and Black, in the novel are) prone.[99]

Ireland addresses a similar debate, but she does so while dismissing sexual difference as an allegorical representation of differing qualities. Winona is replaced by Katherine, who is similarly light-skinned and beautiful and more broadly representative of feminine qualities, as symbolized by her insistence on wearing a corset even though it restricts her fighting abilities ("The day I cannot take down a few shamblers wearing something fashionable is the day I turn in my rifle").[100] Katherine, as she continually reminds Jane, was also the best shot at Miss Preston's, and she uses her rifle and her mollies (a pair of short swords) against shamblers with a rarely matched efficiency.

Her ability to commit violence (mostly against the undead but also, when the occasion calls for it, against living humans) does not detract from her "feminine" role in the novels, as the voice of conscience and empathy, as the character tasked with preventing the more bloody-minded Jane from tipping over into vengeful savagery. Jane takes over the role of Judah, the masculine character whose violent ability is inflamed by racial injustice. Both Hopkins and Ireland recognize that injustice must sometimes be countered with violence, but both writers foreground debates about the use of such violence. And as both Hopkins and Ireland realize, the western form is ready-made for such ethical debates.

The central moment in *Dread Nation*, as it is in *Winona*, that brings together the slave narrative and the western is the deployment of a shared trope between the two genres—the scene in which the hero or heroine is severely beaten. Whipping scenes, vivid and concrete descriptions of savage beatings by overseers or slave owners, are key moments in slave narratives, as important to the emotional argument of the slave narrative as auction-block scenes of family separation, part of the evidence the slave narrative advances of the excessive cruelty of slavery. Such scenes, however, are also important to the western. As Lee Clark Mitchell writes, there is an "almost obsessive recurrence" in westerns "of scenes of men being beaten—or knifed and whipped, propped up, kicked down, kicked in the side, punched in the face, or otherwise lacerated, clubbed, battered, and tortured into unconsciousness."[101] Westerns contain multiple opportunities for achieving and proving manhood, but "one also becomes a man by being punished" and surviving.[102] The recuperation process in westerns is carefully narrated so "that we can see men recover, regaining their strength and resources in the process of once again making themselves into men."[103] The presence of a whipping or beating scene in a Black western is indicative of the intentional hybridity of the text, as it draws from and mixes together specific elements of the conventional scene as it plays out in the separate genres.

Specific to the western's version of the beating or whipping scene is a sequence that narrates the hero's recovery. That recovery is often aided by a feminine presence and by a "restorative female 'gaze' at the male body" that both observes and insures the recovery.[104] The feminine presence is also necessary because it encourages "the return of masculine restraint, of control over emotion and passion, the quality of manliness that enables the frontier hero to embody aspects of masculinity both civilized and savage."[105] Without that feminine presence, the western seems to suggest, the understandable desire for revenge would create a villainous imbalance in the hero, disrupting his ability to render justice (and enact just violence) objectively.

Ireland subverts the beating scene—in both its slave narrative and western versions—in multiple ways. Inserting a heroine rather than a hero into this western scene alters its gender dynamics, suggesting that biological sex is irrelevant to western heroism, as Ireland uses the beating scene to demonstrate the female—not the male—character's toughness and ability to absorb punishment. Scenes of women being beaten, however, are staples of slave narratives, particularly by male writers, and the depiction of the victimization of women is a central element of the rhetoric of abolitionist writing. As McDowell observes, in slave narratives written by male writers, "slave women operate almost totally as physical bodies, as sexual victims."[106] "Black men," McDowell writes, "are largely impotent onlookers, condemned to watch" scenes of abuse that are often described with "strong sexual undercurrents," underscored by descriptions of the victim being stripped of clothing.[107] In her discussion of Douglass's *Narrative*, McDowell argues that his "repetition of the sexualized scene of whipping projects him in a voyeuristic relation to the violence against women, which he watches," even if that spectatorship is accidental (as in the case of Aunt Hester) or compelled against his will (as in moments when all the slaves are forced to watch the punishment of another).[108]

Caught breaking curfew, Jane is "tied to the whipping post in front of the sheriff's office" and sentenced to twenty lashes, a public spectacle during which her shirt is ripped away and her body is exposed to the eyes of the spectators as well as to the leather of the whip.[109] "The whip whistles through the air," Jane observes, "before it carves agony across my back."[110] The scene of whipping continues, with the deputy Bill (mis)counting the lashes as the sheriff strikes, until

Jane is "shaking with pain, delirious with it."[111] In *Dread Nation* Jane remains the point-of-view character during the beating scene, the first-person narrator of her own experience rather than the observer of another's victimization. That shift in point of view disrupts the voyeuristic relations inherent in the structure of scenes of violence or sexualized violence narrated from the perspective of a male observer.

Jane is saved from being whipped to death by the intervention of Katherine, who, in Summerland, is passing as white. As part of the larger plan of escaping the town, Jane has worked to beguile Sheriff Snyder, and she begs for the sheriff to show Jane mercy. If the specific details of the whipping scene recall the slave narrative, Katherine's action suggests the western. The intervention in punishment or execution (most spectacularly in scenes of stopping a hanging by cutting the rope with a fired bullet at the last second) is a staple of westerns, and Katherine fulfills the role of the cowboy hero who stops the execution (even as she uses "feminine wiles" to do so). Most importantly, though, the scene underscores Jane's toughness, her ability to recover from the beating she's received. Noticing the "soft look" the sheriff bestows on Katherine, "just like that, the plan [Jane has] been struggling to come up with for weeks explodes in [her] brain like a stick of dynamite with a too-short fuse."[112] Her body may be damaged, but the sheriff's lash does not affect her ability to think and plan when Katherine provides the opportunity.

However, in spite of her quick mental recovery from the ordeal, *Dread Nation* otherwise follows the western's emphasis on narrating the process of physical recovery, which takes place in the presence of a female restorative gaze, beneath the ministrations of the Duchess (the madam of the town's brothel), who takes Jane in, and Nessie, an African American woman who works at the brothel and befriends Jane. What differs in *Dread Nation* is the male presence in Jane's convalescence—scientist Gideon Carr, whose healing salve aids her recovery and who eventually becomes part of the conspiracy to take down the sheriff. His presence also aids the recovery of Jane's desire and sense of ownership over her own body. After Jane's body has been exposed in public, made into an object for the collective gaze of the gathered crowd, Gideon's presence offers an opportunity to recenter her subjectivity in the story through her own desiring gaze: "I look up just long enough to take in his expression, his eyes sparking with intelligence, his lips pursed in thought. My heart flops like a trout on a riverbank." "I have always been a complete and utter muttonhead for a clever boy," Jane observes, "even when I'm half delirious with pain."[113] We know that Jane has recovered from the experience of being objectified by refusing to remain an object—a refusal signaled by her own acts of looking. In contrast to the beating and recovery scenario that Mitchell describes, the female gaze at the male body is desiring rather than restorative or, perhaps, is restorative because it *is* desiring. The importance of the female gaze is in the effect it has not on the male body but on the female character's psyche—as part of the process of reclaiming a body that has been taken from her by male violence, of becoming once more a desiring subject rather than an acted-upon object.

If Gideon's presence is important to assure the restoration of Jane's ownership of her own body and desire, Katherine plays a role more in keeping with the western's traditional scenario of beating and recovery by aiding the return of "masculine" restraint, the ability of the western hero (and, in this case, heroine) to embody both civilization and savagery in equal measure, a balance that enables the hero to act savagely on behalf of civilization. In *Winona* Hopkins describes a similar scene of whipping, with Winona's brother, Judah, as the one who is stripped and beaten, to the degree that each "merciless lash was engraved . . . in bleeding stripes that called for vengeance."[114] The damage to Judah is physical and psychological. Winona's role is to aid not only his physical recovery but the damage to his humanity, at one point intervening to prevent Judah from an act of violence against one of the men responsible for his beating. "You make yourself as vile as the vilest of them—our enemies," she warns him.[115] Winona's efforts help bend Judah toward justice rather than vengeance, ensuring that Judah emerges at the end of the novel as the proper Kantian agent of objective justice, a true western hero who is able to set aside the desire for personal vengeance in order to do the right thing.

Dread Nation concludes with two distinctively western scenes, each one violently resolving the two primary plot conflicts (the fight against the dead and the fight against racism), and each one turning on Jane's ability to enact justice through violence. Such justice requires Jane's ability to deploy instrumental aggression, violence that is "cool" and calculated, "formulated with forethought and carried out purposefully."[116] As a female character who wields heroic power, Jane's relationship to violence must negotiate gendered norms, and thus it is doubly important that her "cool" be tested through the western's scenario of beating and recovery, so that we can see that biological sex does not undermine her ability to enact the role of western hero. In *Winona* Judah's recovery serves the thematic purpose of countering racist notions of "Black savagery," as it demonstrates his civilized (in terms of racial and gendered beliefs of the novel's era) ability for self-restraint. In a sense, Jane's restoration of intellectual and emotional control demonstrates that her actions are not determined by presumed traits of either race or sex. That control will be further tested in *Deathless Divide*, but the Jane who emerges at the end of *Dread Nation* is the perfectly balanced embodiment of the frontier hero.

Katherine performs a similar role for Jane as Winona does for Judah. In words that echo Winona's, Katherine tells Jane in *Deathless Divide*, "I refuse to believe that we have to be like those we hate in order to carry on."[117] However, femininity is just one part of Katherine's character, and she is no turn-of-the-twentieth-century heroine like Winona. Her means of reminding Jane of her capacity for restraint involve argument, kindness, and a good smack to the face when necessary. "Sometimes a little physical release, directed and controlled," she comments to Jane, "can quiet the heart just a bit." "Heartfelt confessions," Katherine considers, "have never moved Jane the way that actions do, and if I want to help her, if I want to show her that I am her friend, I have to do that in a way that she understands." And as Katherine rightly observes, "If there is anything Jane understands, it is combat."[118] Fortunately for Katherine, one of the things she herself learned at Miss Preston's "was how to fight dirty while wearing a corset."[119] Gender (and sexuality) in Ireland's duology is fluid, with Katherine in particular able to move intentionally between masculine (combat and fighting dirty) and feminine (heartfelt confessions and corsets) modes of discourse and behavior. Ireland's novel has no difficulty in adapting a moral debate (the conflict between violent passion and self-controlled restraint) that the western often embodies through opposing male and female characters by placing that dynamic in the conflict between two female characters.

Given the general incompetence and tendency toward wishful thinking among Summerland's ruling Survivalist Party members, it is no surprise when shamblers break through the town's defensive wall. With a combination of townspeople and African American combatants trained to fight zombies, *Dread Nation* rewrites the classic western's battle scene by replacing the raiding-attacking outlaws, Mexicans, or Native Americans with its horde of shamblers. Jane countermands the sheriff's orders and takes command of the battle ("Ain't no one but the dead dying today!"), effectively defending the town with her careful instructions to her soldiers and her guiding of the direction of the battle (as well as her as usual deadly employment of her sickles).[120] Although the sheriff publicly acknowledges that Jane saved the day, it's also clear that he will not let such an infraction against the racial hierarchy stand, and Jane and Kathleen accordingly plan their escape from Summerland before he can get his revenge. When the sheriff discovers the truth of Katherine's passing, he takes her prisoner, holding her at gunpoint, and we arrive at the second climactic showdown of the novel, in which the combined efforts of Jane and Katherine finally take down the sheriff. Katherine pretends to faint, momentarily distracting the sheriff, and Jane shoots him in the throat, a more or less traditional one-on-one western shootout, with a traditional western weapon (a gun rather than sickles). Through the heroine's ability to employ instrumental violence, the twin villainy of shamblers and white supremacy is defeated, at least temporarily.

JOURNEYING FARTHER WEST IN *DEATHLESS DIVIDE*

Among other themes, *Dread Nation* and *Deathless Divide* are stories about Black migration; even with their zombies, steampunk devices (steam-powered carriages called "ponies"), and rewritten American history, the novels nonetheless depict or reflect multiple aspects of real-life African American history and experience. The characters in Ireland's books are continually on the move, from Baltimore to

Summerland to Nicodemus, and when Nicodemus falls in *Deathless Divide*, Katherine makes her way to San Francisco by way of Fort Riley, Kansas; the Mississippi River; New Orleans; and South America. Jane's route from Nicodemus to California is the more direct (but more dangerous because of the zombies) overland route to San Francisco.[121] Separated during the fall of Nicodemus, Jane and Katherine meet up again as part of a wagon train of Black migrants leaving San Francisco in search of a Black settlement north of Sacramento called Haven. Although Jane is the first-person narrator of *Dread Nation*, the narration of *Deathless Divide* is split between Jane and Katherine, and we move back and forth between the two points of view.

Through their presence and activity within the spaces they occupy—Miss Preston's, Summerland, Nicodemus, and elsewhere—they create within those spaces temporary communities that are repeatedly disrupted by both the westward migration of the zombies and the various actions of racist whites, for whom maintaining the racial hierarchy proves to be a greater priority than survival. Monstrosity in the novels is presented both in the realist mode of African American literature more generally (the depiction of life in a white supremacist society) and in the high-value realism of speculative fiction—the mindless, disruptive zombie hordes that figure exterior forces that threaten Black life in the real world. Jane observes, "Seems to me whenever anyone finds but a little bit of peace, the dead inevitably show up to wreak their special kind of havoc."[122]

As Katherine comments about the mob of white refugees from Summerland gathered outside the Nicodemus jail in the hopes of seeing Jane lynched, "It is monstrous, and yet another reminder that the dead are not the only threat in the world."[123] Shamblers cause the downfall of Nicodemus but only after the town's Black settlers admit the white refugees from Summerland, who, unable to fathom the notion of Black self-governance, ultimately create tension and discord that contributes to the fall. The Nicodemus settlers also make the mistake of taking the advice of the white scientist Gideon Carr, who exploits their trust by convincing them to take part in a scientific experiment (which goes horribly wrong) to test a vaccine that he hopes will protect against the virus that turns the living into the undead.

In *Deathless Divide* the zombies become more clearly a general metaphor for manifest destiny, as they slowly but inexorably make their way west. "Yes, the people of California had fled the dead," Jane notes, "yet here it all was, pursuing them like Pharaoh harrying Moses and the Israelites across Egypt." "They're heading west," Jane comments. "Yep. That's a proper horde," as if moving in a westward direction is a defining characteristic of shamblers gathered en masse.[124] "The promise of California is no more," we're told, "the West will still succumb. The dead always find a way."[125] Like George Romero's zombies going to the mall in *Dawn of the Dead*, the dead just keep moving west, as if driven by some remnant of the ideology of a former life.[126] The zombies are aided in their version of westward expansion by Gideon Carr, who emerges as the mad scientist villain of *Deathless Divide*. Gideon's actions are well intentioned (he wants to perfect an inoculation against the zombie virus), although his methods are careless and vile (taking test subjects against their will and forcing them to endure zombie bites to see if the vaccine protects them from turning); he is ultimately responsible for the zombie invasion of California, as he causes an outbreak in Sacramento when his serum accidently turns the recipients into zombies.

While Katherine arrives in San Francisco aboard ship, Jane fights her way west across the interior of the country. Because of Gideon's inoculation (which is sometimes effective), Jane develops immunity to the bite of the zombies (as she discovers after an attack that ultimately causes her arm to be amputated but leaves her human and alive). An effect of that immunity is that Jane also becomes almost invisible to the zombies, or at least, she no longer triggers the feeding frenzy that other living humans do. In *Deathless Divide* Jane emerges as a full-fledged western hero, her exploits inspiring a series of dime novels, a figure as much out of myth as history. Her missing arm and her invulnerability to shamblers contribute to that mythic figuration. The novel, though, is critical of this version of Jane and of the fully masculinized western hero she has become, one who is as dangerously obsessive in her quest to kill Gideon as Gideon himself is in his scientific pursuits. Kathrine's perspective reveals that critical take on Jane, just as earlier in the story, it's Kathrine who works to feminize—or really, humanize—Jane, so that she doesn't have to, à la Shane, remove herself in order to remove the guns from the valley, wandering off alone into the sunset, an agent of civilization but separate from it.

Jane's reentry into the novel in book 2, "The Road to Perdition," begins with an epigraph from a fictional book called *Western Tales*, volume 23, and we soon learn that the later volumes of *Western Tales* are filled with Jane's post-Nicodemus exploits. "There is no shortage of hard men in the west," the excerpt tells us. "These men kill and rob their way across the unsettled territories, stopped by only two equally powerful forces: the marshal and the bounty hunter."[127] We find Jane outside a nameless saloon in Monterey, California, where she "stomp[s] into the room" and observes her quarry, William Jefferson Perry, sitting in the back corner away from the door.[128] "I draw my pistol and calmly level it at his head," Jane tells us.[129] When Perry's men attempt to sneak up on her from behind, she narrates, "I swing around fast as a jackrabbit and plug both of the men in the middle of their chests."[130]

The Brother from Another Planet suggests a critique of the western's bounty hunter character type by connecting bounty hunters to slave catchers. However, in the history of western cinema, the bounty hunter has emerged as a role frequently associated with African American characters.[131] *Deathless Divide* alludes to that convention by introducing us to a Jane McKeene who has been transformed from Attendant to bounty hunter, doing so through a saloon scene that (once more) suggests the introduction of Clint Eastwood's bounty hunter character in *For a Few Dollars More*. Like Eastwood's bounty hunter, Jane's entry into the saloon is an assertion of dominance. Her preternaturally quick actions (including shooting men who are behind her) likewise suggests the saloon scene in *For a Few Dollars More*. Jane as a bounty hunter is not as cynical as Sergio Leone's characters—she is not just in it for the money. Her quarries tend to be victimizers of women or racist vigilantes, as in the case of the murders of the Turner family, African American settlers killed in their beds by outlaws pretending to need shelter. "It was the kind of crime," Jane observes, "that should have seen them hanged. But killing Negroes wasn't against the law in Colorado Territory."[132]

Jane becomes a notorious figure in the western territories, popularly known as the Devil's Bride. On the cover of the *Abbottsville Eagle*, Jane discovers a picture of herself: "I'm wearing a set of bandoliers and carry an oversized pistol, my lips overly large and my teeth pointed. Nearby is a group of terrified women and children." The "badly executed sketch of yours truly" is a combination of stereotypes: the bandoliers of a bandito, the exaggerated lips of racist drawings of Blacks, the pointed teeth of a monstrosity.[133] In the *Voice of the Negro*, a California African American newspaper, Katherine comes across an installment of the "True Stories of the Wilding West" serial, and she recognizes Jane in the description: "For out of the ashes of America rides an avenging angel, a Negro woman with but a single arm who serves justice by way of pistol and blade."[134] Whites may think of Jane as the Devil's Bride, but women in the West and African Americans in the West see her as an avenging angel, a counter to racial injustice and an agent of vengeance against men who mistreat women.

Jane's fury at Gideon and her by-any-means-necessary (including frequently torturing individuals with knowledge of his whereabouts) approach to tracking him down threaten to transform her from a figure of justice into a mirror image of Gideon. If Jane's adoption of the role of bounty hunter, a role that adds at least a veneer of lawfulness to behavior that is otherwise closer to vigilantism than law and order, enables her to act justly on behalf of those who were wronged, her continuing acts of violence (and her escalating use of excessive violence) threaten to upset the necessary balance between violent capacity and ethical self-restraint. As Jane veers toward a kind of violent hypermasculinity, the female characters in the novel attempt to save her from herself. Jane herself wishes for "just a few hours to feel like a person and not an instrument of destruction."[135] Playing a Winona-like role, Katherine works to help "Jane piece herself together as [they] traveled." When Redfern reappears in the story with a lead on Gideon's whereabouts, Katherine worries all that effort will "begin to come undone as she considers turning back toward the bloody path of revenge."[136] Katherine, unlike Winona, is not constrained by the necessity of performing a nonviolent femininity. When the expected showdown comes, it doesn't play out as we've been led by the novel to expect. Gideon captures Jane and Katherine, and with his gun trained on Jane, she recounts, "A shot rings out, loud and incredibly close, and I have a moment of weightlessness. But then Gideon's eyes widen and he drops his revolver as a crimson rose blossoms on his chest." Jane turns to find that "Katherine still lies on her back, but she holds my pistol."[137] Like the cowboy hero of the conventional western, Katherine acts violently in the service of protecting others, preventing Gideon from killing Jane. However, like Winona and like the character who represents the female presence in the western's scenario of beating and recovering, Katherine also, as it were, protects Jane from herself, pulling her from "the bloody path of revenge" and enabling Jane's restoration of balance. Unlike Winona, Katherine does so not by stopping Jane from acting violently but through acting violently herself. Filling the role of the Kantian moral agent of the classic western in a way that is impossible for Jane—whose desire for personal vengeance overwhelms her ability to perform as an agent of justice—Katherine commits the necessary act of violence that only she can render objectively.

The end of *Deathless Divide* suggests the classic western with its restless hero uncomfortable within the constraints of the civilized community she has worked to protect. "I'm clearing out," Jane declares, "back to murdering and the like, you know how it is."[138] However, unlike Shane, she does not do so alone, as she is joined first by Daniel (who finally emerges unambiguously as an ally) and then by Katherine. If, like the gunslinger at the end of a classic western, Jane finds herself unfit for the civilized society she has helped to save, she does not venture out in search of a new frontier alone.

Afterword

Speculative Wests has been inspired by the rich outburst of speculative western stories that have appeared during the period in which much of the book's writing occurred, from 2016 through 2020. The writing of the book has also taken place in what has been an astonishing period of social and political action, reaction, change, and stubborn resistance to change: the period of the Trump presidency; the Unite the Right Rally in 2017 in Charlottesville, Virginia; the worldwide Black Lives Matter protests sparked by the May 25, 2020, killing of George Floyd in Minneapolis, Minnesota. And for the last two years, this writing has taken place in the context of the worldwide pandemic caused by the novel coronavirus, a disease (COVID-19) that in the United States has been particularly devastating to African American communities, Indigenous communities, and communities of migrants and immigrants (especially those connected to meat-processing plants). And the pandemic has been taking place alongside the slowly unfolding crisis of climate change, another natural disaster exacerbated by denial, wishful thinking, and incompetent response. This brief afterword reflects back on a period of time spent writing about the speculative in a historical moment that too often felt science-fictional.

One of the most affecting images from the pandemic for me, in part because I've been steeped in the imagery of Monument Valley, was a photograph by Kristen Murphy, of the *Deseret News*, that showed Monument Valley Health Center nurse Korene Atene standing at the front of a line of trucks, SUVs, and cars, wearing personal protective equipment and holding a clipboard as she took information from individuals waiting in line for COVID-19 tests.[1] Behind this scene, in the background, were the familiar red rock formations of Monument Valley. At the time, the Navajo Nation had one of the highest per capita infection rates in the country. The uncanniness of the image for me came from the way it intentionally evoked Fordian western imagery and simultaneously suggested the speculative. The masked and goggled faces of Atene and the other nurses and their protective plastic coats recalled to me the space suits of science fiction (and science fact), and the hair coverings worn by two of the nurses similarly offered a visual suggestion of space suit helmets. Even the clipboards, at first glance, seemed uncannily like some sort of futuristic scanner. And given the number of times I've seen Monument Valley represented as a nineteenth-century location, the big black truck in the foreground of the image, as well as the other vehicles, seemed oddly out time, as if some futuristic technology had been transported to an ageless landscape. This photo of a real western location taken during the present moment seemed to realize in visual form so much of what I have been writing about here: the palimpsestic nature of speculative western texts, which can seem to simultaneously depict past, present, and future, as well as the centrality of Native Americans and African Americans and people of color to the stories of the American West, also in the past, present, and future.

Another photograph by Murphy (taken a day later, on April 17, 2020), using a drone for an aerial view, shows from above the line of vehicles with the Monument Valley Health Center in Oljato–Monument Valley, San Juan County, in the midground and, again, the Monument Valley rock formation in the background. An accompanying article in the *Deseret News* observes, "The images evoke western trains, pioneers headed west for a better a life, over the barren land and buttes that marked the landscape."[2] In contrast to the photographs themselves, which evoke multiple moments in time, the comment in the article suggests primarily a backward look, and a nostalgic one at that, one that suggests an understanding of the past that seems to reflect a kind of John Ford version of western history, centered as it is on the pioneers headed west into an empty ("barren") landscape rather than on the Indigenous people who were already (and still are) there. The photographs themselves contest that version of history both by explicitly evoking it through a framing that recalls Ford and by emphasizing another viewpoint, one that includes—and centers—the contemporary Indigenous presence in this place, threatened but still enduring and, most importantly, acting as a community coming together to meet the threat of the pandemic and to insure the future well-being of that community.

Pandemic stories are another subgenre of science fiction, and although I haven't explored that subgenre in much detail here (with the exception of where it intersects with Ireland's *Dread Nation* and *Deathless Divide*), it's a narrative form that lends itself well to western stories.[3] Like climate change science fiction (or cli-fi), it's also a subgenre of science fiction that has become increasingly popular over the last few decades. As Patricia Wald writes in *Contagious: Cultures, Carriers, and the Outbreak Narrative*, we have seen since the last part of the twentieth century an intense interest in stories of "'the coming plague': the species-threatening event forecast by scientists and journalists and dramatized in fiction and film." Although depicting a real-world possibility, "the outbreak narrative—in its scientific, journalistic, and fictional incarnations, follows a formulaic plot that begins with the identification of an emerging infection," follows its global transmission, "and chronicles the epidemiological work that ends with its containment."[4]

As with the zombie film and the postapocalyptic fiction genre in general, the place where speculative "outbreak narratives" converge with the western genre is in their interest in exploring a world reduced to frontier conditions. Elizabeth Outka, in *Viral Modernism*, points out that zombie stories in particular, from the earliest formulations (what she calls "proto-zombies") in the 1920s in the wake of the 1918 influenza pandemic, combine easily with contagion anxieties because they embody "a materialized viral enemy."[5] As Outka writes, "the zombie is a lurching signifier," its characteristics shifting over time, "reflecting the historical contingency of this figure," which responds to "changing cultural needs." Contemporary popular culture versions of the zombie consistently reflect a fear of contagion, and as such, "it's unsurprising that an early form of the viral zombie would emerge in the post-pandemic moment" of the 1920s.[6] If the "outbreak narrative" that Wald describes consistently concludes with the successful containment of the disease resulting from the hard work of teams of scientists and doctors, Outka points out that the stories of the 1920s, following an outbreak that overwhelmed doctors and scientists, who were "largely powerless," generally are more pessimistic.[7] Contemporary zombie stories, even those that were circulating before the COVID-19 epidemic (such as Ireland's *Dread Nation*), seem intent on providing a counterpoint to outbreak narratives that culminate in containment, by depicting a world continuing to exist in the frontier conditions caused by the breakdown of society.[8]

In a recent version of this scenario, director Zack Snyder's film *Army of the Dead* imagines a virally spread zombie outbreak that is only contained by the walling in of Las Vegas, the devastation of which creates a familiarly unfamiliar postwestern landscape of desert, rubble, and the occasional still-standing neon sign. Towering and strangely shaped (due to a combination of original design and extensive damage) casinos replace the rock formations of Monument Valley as a postapocalyptic version of the sublime western landscape. In a moment that directly references the COVID-19 pandemic, we see a soldier using a noncontact thermometer to test the temperature of Las Vegas refugees—a familiar enough scenario over the first year of the COVID-19 pandemic, although, in this case, the soldier is checking for the abnormally *low* temperature of those infected by the virus but not yet turned into the undead. If the destruction of Las Vegas via a nuclear device at the end of the film represents the containment of the threat, the film's coda (in which we see one of the characters starting to turn into a zombie) suggests that such containments are incomplete and temporary.

Mike Chen's 2020 novel *A Beginning at the End*, published early in the year just as global awareness of COVID-19 was starting to expand and set (seemingly prophetically) in a postpandemic San Francisco six years after a devastating disease, offers another speculative vision of a near-future West.[9] In contrast to the "viral zombie" narrative, the epidemic threat in *A Beginning at the End* remains invisible and immaterial, and the social collapse described follows the conventions of science fiction realism (rather than viral zombie horror). The novel offers a plausible speculative exploration of how a pandemic might devastate society, how it might affect the psychology of survivors (who suffer from what the novel terms PASD, Post-Apocalyptic Stress Disorder), and how a tentative return to "normal" from the brink of disaster might occur. As in other narratives of the speculative West discussed here, the story centers on a mixed-race and multiethnic cohort of characters, the white wedding planner Krista Deal, the Japanese American Rob Donelly (widower and father of young daughter Sunny), and the Iranian British immigrant to America Moira Gorman. Each of the characters is affected by past tragedy. Rob struggles with the loss of his wife, Elena (trampled to death in a pandemic-related riot), and with raising a child in a postpandemic society: "There was no manual on the psychological toll of global death and continuous fear of any hint of another pandemic."[10] In addition to the traumatic effect of mass death (reducing the American population by 70 percent) experienced by all the characters, Krista is troubled by a traumatic childhood with an alcoholic mother; and Moira, by a childhood with a manipulative father, whose molding of her into a teen pop star known as Mojo set her on a prepandemic road to alcohol and drug abuse.

The Asian American characters (the Japanese American Rob and daughter Sunny) reflect a central element of American western history, Asian immigration to the West Coast. Considered in genre terms, the most "western" character is Moira, whose story is most reflective of the western and of frontier narratives in general. Johanna Moira Hatfield was born in London to the British Evan Hatfield and "Iranian-born child-prodigy pianist Tala Ahmadi."[11] For Moira, the pandemic provided her with an opportunity to set herself free from her father and the Mojo persona. Using a quarantine order (and an ensuing panic that brought her concert to a halt) as a cover, Moira steps off the concert stage and loses herself in the crowd, leaving Mojo behind forever (or so she hopes). "She'd sprinted out of Madison Square Garden" and "ran to the people that would become her family in a cross-country caravan of sun-beaten cars, surviving on limited fuel and even less food," "a band of overland survivors" moving west (in a caravan of stolen cars rather than the wagon train of the traditional western) who eventually settled in a "Reclaimed Territory commune" located on the abandoned campus of the University of California–Davis.[12] As with other stories of the speculative West, *A Beginning at the End* offers an altered American cartography. The larger political framework of the country remains intact, but the landscape is divided into independently maintained enclaves ("Reclaimed Territory"), reconstituted urban centers connected by police-patrolled and barbed wire–enclosed highways roamed by outlaw gangs, and large swathes of unsettled territory.

By having Moira arrive in America in the performance persona of Mojo, Chen playfully exaggerates and parodies the immigrant's process of acculturation and assimilation, with the social collapse caused by the pandemic adding a Turnerian element to Moria's transformation. "The frontier is the line of most rapid and effective Americanization," Turner writes in "The Significance of the Frontier in American History." And Turner also states in that essay, "The wilderness masters the colonists. It finds him a European in dress, industries, tools, modes of travel, and thought. It takes him from the railroad car and puts him in the birch canoe. It strips off the garments of civilization and arrays him in the hunting shirt and moccasin."[13] On stage performing when the quarantine announcement breaks, Moira, flashing her trademark Mojo smile and wearing a distinctive star created from makeup surrounding one eye, uses the confusion of the announcement to vanish in the panicked crowd, erases the makeup from her face, adopts an American accent, and stops smiling, thus metaphorically stripping "off the garments of civilization." She shifts from technologically sophisticated modes of travel (by air rather than rail) to sometimes walking, sometimes running, and sometimes stealing cars. If she does not array herself in "the hunting shirt and moccasin," her clothing becomes more practical and less decorative, and she picks up a knife and gun and becomes adept at using them both. Joining with a group of others who reject the government confinement of quarantine, she heads out into the "wilderness," the "overland," outside government control.[14] Trained in parkour by the other survivors, former teen star Mojo becomes skilled at "scaling walls, leaping from great heights, vaulting over obstacles, climbing barbed wire fences."[15]

"I want to be no one," Moira tells Santiago, who recruits her to the band of survivors, and she temporarily becomes another western (wo)man without a name, before adapting a false identity (and counterfeiting supporting documents) as Moira Gorman.[16] As she rushes through "the beaten remains of Reno's main strip on Sierra Street," dodging gunfire, a bullet grazes "her bare shoulder during that sprint between a valley of casinos." She takes one in the shoulder like many a cowboy hero before her, while running down a street made into a wilderness "valley" by the collapse of civilization.[17] Traveling east to west, from New York to California, Moira, after a period at the reclaimed settlement at Davis, continues on westward to San Francisco, leaving behind her communal family to join the project of reviving what were urban population centers before the pandemic. Even in her new life in the novel's 2025 present, western elements remain attached to her character. "There's a bounty," she tells Sunny at one point, using a distinctively western name for describing the reward her father has promised for the discovery of Mojo.[18] It is Moira who leads the trio of searchers "into the wilderness of Highway 80," the "mostly empty expanse" between the slowly reviving urban centers, as they try to track down the missing Sunny, using her frontier-learned driving skills to avoid both gunslinging outlaw gangs and government-authorized police outposts.[19]

Reading the book in 2020 and again in 2021, parts of *A Beginning at the End* are eerily familiar: passive aggressive behavior around mask wearing ("The older woman reached into her backpack and pulled out two more disposable masks, then tossed them between Moira and Krista before heading to the café's counter, an audible 'You're putting us all at risk' under her breath"); the psychologically damaging effects of extended quarantines and lockdowns; the traumatic impact of mass death; the fear of the emergence of new and more dangerous viral strains; and even as the development of vaccines promises to bring the crisis to an end, the ongoing vigilance against new outbreaks.[20] In some ways, *A Beginning at the End* follows the contagion narrative structure. But the crack team of doctors is off to the side, and their success comes only after massive failure. And even at the end of the novel, when a new vaccine is developed against an emerging viral strain that once again forces society into lockdown, we're told that "there is no new normal. It's going to keep changing, keep escaping from us." "The future," Rob thinks, "appeared more uncertain than before." However, despite that acknowledgment of uncertainty, *A Beginning at the End*, as the title implies, is ultimately optimistic about facing that uncertain future, because "at least they could do that together."[21] And ultimately, Chen's story is not about the science of controlling the virus but the sociology of repairing human relationships damaged by the epidemic.

Chen's novel asks the question: After years of isolation and social distancing, after years of regarding any encounter with another human being as a potential threat to one's life, how does one even begin to reestablish connections to others? If the novel at its moment of publication seemed particularly prophetic, the question that the novel asks us to contemplate seems all the more relevant now as a massive vaccination campaign that seeks to bring an end to the COVID-19 pandemic occurs simultaneously with the widespread distribution of antivaccination misinformation and extensive vaccination resistance. The popular political mapping of the United States as red states and blue states (indicating affiliation with the Republican or Democratic Parties) is mirrored by 2021 maps that show that political divide reflected in states with low versus high vaccination rates. In the reimagined near-future American West of Chen's novel, his characters guide us toward a more hopeful future, building on a mythology of western transformation that is inclusive and humane, working toward a future outside the "silos with hard delineations" that is as characteristic of the present moment as the 2025 setting of the novel, one that places emphasis on a future created through "blending together" and "symbiotic exchange."[22] If Chen's characters in 2025 don't quite reach that future place, they at least begin a path forward to that more hopeful future, beginning with the potential emergence of a new society in a future West that is imagined as a starting point rather than as a manifest destiny.

Notes

INTRODUCTION

1. Dave Filoni, dir., "The Mandalorian," season 1, episode 1, of *The Mandalorian*, aired November 12, 2019, on Disney+.
2. Sergio Leone, dir., *For a Few Dollars More* (Produzioni Europee Associati, 1965).
3. Clark Johnson, dir., "Nebraska," season 2, episode 8, of *The Walking Dead*, aired February 12, 2012, on AMC.
4. Michael K. Johnson, "Introduction: Television and the American West," *Western American Literature* 47, no. 2 (Summer 2012): 123–31, 123–24.
5. Cynthia J. Miller and A. Bowdoin Van Riper, introduction to *Undead in the West: Vampires, Zombies, Mummies, and Ghosts on the Cinematic Frontier*, ed. Cynthia J. Miller and A. Bowdoin Van Riper (Lanham MD: Scarecrow, 2012), xi–xxvi, xix.
6. Shelley S. Rees, "Frontier Values Meet Big-City Zombies: The Old West in AMC's *The Walking Dead*," in Miller and Van Riper, *Undead in the West*, 80–94, 81.
7. Neil Campbell, "Post-Western Cinema," in *A Companion to the Literature and Culture of the American West*, ed. Nicolas Witschi (West Sussex, UK: Blackwell, 2011), 409–24, 409–10.
8. Miller and Van Riper, *Undead in the West*; Cynthia J. Miller and A. Bowdoin Van Riper, eds., *Undead in the West II: They Just Keep Coming* (Lanham MD: Scarecrow, 2013).
9. Kerry Fine, Michael K. Johnson, Rebecca M. Lush, and Sara L. Spurgeon, eds., *Weird Westerns: Race, Gender, Genre* (Lincoln: University of Nebraska Press, 2020).
10. For a broad overview of weird westerns, see Paul Green, *Encyclopedia of Weird Westerns: Supernatural and Science Fiction Elements in Novels, Pulps, Comics, Films, Television, and Games* (Jefferson NC: McFarland, 2009).

11. Justina Ireland, *Deathless Divide* (New York: HarperCollins, 2020); Rebecca Roanhorse, *Trail of Lightning* (New York: Saga, 2018); Rebecca Roanhorse, *Storm of Locusts* (New York: Saga, 2019); Alfredo Véa, *The Mexican Flyboy* (Norman: University of Oklahoma Press, 2016).

12. Shelley Streeby, "Reading Jaime Hernandez's Comics as Speculative Fiction," in *Altermundos: Latin@ Speculative Literature, Film, and Popular Culture*, ed. Cathryn Josefina Merla-Watson and B. V. Olguín (Los Angeles: UCLA Chicano Studies Research Press, 2017), 72–92, 74–75.

13. Lysa Rivera, "Future Histories and Cyborg Labor: Reading Borderlands Science Fiction after NAFTA," *Science Fiction Studies* 39, no. 3 (November 2012): 415–36, 415.

14. Rivera, "Future Histories," 415.

15. Aimee Bahng, *Migrant Futures: Decolonizing Speculation in Financial Times* (Durham NC: Duke University Press, 2018), 8.

16. Bahng, *Migrant Futures*, 12.

17. Catherine Ramírez, "Afrofuturism/Chicanofuturism: Fictive Kin," *Aztlan* 33, no. 1 (2008): 185–94, 186.

18. For definitional criticism on a variety of futurisms, see, for example, the following writers: Madhu Dubey, "The Future of Race in Afro-Futurist Fiction," in *The Black Imagination: Science Fiction, Futurism and the Speculative*, ed. Sandra Jackson and Julie E. Moody (New York: Peter Lang, 2011), 15–31; Catherine Ramírez, "Afrofuturism/Chicanofuturism"; Grace L. Dillon, "Imagining Indigenous Futurisms," in *Walking the Clouds: An Anthology of Indigenous Science Fiction*, ed. Grace L. Dillon (Tucson: University of Arizona Press, 2012), 1–12; Adilifu Nama, *Black Space: Imagining Race in Science Fiction Film* (Austin: University of Texas Press, 2008); Bahng, *Migrant Futures*, 8.

19. Bahng, *Migrant Futures*, 7.

20. John Rieder, *Colonialism and the Emergence of Science Fiction* (Middletown CT: Wesleyan University Press, 2008), 18.

21. Robert Zemeckis, dir., *Back to the Future III* (Universal City CA: Universal Pictures, 1990).

22. Jim Collins, "Genericity in the Nineties: Eclectic Irony and the New Sincerity," in *Film Theory Goes to the Movies*, ed. Jim Collins, Ava Preacher Collins, and Hilary Radner (New York: Routledge, 1992), 242–63, 249.

23. Daniel H. Wilson, *Robopocalypse* (New York: Vintage, 2011).

24. Rebecca Roanhorse, "Postcards from the Apocalypse," *Uncanny Magazine* 20 (January/February 2018), https://uncannymagazine.com/article/postcards-from-the-apocalypse/.

25. Rieder, *Colonialism and the Emergence of Science Fiction*, 3.

26. Rebecca Roanhorse, "Postcards from the Apocalypse."

27. Wilson, *Robopocalypse*, 310.

28. Wilson, *Robopocalypse*, 313.

29. William R. Handley and Nathaniel Lewis, introduction to *True West: Authenticity and the American West*, ed. William R. Handley and Nathaniel Lewis (Lincoln: University of Nebraska Press, 2004), 1–17, 1.

30. Nathaniel Lewis, "Truth or Consequences: Projecting Authenticity in the 1830s," in Handley and Lewis, *True West*, 21–37, 21, 22, 23.

31. Campbell, "Post-Western Cinema," 410.

32. Campbell, "Post-Western Cinema," 414.

33. Joanna Hearne, *Native Recognitions: Indigenous Cinema and the Western* (Albany: SUNY Press, 2012), 11.

34. Jacques Ranciére, *The Politics of Aesthetics: The Distribution of the Sensible*, ed. and trans. Gabriel Rockhill (London: Bloomsbury, 2004), 8.

35. Ranciére, *The Politics of Aesthetics*, 35.

36. Bahng, *Migrant Futures*, 10–11.

37. Lamont's *Westerns: A Women's History* documents the way "the popular western, widely considered a male-authored tradition, was founded as much by women writers as by men and played a significant role in American women's literary history at the turn of the century." As writers of westerns, "women were active at every turn during the period, between roughly 1880 and 1940, when the American frontier myth, after years of ghettoization in the dime novel, was supposedly 'reborn' as a dominant myth of American identity." Victoria Lamont, *Westerns: A Women's History* (Lincoln: University of Nebraska Press, 2016), 1. Bahng, *Migrant Futures*, 2.

38. Neil Campbell, *Affective Critical Regionality* (London: Rowman and Littlefield, 2016), 3.

39. Campbell, *Affective Critical Regionality*, 20.

40. Michael K. Johnson, *Hoo-Doo Cowboys and Bronze Buckaroos: Conceptions of the African American West* (Jackson: University Press of Mississippi, 2014); Neil Campbell, *Post-Westerns: Cinema, Region, West* (Lincoln: University of Nebraska Press, 2013).

41. Campbell, *Affective Critical Regionality*, 2.

42. Campbell, *Affective Critical Regionality*, 173.

43. Emily Lutenski, *West of Harlem: African American Writers and the Borderlands* (Lawrence: University Press of Kansas, 2015).

44. Lutenski, *West of Harlem*, 95; see also Arna Bontemps, *God Sends Sunday* (New York: Washington Square Press, 1959).

45. Bahng, *Migrant Futures*, ix.

46. Bahng, *Migrant Futures*, x.

47. Kellie Jones, *South of Pico: African American Artists in Los Angeles in the 1960s and 1970s* (Durham NC: Duke University Press, 2017).

48. For a more extensive overview of the intersections between African American studies, place studies, and western studies, see the introduction to "New Directions in Black Western Studies," which I draw on here. Kalenda Eaton, Michael K. Johnson, Jeannette Eileen Jones, introduction to "New Directions in Black Western Studies," special issue, *American Studies* 58, no. 3 (2019): 5–14; Jones, *South of Pico*, 5.

49. Jones, *South of Pico*, 7.

50. Maurice Broaddus, *Buffalo Soldier* (New York: Tom Doherty Associates, 2017), 7.

51. Broaddus, *Buffalo Soldier*, 31.

52. Broaddus, *Buffalo Soldier*, 56.

53. Broaddus, *Buffalo Soldier*, 90.

54. Sara Spurgeon, "Indianizing the Western: Semiotic Tricksterism in William Sanders's *Journey to Fusang*," in Fine et al., *Weird Westerns*, 150–73, 151–52. For a general definitional overview of alternate history as a science fiction subgenre, see Karen Hellekson, *The Alternate History: Refiguring Historical Time* (Kent OH: Kent State University Press, 2001).

55. Spurgeon, "Indianizing the Western," 152.

56. Indigenous writers working in speculative fiction have also used alternative history to imagine decolonized versions of the history of North America, as Sara Spurgeon notes in "Indianizing the Western: Semiotic Tricksterism in William Sanders's *Journey to Fusang*." See also Sara Spurgeon, "The Bomb Was like the Indians: Trickster Mimetics and Native Sovereignty in *The Indians Won*," *American Quarterly* 66, no. 4 (2014), 999–1020.

57. Campbell, *Affective Critical Regionality*, 3.

58. Daniel H. Wilson, "A History of Barbed Wire," in *A People's Future of the United States*, ed. Victor LaVille and John Joseph Adams (New York: One World, 2019), 339–50, 347.

59. Broaddus, *Buffalo Soldier*, 57.

60. Campbell, *Affective Critical Regionality*, 124.

61. Bahng, *Migrant Futures*, 57.

62. Campbell, *Affective Critical Regionality*, 174.

63. Campbell, *Affective Critical Regionality*, 175.

64. Seo-Young Chu, *Do Metaphors Dream of Literal Sheep? A Science-Fictional Theory of Representation* (Cambridge MA: Harvard University Press, 2010), 7, 10.

65. Bahng, *Migrant Futures*, 66.

66. Maureen Moynagh, "Speculative Pasts and Afro-Futures: Nalo Hopkinson's Trans-American Imaginary," *African American Review* 51, no. 3 (Fall 2018): 211–22, 220.

67. Bahng, *Migrant Futures*, 23, 7.

68. Catherine Ramírez, "Afrofuturism/Chicanofuturism," 186.

69. Miller and Van Riper, *Undead in the West*; Miller and Van Riper, *Undead in the West II*.

70. Fine et al., *Weird Westerns*.

71. Carl Abbott, *Frontiers Past and Future: Science Fiction and the American West* (Lawrence: University Press of Kansas, 2006); William H. Katerberg, *Future West: Utopia and Apocalypse in Frontier Science Fiction* (Lawrence: University Press of Kansas, 2008). One subgenre of science fiction that I don't address extensively here is cli-fi (science fiction related to climate change), in part because that is one type of speculative literature that has already become a robust topic area for western studies, as thoroughly documented in a 2021–22 special issue of *Western American Literature*; see Daniel D. Clausen, ed., "California, Cli-Fi, and Climate Crisis," special issue, *Western American Literature* 56, nos. 3–4 (Winter 2021–22).

72. N. K. Jemisin, *The Fifth Season* (New York: Orbit, 2015).

73. Keith Clavin and Christopher J. La Casse, "Triggered: The Post-Traumatic Woman and Narratology in HBO's *Westworld*," in *Women's Space: Essays on Female Characters in the 21st Century Science Fiction Western*, ed. Melanie A. Marotta (Jefferson NC: McFarland, 2019), 177–94, 183.

74. Bahng, *Migrant Futures*, 8.

75. Nanobah Becker, dir., *The 6th World: An Origin Story*, season 3, episode 6, of *FutureStates*, aired May 8, 2012, on PBS; Roanhorse, *Trail of Lightning*; Roanhorse, *Storm of Locusts*.

76. Véa, *The Mexican Flyboy*.

77. Campbell, "Post-Western Cinema," 410.

78. John Sayles, dir., *The Brother from Another Planet* (New York: Cinecom Pictures, 1984); Justina Ireland, *Dread Nation* (New York: HarperCollins, 2018); Justina Ireland, *Deathless Divide* (New York: HarperCollins, 2020); Charlotte Nicole Davis, *The Good Luck Girls* (New York: Tom Doherty Associates, 2019).

79. Mike Chen, *A Beginning at the End* (Toronto ON: Mira, 2020).

1. RACE, TIME TRAVEL, AND THE WESTERN

1. Thor Freudenthal, dir., "The Magnificent Eight," season 1, episode 11, of *Legends of Tomorrow*, aired April 14, 2016, on CW; Cherie Nowlan, dir., "Outlaw Country," season 2, episode 6, of *Legends of Tomorrow*, aired November 17, 2016, on CW; Dermott Downs, dir., "The Good, the Bad and the Cuddly," season 3, episode 18, of *Legends of Tomorrow*, aired April 9, 2018, on CW.

2. John Terlesky, dir., "The Alamo," season 1, episode 5, of *Timeless*, aired October 31, 2016, on NBC; John F. Showalter, dir., "The Murder of Jesse James," season 1, episode 12, of *Timeless*, aired January 23, 2017, on NBC.

3. There is a direct nod to *Hidden Figures* in the episode "Space Race." Theordore Melfi, dir., *Hidden Figures* (Los Angeles: Fox 2000 Pictures, 2016); Charles Beeson, dir., "Space Race," season 1, episode 8, of *Timeless*, aired November 28, 2016, on NBC.

4. Alan Crosland, dir., "The 7th Is Made Up of Phantoms," season 5, episode 10, of *The Twilight Zone*, aired December 6, 1963, on CBS; Virgil W. Vogel, dir., "Billy and Bully," season 1, episode 3, of *Voyagers*, aired October 24, 1982, on NBC; Oscar L. Costo, dir., "The Good, the Bad, and the Wealthy," season 2, episode 4, of *Sliders*, aired March 22, 1996, on Fox; *The Adventures of Brisco County, Jr.*, aired 1993–94 on Fox.

5. Rex Tucker, dir., "A Holiday for the Doctor," season 3, episode 34, of *Doctor Who*, aired April 30, 1966, on BBC; Vincent McEevty, dir., "Spectre of the Gun," season 3, episode 6, of *Star Trek*, aired October 25, 1968, on NBC; Patrick Stewart, dir., "A Fistful of Datas," season 6, episode 8, of *Star Trek: The Next Generation*, aired November 7, 1992, syndicated.

6. Christopher Priest and Jorge Lucas, "Saddles Ablaze, Part 1," *Black Panther* 46 (New York: Marvel Comics, 1998); Christopher Priest and Jorge Lucas, "Saddles Ablaze, Part 2," *Black Panther* 47 (New York: Marvel Comics, 1998); *Black Panther by Christopher Priest: The Complete Collection*, vol. 3 (New York: Marvel Worldwide, 2016).

7. Dan Riba, dir., "The Once and Future Thing, Part One: Weird Western Tales," written by Dwayne McDuffie, season 1, episode 12, of *Justice League Unlimited*, aired January 1, 2005, on Cartoon Network. McDuffie was a writer and editor at Marvel Comics, a freelance writer for Marvel and DC, and the primary writer for the *Justice League* and *Justice League Unlimited* animated series. He was also one of the founders of the African American–centered Milestone Comics.

8. Sergio Leone, dir., *Once upon a Time in the West* (Los Angeles: Paramount, 1968).

9. See Johnson, *Hoo-Doo Cowboys*, 154–85, for a discussion of Woody Strode's western films.

10. Nathan Juran, dir., "Billy the Kid," season 1, episode 22, of *The Time Tunnel*, aired February 10, 1967, on ABC.

11. *Outlaws*, aired 1986–87 on CBS.

12. Nathan Edmonson and Dalibor Talajić, *Red Wolf: Man out of Time* (New York: Marvel Worldwide, 2016).

13. Gerry Conway, "Crisis from Tomorrow," *Justice League of America* 160 (New York: DC Comics, November 1978).

14. William Gereghty, dir., "Serenity," season 5, episode 12, of *MacGyver*, aired January 8, 1990, on ABC.

15. Charles E. Cullen, dir., *A Modern Day Western: The Sanchez Saga* (Cullen Studios, 1997).

16. Lil Nas X, "Lil Nas X—Old Town Road (Official Movie) ft. Billy Ray Cyrus," May 17, 2019, dir. Calmatic, YouTube video, 5:08, https://www.youtube.com/watch?v=w2Ov5jzm3j8.

17. Dillon, "Imagining Indigenous Futurisms," 3.

18. Dillon, "Imagining Indigenous Futurisms," 3, 4.

19. Dillon, "Imagining Indigenous Futurisms," 15.

20. Gerald Vizenor, "Custer on the Slipstream," in Dillon, *Walking the Clouds*, 17–25.

21. Sherman Alexie, *Flight* (New York: Black Cat, 2007).

22. Katherena Vermette, *Pemmican Wars*, vol. 1 of *A Girl Called Echo* (Winnipeg MB: Highwater Press, 2017), 2.

23. Dillon, "Imagining Indigenous Futurisms," 4.

24. Rex Tucker, dir., "A Holiday for the Doctor," season 3, episode 34, of *Doctor Who*, aired April 30, 1966, on BBC.

25. Stuart Hardy, dir., "A Town Called Mercy," season 7, episode 2, of *Doctor Who*, aired September 15, 2012, on BBC.

26. Zemeckis, *Back to the Future III*.

27. The *Supernatural* episode "Frontierland" follows this pattern to the letter, down to the name Clint Eastwood, whose serape Dean Winchester dons along with his name. Don Bee, dir., "Frontierland," season 6, episode 18, of *Supernatural*, aired April 22, 2011, on CW.

28. Collins, "Genericity in the Nineties," 249.

29. Mel Brooks, dir., *Blazing Saddles* (Burbank CA: Warner Brothers, 1974).

30. James Bagdonas, dir., "Tempus Fugtive," season 2, episode 18, of *Lois and Clark: The New Adventures of Superman*, aired March 26, 1995, on ABC.

31. Costo, "The Good, the Bad, and the Wealthy."

32. Sergio Leone, dir., *The Good, the Bad, and the Ugly* (Produzioni Europee Associati, 1966); George Stevens, dir., *Shane* (Los Angeles: Paramount, 1953); John Ford, dir., *The Man Who Shot Liberty Valance* (Los Angeles: Ford Productions–Paramount, 1962).

33. Dubey, "The Future of Race in Afro-Futurist Fiction," 16.

34. Pauline Hopkins, *Winona: A Tale of Negro Life in the South and the Southwest*, in *The Magazine Novels of Pauline Hopkins*, Schomburg Library of Nineteenth-Century Black Women Writers edition (New York: Oxford University Press, 1988), 285–437, originally published in *Colored American Magazine* 5, nos. 1–6 (May–October 1902); all references will refer to the Oxford University Press compiled edition.

35. Nama, *Black Space*; Isiah Lavender III, *Race in American Science Fiction* (Bloomington: Indiana University Press, 2011).

36. André M. Carrington, *Speculative Blackness: The Future of Race in Science Fiction* (Minneapolis: University of Minnesota Press, 2016), 2.

37. Carrington, *Speculative Blackness*, 15.

38. Carrington, *Speculative Blackness*, 13.

39. Carrington, *Speculative Blackness*, 27.

40. Nama, *Black Space*, 124.

41. Avery Brooks, dir., "Far beyond the Stars," season 6, episode 13, of *Star Trek: Deep Space Nine*, aired February 11, 1998, syndicated.

42. Carrington, *Speculative Blackness*, 171.

43. Carrington, *Speculative Blackness*, 159.

44. See Constance Penley, "Time Travel, Primal Scene and the Critical Dystopia," in *Alien Zone: Cultural Theory and Contemporary Science Fiction Cinema*, ed. Annette Kuhn (London: Verso, 1990), 116–27.

45. John Sturges, dir., *The Magnificent Seven* (Los Angeles: Mirisch Company, 1960).

46. The other actors are Arthur Darvill (Rip Hunter), Victor Garber (Martin Stein), Caity Lotz (Sara Lance), Brandon Routh (Ray Palmer), Wentworth Miller (Leonard Snart), and Dominic Purcell (Mick Rory).

47. See Green, *Encyclopedia of Weird Westerns*, 55–56, 109.

48. Anna Deavere Smith, *Twilight: Los Angeles, 1992* (New York: Anchor, 1994), premiere performance, March 24, 1994, Mark Taper Forum, Los Angeles.

49. Green, *Encyclopedia of Weird Westerns*, 150.

50. Carrington, *Speculative Blackness*, 180.

51. Carrington, *Speculative Blackness*, 26.

52. Octavia Butler, *Kindred* (Garden City NY: Doubleday, 1979); Haile Gerima, dir., *Sankofa* (London: Channel Four Films, 1993).

53. Ytasha L. Womack, *Afrofuturism: The World of Black Science Fiction and Fantasy Culture* (Chicago: Lawrence Hill, 2013), 158.

54. Michelle Commander, *Afro-Atlantic Flight: Speculative Returns and the Black Fantastic* (Durham NC: Duke University Press, 2017), 54, 33.

55. Commander, *Afro-Atlantic Flight*, 30.

56. Holly Dale, dir., "Stranded," season 1, episode 7, of *Timeless*, aired November 21, 2016, on NBC.

57. Carrington, *Speculative Blackness*, 190.

58. Commander, *Afro-Atlantic Flight*, 3.

59. Arthur H. Nadel, dir., "The Most Amazing Man," season 5, episode 9, of *The Rifleman*, aired November 26, 1962, on ABC; Ted Post, dir., "The Incident of the Buffalo Soldier," season 3, episode 10, of *Rawhide*, aired March 24, 1961, on CBS.

60. Johnson, *Hoo-Doo Cowboys*, 154–55, 159–60.

61. Art Burton suggests this in his biography of Reeves, *Black Gun, Silver Star*, as well as in several interviews for articles. See, for example, Sheena McKenzie, "Was an African American Cop the Real Lone Ranger?," CNN, August 6, 2013, https://www.cnn.com/2013/08/06/sport/lone-ranger -african-american-reeves/index.html. Art Burton, *Black Gun, Silver Star: The Life and Legend of Frontier Marshal Bass Reeves* (Lincoln: University of Nebraska Press, 2006). Although Burton is careful in noting in his book that his speculation is based on coincidental similarities between the real-life historical figure (whose actual accomplishments Burton's book carefully documents) and the twentieth-century fictional character, journalists and bloggers who have drawn from the story have dispensed with that nuance.

62. Martin Grams, "Myth Debunked: Bass Reeves Was NOT the Lone Ranger," *Martin Grams* (blog), February 9, 2018, http://martingrams.blogspot.com /2018/02/myth-debunked-bass-reeves-was-not.html.

63. Daw-Nay Evans, "The Duty of Reason: Kantian Ethics in High Noon," in *The Philosophy of the Western*, ed. Jennifer L. McMahon and B. Steve Csaki (Lexington: University of Kentucky Press, 2010), 171–83, 171.

64. Daw-Nay Evans, "The Duty of Reason," 173.

65. Daw-Nay Evans, "The Duty of Reason," 180.

66. Fred Zinneman, dir., *High Noon* (Los Angeles: Stanley Kramer Productions, 1952).

67. See Johnson, *Hoo-Doo Cowboys*, 174.

68. Jack Arnold, dir., *Boss*, screenplay by Fred Williamson (Los Angeles: Dimension Pictures, 1974).

69. Brooks, *Blazing Saddles*.

70. Quentin Tarantino, dir., *Django Unchained* (Culver City CA: Columbia Pictures, 2012).

2. TRAUMA, TIME TRAVEL, AND VIOLENCE

1. Karen Grigsby Bates, "Chicago's Red Summer," featuring Eve Ewing, *Codeswitch* (podcast), NPR, July 27, 2019, https://www.npr.org/transcripts /744450509. See also Stefon Bristol, dir., *See You Yesterday* (Brooklyn NY: 40 Acres and a Mule Filmworks, 2019), on Netflix.

2. Chu, *Do Metaphors Dream*, 156.

3. Eve Ewing, in Grigsby Bates, "Chicago's Red Summer."

4. Chu, *Do Metaphors Dream*, 156.

5. Bessel A. van der Kolk and Onno van der Hart, "The Intrusive Past: The Flexibility of Memory and the Engraving of Trauma," in *Trauma: Explora-*

tions in Memory, ed. Cathy Caruth (Baltimore MD: Johns Hopkins Press, 1995), 158–82, 176.

6. Cathy Caruth, "Recapturing the Past: Introduction," in Caruth, *Trauma*, 151–57, 152.

7. Chu, *Do Metaphors Dream*, 156.

8. Kurt Vonnegut, *Slaughterhouse-Five* (1969; repr., New York: Random House, 2009), 29.

9. Chu, *Do Metaphors Dream*, 176.

10. Caruth, "Recapturing the Past," 153.

11. Cathy Caruth, *Unclaimed Experience: Trauma, Narrative, and History* (Baltimore MD: Johns Hopkins University Press, 1996).

12. Clavin and La Casse, "Triggered," 184.

13. Michelle Balaev, "Literary Trauma Theory Reconsidered," in *Contemporary Approaches in Literary Trauma Theory*, ed. Michelle Balaev (London: Palgrave McMillan, 2014), 1–14, quoted in Clavin and La Casse, "Triggered," 185.

14. Clavin and La Casse, "Triggered," 185.

15. Tim O'Brien, *The Things They Carried* (1990; repr., Boston: Mariner Books, 2009); Art Spiegelman, *The Complete Maus: A Survivor's Tale* (New York: Pantheon, 1996; originally serialized in *Raw* magazine vol. 1, no. 2–vol. 2, no. 3, 1980–91).

16. For an overview of those techniques, see Joshua L. Charlson, "Framing the Past: Postmodernism and the Making of Reflective Memory in Art Spiegelman's *Maus*," *American Quarterly* 57, no. 3 (Autumn 2001): 91–120; Janet Ewert, "Art Spiegelman's *Maus* and the Graphic Narrative," in *Narrative across Media: The Language of Storytelling*, ed. Marie-Laure Ryan (Lincoln: University of Nebraska Press, 2004), 178–93.

17. Alan Gibbs, *Contemporary American Trauma Narratives* (Edinburgh: Edinburgh University Press, 2014), quoted in Clavin and La Casse, "Triggered," 185.

18. Clavin and La Casse, "Triggered," 185.

19. Caruth, "Recapturing the Past," 154.

20. For example, Sherman Alexie's novel of time travel and trauma, *Flight*, begins with an epigraph from *Slaughterhouse-Five*.

21. Clavin and La Casse, "Triggered," 185; Chu, *Do Metaphors Dream*, 7.

22. Bridget Carpenter, creator, *11.22.63* (Santa Monica CA: Bad Robot; Burbank CA: Warner Bros. Television, 2016), on Hulu.

23. Constance Penley, "Time Travel, Primal Scene and the Critical Dystopia," in *Alien Zone: Cultural Theory and Contemporary Science Fiction Cinema*, ed. Annette Kuhn (London: Verso, 1990), 116–27, 120.

24. Penley, "Time Travel," 121.

25. Penley, "Time Travel," 121–22.

26. Raúl Ramos, "The Alamo Is a Rupture," *Guernica*, February 19, 2019, https://www.guernicamag.com/the-alamo-is-a-rupture-texas-mexico-imperialism-history/.

27. Cathryn Josefina Merla-Watson, "(Trans)Mission Possible: The Coloniality of Gender, Speculative Rasquachismo, and Altermundos in Luis Valedera's Chican@futurist Visual Art," in Merla-Watson and Olguín, *Altermundos*, 352–70, 357.

28. Raúl Ramos, "The Alamo Is a Rupture."

29. John Terlesky, dir., "The Alamo," season 1, episode 5, of *Timeless*, aired October 31, 2016, on ABC.

30. Roberta E. Pearson, "The Twelve Custers, or, Video History," in *Back in the Saddle Again: New Essays on the Western*, ed. Edward Buscombe and Roberta E. Pearson (London: BFI Publishing, 1998), 197–213, 199.

31. Ric Burns, dir., *The Way West: How the West Was Won and Lost, 1845–1893*, American Experience (Arlington VA: PBS, 1995), originally aired season 7, episodes 8–9, of *American Experience*, May 8–9, 1995, on PBS, quoted in Pearson, "The Twelve Custers," 200.

32. Pearson, "The Twelve Custers," 209–10.

33. Pearson, "The Twelve Custers," 210.

34. Alan Crosland Jr., dir., "The 7th Is Made Up of Phantoms," season 5, episode 10, of *The Twilight Zone*, aired December 6, 1963, on CBS.

35. Charlson, "Framing the Past," 115.

36. Charlson, "Framing the Past," 115.

37. Ramos, "The Alamo Is a Rupture."

38. Sobey Marin, dir., "The Alamo," season 1, episode 13, of *The Time Tunnel*, aired December 9, 1966, on ABC.

39. Murray Golden, dir., "Massacre," season 1, episode 8, of *The Time Tunnel*, aired October 28, 1966, on ABC.

40. Alexie, *Flight*. As Grace L. Dillon writes, "Incorporating time travel, alternate realities, parallel universes and multiverses, and alternative histories is a hallmark of Native storytelling tradition, while viewing time as pasts, presents, and futures that flow together like currents in a navigable stream is central to Native epistemologies." For a thorough overview of the use of slipstream time travel in the work of a wider range of Native American novels, see Grace L. Dillon, "Native Slipstream: Blackfeet Physics in *The Fast Red Road*," in *The Fictions of Stephen Graham Jones: A Critical Companion*, ed. Billy J. Stratton (Albuquerque: University of New Mexico Press, 2016), 343–55, 345.

41. Alexie, *Flight*, 31.

42. Alexie, *Flight*, 72.

43. Alexie, *Flight*, 74, 75.

44. Alexie, *Flight*, 76–77.

45. Alexie, *Flight*, 87.

46. Alexie, *Flight*, 158.

47. Howard F. Stein, "A Mosaic of Transmissions after Trauma," in *Lost in Transmission: Studies of Trauma across Generations*, ed. M. Gerard Fromm (London: Routledge, 2012), 173–201, 173.

48. M. Gerard Fromm, introduction to *Lost in Transmission*, xv–xxii, xix.

49. Fromm, introduction, xxi.

50. Fromm, introduction, xvi.

51. Stein, "A Mosaic of Transmissions after Trauma," 173.

52. Fromm, introduction, xxi.

53. Chu, *Do Metaphors Dream*, 156.

54. Nicole Kassell, dir., "It's Summer and We're Running Out of Ice," season 1, episode 1, of *Watchmen*, aired October 20, 2019, on HBO.

55. Showalter, "The Murder of Jesse James."

56. Bass Reeves certainly has become a feature of speculative westerns. Bass Reeves (Adrian Holmes) appears as a kind of ghostly time traveler to the present in an episode of *Wynonna Earp*, "Everybody Knows." The time travelers of *Legends of Tomorrow* encounter Bass Reeves when they journey back in time to Oklahoma Territory in "Stressed Western" (where the role is played by David Ramsey, who also directed the episode). See Rebecca Lush, "Racial Metaphors and Vanishing *indians* in *Wynonna Earp*, *Buffy the Vampire Slayer*, and Emma Bull's *Territory*," in Fine et al., *Weird Westerns*, 255–85; Paolo Barzman, dir., "Everybody Knows," season 2, episode 7, of *Wynonna Earp*, aired July 27, 2017, on SyFy; David Ramsey, dir., "Stressed Western," season 6, episode 8, of *Legends of Tomorrow*, aired June 27, 2021, on CW.

57. Stephen Williams, dir., "This Extraordinary Being," season 1, episode 6, of *Watchmen*, aired November 24, 2019, on HBO.

58. Freudenthal, "The Magnificent Eight."

59. Fromm, introduction, xxi.

60. Williams, "This Extraordinary Being."

61. The traumatic history of the Tulsa race massacre is also a feature of the HBO series *Lovecraft Country*, which also involves an episode ("Rewind: 1921") involving time travel back to the event and which similarly uses time travel as a narrative device for investigating individual and collective trauma. Jeffrey Nachmanoff, dir., "Rewind: 1921," season 1, episode 9, of *Lovecraft Country*, aired October 11, 2020, on HBO.

62. M. Gerard Fromm, "Treatment Resistance and the Transmission of Trauma," in Fromm, *Lost in Transmission*, 99–115, 104.

63. In "Family Pictures: *Maus*, Mourning, and Post-Memory," Marianne Hirsch notes the use of a parallel technique in Spiegelman's *Maus*, the insertion of photographs in a visual narrative that consists primarily of drawn illustrations, as an aesthetic strategy (the sudden and shocking contrast between two forms of visual media) for representing "unassimilated and unassimilatable memories." Marianne Hirsch, "Family Pictures: *Maus*, Mourning, and Post-Memory," *Discourse* 15, no. 2 (Winter 1992–93): 3–29, 16.

64. Fromm, "Treatment Resistance and the Transmission of Trauma," 104.

65. Frederick E. O. Toye, dir., "See How They Fly," season 1, episode 9, of *Watchmen*, aired December 15, 2019, on HBO.

3. ALTERNATE CARTOGRAPHIES OF THE WEST(ERN)

1. Campbell, *Affective Critical Regionality*, 124.

2. Hearne, *Native Recognitions*, 182.

3. Zemeckis, *Back to the Future III*.

4. R. Barton Palmer, *Shot on Location: Postwar American Cinema and the Exploration of Real Place* (New Brunswick NJ: Rutgers University Press, 2016), 77.

5. Salma Monani, "Science Fiction, Westerns, and the Vital Cosmo-Ethics of *The 6th World*," in *Ecocriticism and Indigenous Studies: Conversations from Earth to Cosmos*, ed. Salma Monani and Joni Adamson (New York: Routledge, 2017), 44–61, 49.

6. R. Barton Palmer, *Shot on Location*, 89.

7. Monani, "Science Fiction," 49.

8. Hearne, *Native Recognitions*, 202.

9. Riba, "The Once and Future Thing, Part One."

10. Palmer, *Shot on Location*, 81.

11. Matt Shakman, dir., "The Spoils of War," season 7, episode 4, of *Game of Thrones*, aired August 6, 2017, on HBO.

12. Monani, "Science Fiction," 57.

13. Hearne, *Native Recognition*, 182.

14. Ramona Emerson, dir., *Opal* (Reel Indian Pictures, 2012); Susan Bernardin, "It's a Good Day to Bike: Indigenous Futures in Ramona Emerson's *Opal*," *Western American Literature* 49, no. 1 (Spring 2014): 89–112, 95.

15. Michael Winner, dir., *Chato's Land* (Scimitar Films, 1972).

16. Bernardin, "It's a Good Day to Bike," 106.

17. Hearne, *Native Recognition*; James Young Deer, dir., *White Fawn's Devotion* (Pathé Frères, 1910); Cecil B. Demille and Oscar C. Apfel, dirs., *The Squaw Man* (Jesse L. Lasky, Feature Play Company, 1914); George B. Seitz, dir., *The Vanishing American* (Famous Players-Lasky, 1925); Richardson Morse,

dir., *House Made of Dawn* (1972); Chris Eyre, dir., *Smoke Signals* (Miramax, 1998); Chris Eyre, dir., *Skins* (Starz Encore Entertainment, 2002).

18. Hearne, *Native Recognitions*, 40.

19. Bernardin, "It's a Good Day to Bike," 96.

20. Bernardin, "It's a Good Day to Bike," 98–99.

21. Becker, *The 6th World*; Roanhorse, *Trail of Lightning*; Roanhorse, *Storm of Locusts*.

22. Bernardin, "It's a Good Day to Bike," 106.

23. Hearne, *Native Recognitions*, 182.

24. Stanley Kubrick, dir., *2001: A Space Odyssey* (Stanley Kubrick Productions, 1968); Michael Bay, dir., *Transformers: Age of Extinction* (Pawtucket RI: Hasbro Films, 2014).

25. Abbott, *Frontiers Past and Future*, 20.

26. Monani, "Science Fiction," 48.

27. Monani, "Science Fiction," 50.

28. Monani, "Science Fiction," 45.

29. Monani, "Science Fiction," 50.

30. Monani, "Science Fiction," 48.

31. Monani, "Science Fiction," 54.

32. Monani, "Science Fiction," 55.

33. Campbell, *Affective Critical Regionality*, 30.

34. Campbell, *Affective Critical Regionality*, 42.

35. Campbell, *Affective Critical Regionality*, 201.

36. Cynthia Fowler, "Aboriginal Beauty and Self-Determination: Hulleah Tsinhnahjinnie's Photographic Projects," in *Visualities: Perspectives on Contemporary American Indian Film and Art*, ed. Denise K. Cummings (East Lansing: Michigan State University Press, 2011), 189–206, 201.

37. Luci Tapahonso, *Blue Horses Rush In* (Tucson: University of Arizona Press, 1997).

38. Fowler, "Aboriginal Beauty," 196.

39. Fowler, "Aboriginal Beauty," 199, 202.

40. Fowler, "Aboriginal Beauty," 202.

41. Campbell, *Affective Critical Regionality*, 42, 201.

42. Rebecca Roanhorse, "Welcome to Your Authentic American Indian Experience," *Apex*, August 8, 2017, https://apex-magazine.com/welcome-to-your-authentic-indian-experience/.

43. Lila Shapiro, "The Sci-Fi Author Reimagining Native History," *Vulture*, October 20, 2020, https://www.vulture.com/article/rebecca-roanhorse-black-sun-profile.html.

44. Shapiro, "The Sci-Fi Author Reimagining Native History."

45. Shapiro, "The Sci-Fi Author Reimagining Native History."

46. Shapiro, "The Sci-Fi Author Reimagining Native History"; Rebecca Roan-horse, *Black Sun* (New York: Saga Press, 2020).

47. Saad Bee Hozho, "The *Trail of Lightning* Is an Appropriation of Diné Beliefs," *Indian Country Today*, November 5, 2018. For a critique of that response, see Adrian L. Jawort (Northern Cheyenne), "The Dangers of the Appropri-ation Critique," *Los Angeles Review of Books*, October 5, 2019, https://www .lareviewofbooks.org/article/the-dangers-of-the-appropriation-critique.

48. Nick Martin, "Reckoning with Anti-Blackness in Indian Country," *New Republic*, July 3, 2020, https://newrepublic.com/article/158294/reckoning -anti-blackness-indian-country.

49. Dillon, "Imagining Indigenous Futurisms."

50. Catherine Ramírez, "Afrofuturism/Chicanofuturism."

51. Joy Sanchez-Taylor, "Alternative Futurisms: Tananarive Due's African Immortal Series," *Extrapolation* 61, nos. 1–2 (2020): 91–108, 105.

52. Sanchez-Taylor, "Alternative Futurisms," 91, 91–92.

53. Sanchez-Taylor, "Alternative Futurisms," 91.

54. Sanchez-Taylor, "Alternative Futurisms," 91–92.

55. Roanhorse, *Trail of Lightning*, 22.

56. Roanhorse, *Trail of Lightning*, 23.

57. Campbell, *Affective Critical Regionality*, 42.

58. Roanhorse, *Trail of Lightning*, 23.

59. Roanhorse, *Storm of Locusts*, 12.

60. Gerald Robert Vizenor, *The Heirs of Columbus* (Middletown CT: Wes-leyan University Press, 1991).

61. Andrew Uzendoski, "Speculative States: Citizenship Criteria, Human Rights, and Decolonial Legal Norms in Gerald Vizenor's *The Heirs of Colum-bus*," *Extrapolation* 27, nos. 1–2 (Spring/Summer 2016): 21–49, 42–43.

62. Campbell, *Affective Critical Regionality*, 128.

63. Roanhorse, *Storm of Locusts*, 27.

64. Roanhorse, *Storm of Locusts*, 94.

65. Shoshi Parks, "A Route 66 Trip through Indigenous Homelands," *Yes Mag-azine*, May 13, 2019, https://www.yesmagazine.org/issue/travel/opinion /2019/05/13/decolonize-america-road-trip-indigenous-homelands.

66. Parks, "A Route 66 Trip." See also Lisa Hicks Snell, *American Indians and Route 66* (Albuquerque NM: American Indian Alaska Native Tourism Asso-ciation, 2016), https://www.aianta.org/wp-content/uploads/2020/03 /American_Indians_Route66.pdf; Ron Warnick, "'American Indians and Route 66' Guide Published," Route 66 News, April 18, 2016, https://www .route66news.com/2016/04/18/american-indians-route-66-guide/.

67. Roanhorse, *Storm of Locusts*, 235.

68. Roanhorse, *Storm of Locusts*, 174.

69. Roanhorse, *Storm of Locusts*, 300.

70. George Miller, dir., *Mad Max: Fury Road* (Sydney, Australia: Kennedy Miller Mitchell Productions, 2015).

71. Roanhorse, "Welcome to Your Authentic American Indian Experience."

72. Mourning Dove, *Cogewea, the Half Blood: A Depiction of the Great Montana Cattle Range* (Boston: Four Seas, 1927; Lincoln: University of Nebraska Press, 1981).

73. Lamont, *Westerns*, 78.

74. Lamont, *Westerns*, 78, 82.

75. Kirby Brown, *Stoking the Fire: Nationhood in Cherokee Writing, 1907–1970* (Norman: University of Oklahoma Press, 2018), 40.

76. John Rollin Ridge, *The Life and Adventures of Joaquín Murieta: The Celebrated California Bandit* (W. R. Cook, 1854; New York: Penguin, 2018); Alice Callahan, *Wynema: A Child of the Forest* (Chicago: H. J. Smith, 1891; Lincoln: University of Nebraska Press, 1997); John Milton Oskison, *Black Jack Davy* (New York: Appleton, 1926).

77. Louise Erdrich was honored with the Wister Award in 2017, Robert Conley in 2014, N. Scott Momaday in 2010. Western Writers of America, "The Owen Wister Award," accessed May 31, 2021, https://westernwriters.org/the-owen-wister-award/.

78. Most recently, Robert Conley won the 1995 Spur Award for Best Western Novel, for *The Dark Island* (New York: Doubleday, 1995). Fred Grove's most recent win was the 1982 Spur Award for Best Western Novel, for *Match Race* (New York: Doubleday, 1982). Western Writers of America, "Winners," accessed May 31, 2021, https://westernwriters.org/winners/.

79. David Heska Wanbli Weiden, *Winter Counts* (New York: HarperCollins, 2020).

80. Brown, *Stoking the Fire*, 41.

81. Collins, "Genericity in the Nineties," 249.

82. Roanhorse, *Trail of Lightning*, 24.

83. Roanhorse, *Trail of Lightning*, 257.

84. Roanhorse, *Trail of Lightning*, 219.

85. Roanhorse, *Trail of Lightning*, 252.

86. Roanhorse, *Trail of Lightning*, 88–89.

87. Roanhorse, *Trail of Lightning*, 105.

88. Roanhorse, *Trail of Lightning*, 105.

89. Hearne, *Native Recognitions*, 265–66; Eyre, *Smoke Signals*.

90. Hearne, *Native Recognitions*, 266–67.

91. Hearne, *Native Recognitions*, 266.

92. Hearne, *Native Recognitions*, 267.

93. Eyre, *Skins*.

94. Hearne, *Native Recognitions*, 284.

95. Roanhorse, *Trail of Lightning*, 105.

96. Roanhorse, *Trail of Lightning*, 106.

97. Roanhorse, *Trail of Lightning*, 107.

98. Roanhorse, *Trail of Lightning*, 105.

99. Roanhorse, *Trail of Lightning*, 233.

100. Roanhorse, *Trail of Lightning*, 262.

101. Roanhorse, *Trail of Lightning*, 264.

102. Roanhorse, *Trail of Lightning*, 265.

103. Roanhorse, *Trail of Lightning*, 268.

104. Roanhorse, *Trail of Lightning*, 109.

4. SPECULATIVE BORDERLANDS I

1. Alex Rivera, dir., *Sleep Dealer* (New York City: Likely Story, 2008).

2. Bahng, *Migrant Futures*, 72.

3. Curtis Marez, *Farm Worker Futurism: Speculative Technologies of Resistance* (Minneapolis: University of Minnesota Press, 2016). See also John Carlos Frey, dir., *The Gatekeeper* (Los Angeles: Gatekeeper Productions, 2002); Rosaura Sánchez and Beatrice Pita, *Lunar Braceros: 2125–2148* (2009; repr., Moorpark CA: Floricanto Press, 2019). The quoted phrase "cognitive estrangement" is a reference to Darko Suvin's influential *Metamorphoses of Science Fiction: On the Poetics and History of a Literary Genre* (New Haven CT: Yale University Press, 1979). Variations of this phrase and concept appear throughout *Speculative Wests*, as it has been a central concept in science fiction studies for decades.

4. In replacing the "a/o" in Latina/o and Chicana/o with an at sign, I'm following what seems to be the predominant practice in studies of Latin@ and Chican@ futurism.

5. Matthew David Goodwin, introduction to *Latin@ Rising: An Anthology of Latin@ Science Fiction and Fantasy* (San Antonio TX: Wings Press, 2017), ix–xiii, xii.

6. Chu, *Do Metaphors Dream*, 10.

7. Lysa M. Rivera, "*Mestizaje* and Heterotopia in Ernest Hogan's *High Aztech*," in *Black and Brown Planets: The Politics of Race in Science Fiction*, ed. Isiah Lavendar III (Jackson: University Press of Mississippi, 2014), 146–62, 159. See also Ernest Hogan, *High Aztech* (1990; repr., San Francisco: Strange Particle Press, 2016).

8. Catherine Ramírez, "Afrofuturism/Chicanofuturism," 187.

9. Rivera, "*Mestizaje* and Heterotopia," 147.

10. José Vasconcelos, *The Cosmic Race / La raza cósmica* (1925; repr., Baltimore MD: Johns Hopkins University Press, 1997), quoted in Rivera, "*Mestizaje* and Heterotopia," 148.

11. Rivera, "*Mestizaje* and Heterotopia," 154.

12. Rivera, "*Mestizaje* and Heterotopia," 155.

13. Mary Louise Pratt, "Arts of the Contact Zone," *Profession* 91 (1991): 33–40, 33.

14. Silvia Moreno-Garcia, *Gods of Jade and Shadow* (New York: Random House, 2019).

15. Rivera, "*Mestizaje* and Heterotopia," 152.

16. Rivera, "*Mestizaje* and Heterotopia," 155.

17. Rivera, "*Mestizaje* and Heterotopia," 156. See also Fernando Ortiz, *Cuban Counterpoint: Tobacco and Sugar* (Durham NC: Duke University Press, 1995).

18. Moreno-Garcia, *Gods of Jade and Shadow*, 111.

19. Moreno-Garcia, *Gods of Jade and Shadow*, 204.

20. Moreno-Garcia, *Gods of Jade and Shadow*, 247.

21. Moreno-Garcia, *Gods of Jade and Shadow*, 332.

22. Moreno-Garcia, *Gods of Jade and Shadow*, 323–24.

23. Bahng, *Migrant Futures*, 66.

24. Moreno-Garcia, *Gods of Jade and Shadow*, 188.

25. Moreno-Garcia, *Gods of Jade and Shadow*, 334.

26. Of the writers examined here, Rudolfo Anaya is no doubt the best known, with a long and renowned literary career. One of my reasons for focusing on the ChupaCabra series is that very little has been written about those particular books. Another of Anaya's popular-genre experiments, a series of novels centered on New Mexico private detective Sonny Baca, similar to the ChupaCabra series, crosses multiple genres. The third book in the Baca series, *Shaman Winter*, involves slipstream time travel, with Baca traveling back in time through dreaming. Like *ChupaCabra Meets Billy the Kid*, there's even a time-travel encounter with the famous outlaw. For a general critical overview of Anaya's work, see Roberto Cantú, ed., *The Forked Juniper: Critical Perspectives on Rudolfo Anaya* (Norman: University of Oklahoma Press, 2016). See also Rudolfo Anaya, *Shaman Winter* (New York: Grand Central Publishing, 1999).

27. Véa, *The Mexican Flyboy*.

28. Micah K. Donohue, "'He's a Ghost. But He's out There': Borderlands Science Fiction and the Gothic in *No Country for Old Men*," *Western American Literature* 55, no. 3 (Fall 2020): 261–87, 263, 264.

29. Rudolfo Anaya, *ChupaCabra Meets Billy the Kid* (Norman: University of Oklahoma Press, 2018).

30. Rudolfo Anaya, *ChupaCabra and the Roswell UFO* (Albuquerque: Univer-

sity of New Mexico Press, 2008); Rudolfo Anaya, *Curse of the ChupaCabra* (Albuquerque: University of New Mexico Press, 2006).

31. Anaya, *Curse of the ChupaCabra*, 4.

32. Anaya, *Curse of the ChupaCabra*, 165.

33. Anaya, *ChupaCabra Meets Billy the Kid*, 37.

34. Anaya, *ChupaCabra Meets Billy the Kid*, 38.

35. Anaya, *ChupaCabra Meets Billy the Kid*, 41.

36. Anaya, *Curse of the ChupaCabra*, 149.

37. Anaya, *Curse of the ChupaCabra*, 126.

38. William A. Calvo-Quirós, "The Emancipatory Power of the Imaginary: Defining Chican@ Speculative Productions," in Merla-Watson and Olguín, *Altermundos*, 39–54, 51. See also William A. Calvo-Quirós, "Chupacabras: The Strange Case of Carlos Salinas de Gortari and His Transformation into the Chupatodo," in *Crossing the Borders of Imagination*, ed. Maria del Mar Ramon Torrijos (Madrid: Instituto Franklin de Estudios Norteamericanos, Universidad de Alcala, 2014), 95–108.

39. Bahng, *Migrant Futures*, 55.

40. Anaya, *Curse of the ChupaCabra*, 129.

41. Bahng, *Migrant Futures*, 77.

42. Anaya, *ChupaCabra and the Roswell UFO*, 7.

43. Anaya, *ChupaCabra and the Roswell UFO*, 77.

44. Anaya, *ChupaCabra and the Roswell UFO*, 87.

45. Anaya, *ChupaCabra and the Roswell UFO*, 88.

46. Anaya, *ChupaCabra and the Roswell UFO*, 99.

47. Anaya, *ChupaCabra and the Roswell UFO*, 109.

48. Campbell, *Post-Westerns*, 204. See also Gilles Deleuze, *Cinema 2: The Time Image* (London: Athlone Press, 1989); John Sayles, dir., *Lone Star* (Beverly Hills CA: Castle Rock Entertainment, 1996).

49. Anaya, *ChupaCabra Meets Billy the Kid*, 44, 46.

50. Anaya, *ChupaCabra Meets Billy the Kid*, 56.

51. Anaya, *ChupaCabra Meets Billy the Kid*, 22.

52. Anaya, *ChupaCabra Meets Billy the Kid*, 116.

53. Anaya, *ChupaCabra Meets Billy the Kid*, 44.

54. Anaya, *ChupaCabra Meets Billy the Kid*, 54.

55. Anaya, *ChupaCabra Meets Billy the Kid*, 83.

56. Anaya, *ChupaCabra Meets Billy the Kid*, 98.

57. Anaya, *ChupaCabra Meets Billy the Kid*, 70; see also Robert Heinlein, *Stranger in a Strange Land* (New York: G. P. Putnam's Sons, 1961).

58. Anaya, *ChupaCabra Meets Billy the Kid*, 31.

59. Anaya, *ChupaCabra Meets Billy the Kid*, 59.

60. Anaya, *ChupaCabra Meets Billy the Kid*, 53, 39.

61. Erin Murrah-Mandril, *In the Mean Time: Temporal Colonization and the Mexican American Literary Tradition* (Lincoln: University of Nebraska Press, 2020), 4.

62. Murrah-Mandril, *In the Mean Time*, 13.

63. John L. O'Sullivan, "The Great Nation of Futurity," *United States Magazine and Democratic Review* 6, no. 23 (1839): 426–30, quoted in Murrah-Mandril, *In the Mean Time*, 8.

64. Murrah-Mandril, *In the Mean Time*, 9.

65. Murrah-Mandril, *In the Mean Time*, 117.

66. Frederick Jackson Turner, "Significance of the Frontier in American History" (1893), in *History, Frontier, and Section: Three Essays by Frederick Jackson Turner*, ed. Martin Ridge (Albuquerque: University of New Mexico Press, 1993), 59–91, quoted in Murrah-Mandril, *In the Mean Time*, 9.

67. Murrah-Mandril, *In the Mean Time*, 117.

68. Murrah-Mandril, *In the Mean Time*, 117–18.

69. Murrah-Mandril, *In the Mean Time*, 9.

70. Fred Zinneman, dir., *High Noon* (Stanley Kramer Productions, 1952).

71. Murrah-Mandril, *In the Mean Time*, 16.

72. Murrah-Mandril, *In the Mean Time*, 17, 12.

73. Murrah-Mandril, *In the Mean Time*, 22–23.

74. Anaya, *ChupaCabra Meets Billy the Kid*, 39.

75. Anaya, *ChupaCabra Meets Billy the Kid*, 109.

76. Anaya, *ChupaCabra Meets Billy the Kid*, 134.

77. Anaya, *ChupaCabra Meets Billy the Kid*, 49.

78. Anaya, *ChupaCabra Meets Billy the Kid*, 66.

79. Anaya, *ChupaCabra Meets Billy the Kid*, 129.

80. Murrah-Mandril, *In the Mean Time*, 29.

81. Chela Sandoval, *Methodology of the Oppressed* (Minneapolis: University of Minnesota Press, 2000); Murrah-Mandril, *In the Mean Time*, 12.

82. Murrah-Mandril, *In the Mean Time*, 15.

83. Anaya, *ChupaCabra Meets Billy the Kid*, 149.

84. Michel Foucault, "Of Other Spaces: Utopias and Heterotopias," trans. Jay Miskowiec, *Diacritics* 16, no. 1 (1986): 1–9, 3, 4.

85. Foucault, "Of Other Spaces," 7.

86. Anaya, *ChupaCabra Meets Billy the Kid*, 151.

5. SPECULATIVE BORDERLANDS II

1. At the time of this writing, only the first season of *Undone* had aired, and thus my discussion here is limited to the events of that season.

2. Pratt, "Arts of the Contact Zone," 33.

3. Véa, *The Mexican Flyboy*.

4. Murrah-Mandril, *In the Mean Time*, 14, 15; Chu, *Do Metaphors Dream*, 7, 10.

5. Lutenski, *West of Harlem*, 94.

6. Hisko Hulsing, dir., "The Crash," season 1, episode 1, of *Undone*, aired September 13, 2019, on Amazon Prime.

7. Hisko Hulsing, dir., "The Hospital," season 1, episode 2, of *Undone*, aired September 13, 2019, on Amazon Prime.

8. Gloria E. Anzaldúa, *Borderlands / La Frontera: The New Mestiza* (San Francisco: Aunt Lute, 1987). The term *nepantla* has Nahuatl origins and refers to a middle or between state.

9. Susana Ramírez, "Recovering Gloria Anzaldúa's Sci-Fi Roots: Nepantler@ Visions in the Unpublished and Published Speculative Precursors to *Borderlands*," in Merla-Watson and Olguín, *Altermundos*, 55–71, 60, 61.

10. Susana Ramírez, "Recovering Gloria Anzaldúa's Sci-Fi Roots," 61.

11. Hisko Hulsing, dir., "The Wedding," season 1, episode 7, of *Undone*, aired September 13, 2019, on Amazon Prime.

12. Hisko Hulsing, dir., "Alone in This (You Have Me)," season 1, episode 5, of *Undone*, aired September 13, 2019, on Amazon Prime.

13. Véa, *The Mexican Flyboy*, 47, 40.

14. Véa, *The Mexican Flyboy*, 64.

15. Véa, *The Mexican Flyboy*, 67.

16. Véa, *The Mexican Flyboy*, 68.

17. Véa, *The Mexican Flyboy*, 68, 69.

18. Véa, *The Mexican Flyboy*, 71.

19. Véa, *The Mexican Flyboy*, 72.

20. Merla-Watson, "(Trans)Mission Possible," 355.

21. Merla-Watson, "(Trans)Mission Possible," 359. See Tomás Ybarra-Frausto, "Rasquachismo: A Chicano Sensibility," in *Chicano Art: Resistance and Affirmation, 1965–1985*, ed. Richard Griswold del Castillo, Teresa McKenna, and Yvonne Yarbro-Bejarano (Los Angeles: Wight Art Gallery, University of California, 1991), 155–62.

22. Merla-Watson, "(Trans)Mission Possible," 359.

23. Véa, *The Mexican Flyboy*, 234.

24. Véa, *The Mexican Flyboy*, 49.

25. Christopher Conway, *Heroes of the Borderlands: The Western in Mexican Film, Comics, and Music* (Albuquerque: University of New Mexico Press, 2019).

26. Conway, *Heroes of the Borderlands*, 192.

27. Conway, *Heroes of the Borderlands*, 191, 192.

28. Chela Sandoval, *Methodology of the Oppressed* (Minneapolis: University of Minnesota Press, 2000), quoted in Murrah-Mandril, *In the Mean Time*, 112.

29. Véa, *The Mexican Flyboy*, 35.

30. Véa, *The Mexican Flyboy*, 134. A veteran of the Vietnam War himself, Alfredo Véa has written about war trauma in other novels as well, including what is probably his best-known novel, *Gods Go Begging*. Brian Williams describes how, in that novel, Véa "directly addresses the dominant tropes of the therapeutic Vietnam novel, inventing alternative narration to produce complex concepts of community invested in a more nuanced understanding of nationhood and national trauma." *The Mexican Flyboy* continues Véa's experimentation with narrative form as a means of conveying the experience of trauma and healing. See Alfredo Véa, *Gods Go Begging* (New York: Plume, 1999); Brian Williams, "'In This Same Shamble of Strewn Bone': *Gods Go Begging* and the Community of Loss," *Critique: Studies in Contemporary Fiction* 54, no. 3 (2013): 316–34, 317.

31. Véa, *The Mexican Flyboy*, 266.

32. Véa, *The Mexican Flyboy*, 193.

33. Véa, *The Mexican Flyboy*, 193.

34. Véa, *The Mexican Flyboy*, 109.

35. Véa, *The Mexican Flyboy*, 110.

36. Véa, *The Mexican Flyboy*, 220.

37. Campbell, *Affective Critical Regionality*, 10.

38. Véa, *The Mexican Flyboy*, 44.

39. Véa, *The Mexican Flyboy*, 39.

40. Véa, *The Mexican Flyboy*, 46.

41. Véa, *The Mexican Flyboy*, 39.

42. Véa, *The Mexican Flyboy*, 12.

43. Véa, *The Mexican Flyboy*, 38.

44. Véa, *The Mexican Flyboy*, 40, 41.

45. Campbell, *Affective Critical Regionality*, 1.

46. Campbell, *Affective Critical Regionality*, 10; Tim Ingold, *The Life of Lines* (London: Routledge, 2015).

47. Campbell, *Affective Critical Regionality*, 17.

48. Véa, *The Mexican Flyboy*, 139.

49. Véa, *The Mexican Flyboy*, 140, 144.

50. Véa, *The Mexican Flyboy*, 263.

51. Véa, *The Mexican Flyboy*, 62.

52. Campbell, *Affective Critical Regionality*, 219.

53. Véa, *The Mexican Flyboy*, 266.

54. Fromm, introduction to *Lost in Transmission*, xix.

55. Campbell, *Post-Westerns*, 204; see also Deleuze, *Cinema 2*; Sayles, *Lone Star*.

56. Véa, *The Mexican Flyboy*, 95–96.

57. Véa, *The Mexican Flyboy*, 96.

58. Véa, *The Mexican Flyboy*, 42.

59. Véa, *The Mexican Flyboy*, 151.

60. Véa, *The Mexican Flyboy*, 165–66.

61. Véa, *The Mexican Flyboy*, 167.

62. Véa, *The Mexican Flyboy*, 168.

63. Véa, *The Mexican Flyboy*, 171.

64. Véa, *The Mexican Flyboy*, 175.

65. Véa, *The Mexican Flyboy*, 315.

66. Véa, *The Mexican Flyboy*, 313.

67. Véa, *The Mexican Flyboy*, 233.

68. Véa, *The Mexican Flyboy*, 244.

69. Véa, *The Mexican Flyboy*, 146.

70. Campbell, *Affective Critical Regionality*, 173.

71. Campbell, *Affective Critical Regionality*, 17.

72. Véa, *The Mexican Flyboy*, 337.

73. Véa, *The Mexican Flyboy*, 310.

74. Véa, *The Mexican Flyboy*, 142.

75. Véa, *The Mexican Flyboy*, 142.

76. Van der Kolk and Onno van der Hart, "The Intrusive Past," 179.

77. Caruth, "Recapturing the Past," in Caruth, *Trauma*, 153.

78. Véa, *The Mexican Flyboy*, 265.

79. Véa, *The Mexican Flyboy*, 291.

80. Véa, *The Mexican Flyboy*, 319.

81. Michel Foucault, "Of Other Spaces: Utopias and Heterotopias," trans. Jay Miskowiec, *Diacritics* 16, no. 1 (1986): 1–9, 3.

82. Foucault, "Of Other Spaces," 7.

83. Jones, *South of Pico*, 7.

84. Véa, *The Mexican Flyboy*, 310.

85. Véa, *The Mexican Flyboy*, 311.

86. Campbell, *Affective Critical Regionality*, 174, 175.

6. SPECULATIVE SLAVE NARRATIVE WESTERNS

1. Dubey, "The Future of Race in Afro-Futurist Fiction," 17. Nnedi Okorafor usefully distinguishes "Afrofuturism" from "Africanfuturism," suggesting that Afrofuturism is more in keeping with an African American context and noting that there is plenty of Black speculative writing (including her own) that is often labeled Afrofuturist that might be more properly termed Africanfuturist: "Africanfuturism is similar to 'Afrofuturism' in the way that blacks on the continent and in the Black Diaspora are all connect by blood, spirit, history and future. The difference is that Afri-

canfuturism is specifically and more directly rooted in African culture, history, mythology and point-of-view as it then branches into the Black Diaspora, and it does not privilege or center the West." Nnedi Okorafor, "Africanfuturism Defined," *Nnedi's Wahala Zone Blog*, October 19, 2019, https://nnedi.blogspot.com/2019/10/africanfuturism-defined.html. My focus in this chapter is specifically on African American texts, but it should be noted that the larger field of Black speculative art is much broader.

2. Isiah Lavender III, *Afrofuturism Rising: The Literary Prehistory of a Movement* (Columbus: The Ohio State University Press, 2019), 20.

3. Lavender, *Afrofuturism Rising*, 9; Mark Dery, "Black to the Future: Interviews with Samuel R. Delaney, Greg Tate, and Tricia Rose," in "Flame Wars: The Discourse of Cyberculture," ed. Mark Dery, special issue, *South Atlantic Quarterly* 92, no. 4 (1993): 735–78, 768.

4. Lavender, *Afrofuturism Rising*, 2.

5. Alondra Nelson, "Introduction: Future Texts," *Social Text* 20, no. 2 (2002): 1–15, quoted in Dubey, "The Future of Race in Afro-Futurist Fiction," 21.

6. Lavender, *Race in American Science Fiction*, 54.

7. Lavender, *Race in American Science Fiction*, 55. *Neo–slave narrative* is a term that has been in use for a number of years. Lavender identifies the source as Bernard Bell's *The Afro-American Novel and Its Tradition*, which uses the term to describe contemporary fictional stories "set in the historical era of slavery to critique the status of race relations and engage in cultural politics. Writers accomplish this task by informing their fiction with the firmly bound characteristics of the slave narrative." Lavender's term *meta–slavery narrative* draws a distinction between these realistic fictional stories and speculative works that engage with slavery. Bernard W. Bell, *The Afro-American Novel and Its Tradition* (Amherst: University of Massachusetts Press, 1987); Lavender, *Race in American Science Fiction*, 57.

8. Lavender, *Race in American Science Fiction*, 60. To name just a few examples of speculative works that incorporate elements of the slave narrative (or of the history of slavery), we might mention Octavia Butler's *Kindred* (New York: Doubleday, 1979) and her Xenogenesis trilogy, *Dawn, Adulthood Rites*, and *Imago* (New York: Grand Central Publishing, 1987–89); Samuel R. Delaney's *Stars in My Pocket like Grains of Sand* (New York: Bantam, 1984); Stephen Barnes's *Lion's Blood* (New York: Warner Aspect, 2002) and *Zulu Heart* (New York: Warner Aspect, 2003); and Colson Whitehead's novel *The Underground Railroad* (New York: Doubleday, 2016).

9. Joshua D. Smith, "*Uncle Tom's Cabin* Showdown: Stowe, Tarantino, and Minstrelsy of the Weird West," in Fine et al., *Weird Westerns*, 313–47; Harriet Beecher Stowe, *Uncle Tom's Cabin; or, Life among the Lowly*, ed. Elizabeth Ammons (New York: Norton, 2010; originally published in

Boston: John P. Jewett, 1852); Quentin Tarantino, dir., *Django Unchained* (Los Angeles: A Band Apart, 2012).

10. Eric Gardner, "Gateways and Borders: Black St. Louis in the 1840s and 1850s," in *Unexpected Places: Relocating Nineteenth-Century African American Literature* (Jackson: University Press of Mississippi, 2009), 22–55, 25.

11. Joshua D. Smith, "*Uncle Tom's Cabin* Showdown," 314.

12. For an overview of the "slave narrative western," see Michael K. Johnson, "The D Is Silent: *Django Unchained* and the African American West," *Safundi* 16, no. 3 (2015): 256–66.

13. Justina Ireland, *Deathless Divide* (New York: HarperCollins, 2020), 553; see also Justina Ireland, *Dread Nation* (New York: HarperCollins, 2018).

14. Hopkins, *Winona*.

15. Paul Bogart and Gordon Douglas, dirs., *The Skin Game* (Burbank CA: Warner Brothers, 1971); Brooks, *Blazing Saddles*; Sidney Poitier, dir., *Buck and the Preacher* (E&R Productions, 1972).

16. Ishmael Reed, *Yellow Back Radio Broke-Down* (1969; repr., McLean IL: Dalkey Archive, 2000).

17. Melanie A. Marotta, "Introduction: Where Are We Going and Where Have We Been?," in Marotta, *Women's Space*, 1–23, 1, 2; Green, *Encyclopedia of Weird Westerns*.

18. To provide a sense of the potential largeness of the field, even limited to television shows that might be considered SF westerns with significant African American characters, we might include consciously hybrid SF westerns such as *The Adventures of Brisco County, Jr.* (which costars Julius Carry as an African American bounty hunter, Lord Bowler) and the Joss Whedon series *Firefly* (which features African American actors as part of the ensemble). Even limiting the time period to 2016–20, we might include *Westworld* (another consciously hybrid narrative that also directly addresses issues of enslavement), as well as several SF frontier narratives that implicitly (and sometimes explicitly) evoke western conventions, such as *Killjoys* (in which frontier bounty hunters range across a planetary system known as the Quad and which includes Afro-British actress Hannah John-Kamen as central character Dutch), *The Expanse* (which replicates the western genre's eastern-western dichotomy as the tension between Earth and the settled and partially settled outer planets and which stars Afro-British actress Dominique Tipper as Naomi Nagata), and the second season of the Netflix series *Altered Carbon* (in which African American actor Anthonie Mackie takes over the role as Kovac and African American actor Simone Messick is featured as the bounty hunter Trepp). See *The Adventures of Brisco Country, Jr.*, aired 1993–94 on Fox; *Firefly*, aired 2002–3 on Fox; *Killjoys*, aired 2013–19 on Space; *The Expanse*,

aired 2015–18 on Syfy and 2019– on Amazon Prime; *Altered Carbon*, aired 2018–20 on Netflix.

19. Sayles, *The Brother from Another Planet*; Ireland, *Dread Nation*; Ireland, *Deathless Divide*; Davis, *The Good Luck Girls*.
20. Lamont, *Westerns*, 1.
21. John Coney, dir., *Space Is the Place* (produced by Jim Newman, 1972).
22. Nama, *Black Space*, 154.
23. Nama, *Black Space*, 154.
24. Ramzi Fawaz, "Space, That Bottomless Pit: Planetary Exile and Metaphors of Belonging in American Afrofuturist Cinema," *Callaloo* 35, no. 4 (2012): 1103–22, 1103.
25. Bahng, *Migrant Futures*, x.
26. Ed Guerrero, *Framing Blackness: The African American Image in Film* (Philadelphia: Temple University Press, 1993), 48.
27. Janani Subramanian, "Alienating Identification: Black Identity in *The Brother from Another Planet* and *I Am Legend*," *Science Fiction Film and Television* 3, no. 1 (2010): 37–56, 38.
28. Fawaz, "Space, That Bottomless Pit," 1109–10.
29. Fawaz, "Space, That Bottomless Pit," 1110.
30. There are multiple versions of Henry Box Brown's story, including theatrical versions involving elaborate panoramas in which Brown performed his own story. The story first appeared in print in the United States (written by and in the voice of abolitionist Charles Stearns) in 1849 under the title *Narrative of Henry Box Brown, Who Escaped from Slavery Enclosed in a Box 3 Feet Long and 2 Wide. Written from a Statement of Facts Made by Himself. With Remarks upon the Remedy for Slavery*. Brown published another version of his story (in which he had more control over the narrative) in England in 1851: *Narrative of the Life of Henry Box Brown. Written by Himself*. Charles Stearns, *Narrative of Henry Box Brown, Who Escaped from Slavery Enclosed in a Box 3 Feet Long and 2 Wide. Written from a Statement of Facts Made by Himself. With Remarks upon the Remedy for Slavery* (Boston: Brown and Stearns, 1849); Henry Brown, *Narrative of the Life of Henry Box Brown. Written by Himself*, ed. and with an introduction by John Ernst (Manchester, UK: Lee and Glynn, 1851; Chapel Hill: University of North Carolina Press, 2008).
31. Lavender compares Brown's experience to that of Harriet Jacobs, who details in her *Incidents in the Life of a Slave Girl* the seven years she spent hiding from her owner in her grandmother's attic crawl space, which she calls a "loophole of retreat." That such extreme actions are necessary is suggestive of what Lavender describes as the "science-fictional existence that blacks have *always* experienced" in America. Lavender, *Afrofutur-*

ism Rising, 9. Colson Whitehead's *The Underground Railroad*—part slave narrative, part alternate history, part *Gulliver's Travels*–inspired satirical allegory—imagines a literal underground railroad of tracks, tunnels, and trains. He also continues the "loophole of retreat" trope when his protagonist, the fugitive slave Cora, finds refuge above a false ceiling in an attic, a "cramped nook" only three feet high with a "hole in the wall that faced the street" that was the "only source of light and air," a tiny space that in its cramped limitations and its "spy hole" reflects back on Jacobs's experience. Whitehead, *The Underground Railroad*, 154. "Brown's and Jacobs's resistance to slavery," Lavender writes, "provokes a uniquely afro-futurist vibe when their separate experiences are framed as self-engineered pocket universes." In those pocket spaces, "they exist outside history, unobserved by all except their readers: victims of slavery determined to escape from their artificial worlds, from a slave world designed to consume them, to live free in a free world." Lavender, *Afrofuturism Rising*, 88. In keeping with this idea, Brother consistently finds such "loopholes of retreat": the spaceship in which he travels, the bar in which he finds refuge, the room filled with malfunctioning video games where he finds employment. He even utilizes a kind of "spy hole" when he removes and hides his eye, using it to perform surveillance on the bad actors in the world he comes to inhabit, much as Cora and Jacobs do in their hidden nooks. And then, like Cora and Jacobs, Brother uses the information gathered to intervene in that world. Lavender, *Afrofuturism Rising*; Whitehead, *The Underground Railroad*.

32. John White, *Westerns* (New York: Routledge, 2011), 8.

33. Stevens, *Shane*; Clint Eastwood, dir., *High Plains Drifter* (Burbank CA: The Malpaso Company, 1973).

34. Cynthia J. Miller, "'So This Zombie Walks into a Bar . . .': The Living, the Undead, and the Western Saloon," in Miller and Van Riper, *Undead in the West*, 3–18, 3, 4.

35. Leone, *For a Few Dollars More*.

36. John Huston, dir., *The Treasure of the Sierra Madre* (Burbank CA: Warner Brothers, 1948).

37. We might make a similar point—regarding the suggestion that in the 1980s (or 1970s) a western with a Black actor in the lead role could appear only through multiple layers of generic disguise—about John Carpenter's contemporary western *Assault on Precinct 13*, which was filmed and set in Los Angeles and features African American actor Austin Stoker as a police officer involved in a last-stand scenario defending a recently closed precinct from violent gang members. John Carpenter, dir., *Assault on Precinct 13* (Hollywood CA: CKK Corporation, 1976).

38. Lamont, *Westerns*, 1. See also Emma Ghent Curtis, *The Administratrix* (New York: John B. Alden, 1889); Owen Wister, *The Virginian* (New York: Macmillan, 1902).

39. Lamont, *Westerns*, 2.

40. Kerry Fine, "She Hits like a Man, but She Kisses like a Girl: TV Heroines, Femininity, Violence, and Intimacy," *Western American Literature* 47, no. 2 (Summer 2012): 153–73, 153. See also *In Plain Sight*, aired 2008–12 on USA Network; *Sons of Anarchy*, aired 2008–14 on Fox.

41. Fine, "She Hits like a Man," 155.

42. Fine, "She Hits like a Man," 155. Stereotypes of African Americans (such as the angry Black man) likewise associate them more with "expressive aggression," and westerns that have included African American characters have sometimes struggled with finding strategies to include Black characters in western violence while negotiating violent stereotypes associated with Black men in particular. Nonetheless, there have been a variety of Black male characters in westerns who have filled the role of western hero, the agent of instrumental aggression. However, in westerns, even speculative westerns, African American women who use instrumental aggression are few and far between, but some examples might include Zoë Washburne (Gina Torres) in the SF western *Firefly*; Maeve (Thandiwe Newton) in *Westworld*; Michonne (Danai Gurira) in *The Walking Dead*; and in *Dread Nation* and *Deathless Divide*, Jane McKeene and Kathleen Devereaux. *Westworld*, aired 2016– on HBO; *The Walking Dead*, aired 2010– on AMC.

43. Lamont, *Westerns*, 4.

44. Curtis, *The Administratrix*, quoted in Lamont, *Westerns*, 28.

45. The original full text of *Winona* is available at the Digital Colored American Magazine website, http://coloredamerican.org/. As a serial, *Winona* appeared in *Colored American Magazine* 5, nos. 1–6 (May–October 1902).

46. Lamont, *Westerns*, 4.

47. Lamont, *Westerns*, 3.

48. Pauline Hopkins, *Hagar's Daughter: A Story of Southern Caste Prejudice*, in *The Magazine Novels of Pauline Hopkins*, 1–284, originally published in *Colored American Magazine* 2, nos. 5–6 (March and April 1901); 3, nos. 1–6 (May–October 1901); 4, nos. 1–4 (November–December 1901; January–March 1902); all references will refer to the Oxford University Press compiled edition. Pauline Hopkins, *Of One Blood: or, the Hidden Self*, in *The Magazine Novels of Pauline Hopkins*, 439–621, originally published in *Colored American Magazine* 6, nos. 1–11 (November–December 1902; January–November 1903).

49. Rachel Ihara, "'The Stimulus of Books and Tales': Pauline Hopkins's Serial Novels for *Colored American Magazine*," in *Transnationalism and American Serial Fiction*, ed. Patricia Okker (New York: Routledge, 2011), 129.

50. Hazel V. Carby, introduction to *The Magazine Novels of Pauline Hopkins*, xxix–l, xxix.

51. Ihara, "'The Stimulus of Books and Tales,'" 129.

52. Nisi Shawl, "Introduction to the Novel: Occult Blood," in *Of One Blood: or, The Hidden Self*, by Pauline Hopkins, Haunted Library of Horror Classics (Naperville IL: Poisoned Pen Press, 2021), xi–xiii, xii.

53. Jalondra A. Davis, "Utopia and the Gendered Past in Pauline Hopkins' *Of One Blood; or, The Hidden Self*," *Journal of Science Fiction* 3, no 1 (March 2019): 7–20, 7.

54. Colleen O'Brien, "'All the Land Had Changed': Territorial Expansion and the Native American Past in Pauline Hopkins's *Winona*," *Studies in American Fiction* 41, no. 1 (2014): 27–48, 27.

55. Lisa McGunigal, "'Shifting' the Black Abolitionist Panorama: Subversive Realism in Pauline Hopkins's *Winona*," *Nineteenth-Century Contexts* 40, no. 5 (2018): 455–72, 455.

56. Lamont, *Westerns*, 7.

57. Lamont, *Westerns*, 7–8.

58. "*The Good Luck Girls*," McMillan Publishers, accessed July 12, 2020, https://us.macmillan.com/books/9781250299703.

59. Clint Eastwood, dir., *Unforgiven* (Burbank CA: Malpaso Productions, 1992).

60. Davis, *The Good Luck Girls*, 22.

61. Lavender, *Race in American Science Fiction*, 55.

62. Davis, *The Good Luck Girls*, 21, 147, 106, 37, 73.

63. As Marotta points out in her discussion of cyberpunk westerns, "Female characters tend to be depicted as prostitutes" (a practice that eventually evolves into more complex characterization, she argues, around the turn of the twenty-first century). Marotta, "Introduction," 11. See also Melanie A. Marotta, "The Reformation of the 'Plastic Girl': Prostitute/Killer and Messenger Characters in Cyberpunk to Post-Cyberpunk," in Marotta, *Women's Space*, 42–58.

64. Davis, *The Good Luck Girls*, 90.

65. John Ford, dir., *My Darling Clementine* (Los Angeles: 20th Century Fox, 1946).

66. Davis, *The Good Luck Girls*, 102.

67. Davis, *The Good Luck Girls*, 176.

68. Davis, *The Good Luck Girls*, 176.

69. Davis, *The Good Luck Girls*, 298.

70. Davis, *The Good Luck Girls*, 183.

71. Davis, *The Good Luck Girls*, 162.

72. Davis, *The Good Luck Girls*, 206.

73. Hopkins, *Winona*, 348.

74. Colleen O'Brien, "'All the Land Had Changed,'" 39.

75. Davis, *The Good Luck Girls*, 179.

76. Davis, *The Good Luck Girls*, 244.

77. Davis, *The Good Luck Girls*, 245.

78. Davis, *The Good Luck Girls*, 340–41.

79. Ihara, "'The Stimulus of Books and Tales,'" 141.

80. Ihara, "'The Stimulus of Books and Tales,'" 137, 141.

81. Ihara, "'The Stimulus of Books and Tales,'" 137.

82. Lavender, *Afrofuturism Rising*, 7.

83. Davis, *The Good Luck Girls*, 342.

84. Davis, *The Good Luck Girls*, 348.

85. Miller and Van Riper, introduction to *Undead in the West*, xix. The question arises with "undead westerns" that retain the basic structuring dichotomies of the classic western as to whether or not they represent a sufficient reimagining of the form. By displacing or replacing the Native American antagonists of classic westerns, undead westerns may "repackage the violence of colonial race war in a form that is ideologically safer." James Hewiston, however, suggests that undead westerns do not automatically replicate imperialistic narratives, arguing that the zombie apocalypse might also serve the purpose of challenging dominant ideology rather than repeating it. Gerry Canavan, "'We Are the Walking Dead': Race, Time, and Survival in Zombie Narrative," *Extrapolation* 51, no. 3 (2010): 431–53, 439; James Hewitson, "Undead and Un-American: The Zombified Other in Weird Western Films," in Miller and Van Riper, *Undead in the West*. An extensive archive of cultural criticism on zombies exists and continues to grow. For an overview, see the essays collected in Sarah Juliet Lauro, ed., *Zombie Theory: A Reader* (Minneapolis: Minnesota University Press, 2017).

86. Ireland, *Dread Nation*, 35. Robin Means Coleman, in *Horror Noire: Blacks in American Horror Films from the 1890s to Present*, similarly finds that the horror genre "'speaks' difference" in allegorical ways by "marking Black people and culture as Other," as the source of the horrific, as in films that use voodoo practices as the cause of the horror unleashed or in the coding of the monster as racial other. However, as Coleman points out, there have nonetheless been points of resistance within the genre of the horror film—from *Tales from the Hood* (1995) to *Get Out* (2017). Robin Means Coleman, *Horror Noire: Blacks in American Horror Films from the*

1890s to Present (New York: Routledge, 2011), 2. See also John Cussans, *Undead Uprising: Haiti, Horror, and the Zombie Complex* (London: Strange Attractor, 2017).

87. Ireland, *Dread Nation*, 35.

88. Ireland, *Dread Nation*, 10.

89. For critique of Native American representation in *Dread Nation* and its portrayal of the boarding school system, see Debbie Reese's (Nambe Pueblo) blog post "Twitter Thread on Justina Ireland's DREAD NATION," *American Indians in Children's Literature* (blog), May 1, 2018, https://americanindiansinchildrensliterature.blogspot.com/2018/05/twitter-thread-on-justina-irelands.html.

90. Ireland, *Dread Nation*, 130.

91. Ireland, *Dread Nation*, 109.

92. Ireland, *Dread Nation*, 116.

93. Ireland, *Dread Nation*, 201.

94. Ireland, *Dread Nation*, 260.

95. Ireland, *Dread Nation*, 15.

96. Ireland, *Dread Nation*, 433.

97. Colleen O'Brien, "'All the Land Had Changed,'" 28–29.

98. Sanchez-Taylor, "Alternative Futurisms," 91–92.

99. For discussions of gender and justice in the novel, see Michael K. Johnson, *Black Masculinity and the Frontier Myth in American Literature* (Norman: University of Oklahoma Press, 2002), 117–46; see also Martha H. Patterson, "'kin o' rough jestice fer a parson': Pauline Hopkins's *Winona* and the Politics of Reconstructing History," *African American Review* 32, no. 3 (Fall 1998): 445–60.

100. Ireland, *Dread Nation*, 437.

101. Lee Clark Mitchell, *Westerns: The Making of the Man in Fiction and Film* (Chicago: University of Chicago Press, 1996), 169.

102. Mitchell, *Westerns*, 170.

103. Mitchell, *Westerns*, 179.

104. Mitchell, *Westerns*, 179.

105. Johnson, *Black Masculinity*, 127.

106. Deborah E. McDowell, "In the First Place: Making Frederick Douglass and the Afro-American Tradition," in *African American Autobiography*, ed. William L. Andrews (Englewood Cliffs NJ: Prentice Hall, 1993), 36–58, 48.

107. McDowell, "In the First Place," 48, 50.

108. McDowell, "In the First Place," 50; see also Frederick Douglass, *Narrative of the Life of Frederick Douglass, An American Slave Written by Himself* (New York: Signet/New American Library, 1968).

109. Ireland, *Dread Nation*, 313.

110. Ireland, *Dread Nation*, 319.

111. Ireland, *Dread Nation*, 320.

112. Ireland, *Dread Nation*, 322.

113. Ireland, *Dread Nation*, 327.

114. Hopkins, *Winona*, 328.

115. Hopkins, *Winona*, 422.

116. Fine, "She Hits like a Man," 155.

117. Ireland, *Deathless Divide*, 79.

118. Ireland, *Deathless Divide*, 79.

119. Ireland, *Deathless Divide*, 82.

120. Ireland, *Dread Nation*, 389.

121. As an alternate history, *Deathless Divide* reimagines western history (and California history specifically) through a speculative cartography that reflects an alternate process of settlement and development. White migration to the West has been disrupted by the rising of the dead, leaving California settlement to Asian immigration and to the pervasive influence of "Californios," Mexican migrants, long-established settlers of Spanish and of mixed Spanish and Indigenous background. That alternate history is reflected in the architecture and in the language, as Chinese and Spanish become the primary spoken languages in this version of California. "San Francisco's architecture," Katherine observes, "is part Spanish and part Chinese, and it is beautiful. I have never seen anything like it." However, Katherine discovers that multicultural San Francisco is built on its own practices of exclusion. Blacks are forced into segregated housing and worse, "squats" and "a collection of tents and haphazard structures," and occasionally subjected to vigilante attempts to burn down their neighborhoods. Ireland, *Deathless Divide*, 305, 311.

122. Ireland, *Deathless Divide*, 420.

123. Ireland, *Deathless Divide*, 133.

124. Ireland, *Deathless Divide*, 437.

125. Ireland, *Deathless Divide*, 456.

126. George Romero, dir., *Dawn of the Dead* (New York: Laurel Group, 1978). As Hewitson writes, there's a distinction "between the zombies that appear in Haitian folklore—popularized in American films of the early and mid-twentieth century—and the current image of zombies as flesh-eating ghouls that originated with George Romero's *Night of the Living Dead* (1968) and its sequels. Romero's zombies are damaged, decaying, animated corpses, fixated on eating living humans. Haitian zombies, however, are reanimated corpses disinterred by a voodoo priest and turned into slaves: they act as mindless automatons, obeying their masters without question." Haitian folklore-influenced zombies may metaphorically suggest

the experience of slavery. Generally speaking, zombies in Ireland's duology suggest the influence of the Romero-style zombie. James Hewitson, "Undead and Un-American," 172–73.

127. Ireland, *Deathless Divide*, 286.
128. Ireland, *Deathless Divide*, 288.
129. Ireland, *Deathless Divide*, 289.
130. Ireland, *Deathless Divide*, 291.
131. See Johnson, *Hoo-Doo Cowboys*, 173–82. See note 18 in this chapter for numerous examples of Black bounty hunter characters in television's speculative westerns.
132. Ireland, *Deathless Divide*, 327.
133. Ireland, *Deathless Divide*, 482.
134. Ireland, *Deathless Divide*, 397.
135. Ireland, *Deathless Divide*, 443.
136. Ireland, *Deathless Divide*, 493.
137. Ireland, *Deathless Divide*, 524.
138. Ireland, *Deathless Divide*, 546.

AFTERWORD

1. Doug Wilks, "Inside the Newsroom: The Power of a Story and Iconic Photos of the West," *Deseret News* (Salt Lake City UT), April 25, 2020, https://www.deseret.com/opinion/2020/4/25/21236405/coronavirus-covid-19-navajo-testing-healthcare-pandemic-media-photos-newsroom.
2. Wilks, "Inside the Newsroom."
3. Early in the pandemic, novelist Ted Chiang observed, "While there has been plenty of fiction written about pandemics, I think the biggest difference between those scenarios and our reality is how poorly our government has handled it. If your goal is to dramatize the threat posed by an unknown virus, there's no advantage in depicting the officials responding as incompetent, because that minimizes the threat. . . . A pandemic story like that would be similar to what's known as an 'idiot plot,' a plot that would be resolved very quickly if your protagonist weren't an idiot." That interview with Chiang partially inspired this afterword comparing my lived experience with fictional representations of pandemics. Ted Chiang, "Ted Chiang Explains the Disaster Novel We All Suddenly Live In," interview by Halimah Marcus, *Electric Lit*, March 31, 2020, https://electricliterature.com/ted-chiang-explains-the-disaster-novel-we-all-suddenly-live-in/.
4. Priscilla Wald, *Contagious: Cultures, Carriers, and the Outbreak Narrative* (Durham NC: Duke University Press, 2008), 1, 2.
5. Elizabeth Outka, *Viral Modernism: The Influenza Pandemic and Interwar Literature* (New York: Columbia University Press, 2020), 200.

6. Outka, *Viral Modernism*, 216.

7. Outka, *Viral Modernism*, 201.

8. See also Dahlia Schweitzer's *Going Viral* for an extended discussion of "viral zombies" in relation to the outbreak narrative. Dahlia Schweitzer, *Going Viral: Zombies, Viruses, and the End of the World* (New Brunswick NJ: Rutgers University Press, 2018).

9. Chen, *A Beginning at the End*.

10. Chen, *A Beginning at the End*, 25.

11. Chen, *A Beginning at the End*, 61.

12. Chen, *A Beginning at the End*, 30, 53.

13. Frederick Jackson Turner, "The Significance of the Frontier in American History," in *Rereading Frederick Jackson Turner*, ed. John Mack Faragher (New York: Henry Holt, 1994; originally published in 1893), 31–60, 33.

14. Chen, *A Beginning at the End*, 287.

15. Chen, *A Beginning at the End*, 68.

16. Chen, *A Beginning at the End*, 294.

17. Chen, *A Beginning at the End*, 299–300.

18. Chen, *A Beginning at the End*, 162.

19. Chen, *A Beginning at the End*, 300, 301.

20. Chen, *A Beginning at the End*, 27.

21. Chen, *A Beginning at the End*, 375.

22. Chen, *A Beginning at the End*, 391.

Index

IN THE POSTWESTERN HORIZONS SERIES

CPSIA information can be obtained
at www.ICGtesting.com
Printed in the USA
LVHW101306250123
737850LV00003B/163

9 781496 234582